Daily
Wisdom
for
MEN

2016 Devotional Collection

BARBOUR BOOKS
An Imprint of Barbour Publishing, Inc.

Print ISBNs 978-1-63409-316-3, 978-1-63409-706-2

eBook Editions:
Adobe Digital Edition (.epub) 978-1-63409-609-6
Kindle and MobiPocket Edition (.prc) 978-1-63409-610-2

Published by Barbour Books, an imprint of Barbour Publishing, Inc., P.O. Box 719, Uhrichsville, Ohio 44683, www.barbourbooks.com

Our mission is to publish and distribute inspirational products offering exceptional value and biblical encouragement to the masses.

Member of the
Evangelical Christian
Publishers Association

Printed in China.

GOD IS THERE FOR YOU

The righteous cry out, and the LORD hears them;
he delivers them from all their troubles.
PSALM 34:17 NIV

Those who have lived the Christian life for any length of time have likely had a good chance to learn an important lesson about a life of faith, namely that God never promised that it would be easy or that there wouldn't be times of difficulty.

Indeed, any effort to find a scriptural promise telling us that the Christian life is a trouble-free life would end in frustration and failure. In fact, Jesus promised quite the opposite when He said, "In this world you will have trouble. But take heart! I have overcome the world" (John 16:33 NIV).

Yes, in this world, we're going to face times of trouble. But there is one promise God has made repeatedly in His written Word for believers facing times of difficulty. Time and time again, He tells us, *"I'll be there for you."*

God is our loving heavenly Father, and He's also a devoted Friend who is there for us in our times of greatest trouble. And not only that, He provides us all we need to emerge from the difficult times as overcomers.

With a Friend like Him, who needs. . .*anything else*?

HOW MUCH IS "ENOUGH"?

*Whoever loves money never has enough;
whoever loves wealth is never satisfied with
their income. This too is meaningless.*
ECCLESIASTES 5:10 NIV

The 1987 movie *Wall Street* contains an often-quoted line, spoken by the aptly named character Gordon Gecko, who said, "Greed, for lack of a better word, is good."

But the Bible warns that greed is not good, that greed is a destructive force in the life of any man—especially a man of God.

The apostle Paul wrote that "the love of money is a root of all kinds of evil" and that some who have an insatiable desire have "wandered from the faith and pierced themselves with many griefs" (1 Timothy 6:10 NIV).

God is not against earning money—even against accruing wealth—as long as we do it through righteous means and with righteous motivation. In fact, the Bible repeatedly encourages God's people to work hard so that they may prosper. What God is against—passionately against—is making money an idol, a life's focus ahead of family and, yes, ahead of God Himself.

So approach your work with passion. Work hard to provide well for yourself and your family. But never lose sight of the fact that your ultimate satisfaction, your ultimate source of all good things, is your heavenly Father.

GOD-HONORING HUMILITY

*Humble yourselves, therefore, under God's mighty
hand, that he may lift you up in due time.*
1 PETER 5:6 NIV

It's probably fair to say that pride is at the heart of nearly every sin we can commit against God and against others. Pride causes people to boast about themselves and to tear others down. Pride causes people to believe they can do for themselves what God has promised to do for them, and that leads to a lack of prayer. Pride causes conflicts between people, and it keeps us from confessing our sins to one another and to God so that we can be reconciled.

This list of the terrible results of human pride could go on and on, but when you read it, it is no small wonder that God has said, *"I hate pride"* (see Proverbs 8:13).

God hates human pride, but He loves humility, which can be defined as the acknowledgment that apart from Him, we are nothing and can do nothing of value. When we are humble, in effect we are confessing that we have nothing to offer God apart from what He has already done.

So build your life on the words of the apostle Peter. Humble yourself before God. Don't seek to be exalted on your own but wait patiently for God to give you what you are due.

READ YOUR BIBLE!

Your word is a lamp for my feet, a light on my path.
PSALM 119:105 NIV

Life is busy, isn't it? We spend 8-plus hours a day, 5-plus days a week working, and then we have to make time for family, for friends, and for church and church-related activities. Sometimes we're squeezed for time, and one of the first casualties is time alone with God in prayer and Bible reading.

The psalmist who wrote today's verse understood that the Word of God gives believers direction and lights the way as we follow its leading. But the apostle Paul had much more to say about what the Bible does for us: "All Scripture is God-breathed and is useful for teaching, rebuking, correcting and training in righteousness, so that the servant of God may be thoroughly equipped for every good work" (2 Timothy 3:16–17 NIV).

So the words recorded in scripture lead and guide us, instruct us, rebuke and correct us, and teach us what it means to be righteous. Can there be any question as to how important it is that we spend time reading God's Word?

Reading books and other material about the Bible is a good thing, and attending group Bible studies is probably even better. But nothing should ever take the place of spending time alone with God, reading and meditating on His written Word.

YOUR CONSCIENCE CAN BE YOUR GUIDE

*Holding on to faith and a good conscience,
which some have rejected and so have
suffered shipwreck with regard to the faith.*

1 TIMOTHY 1:19 NIV

God has given human beings the wonderful gift of a conscience—a sense of right and wrong. But the human conscience was exposed to damage when sin entered into the human experience, when Adam and Eve chose to disobey the one commandment God had given them (see Genesis 3). Since that moment, sin has damaged the conscience of every human being.

When you first received the free gift of salvation through Jesus Christ, God placed His Holy Spirit within you. Part of the Holy Spirit's role in your Christian life is to alert you when you're about to make a choice that doesn't please God. That is partly what Jesus meant when He told His followers that the Spirit would "guide you into all the truth" (John 16:13 NIV).

When God's Holy Spirit is inside you, He allows you to better understand the truths of scripture, which are the basis for every decision we make. And when we have the Spirit playing that role in our lives, we can safely allow our conscience to be our guide.

LEARNING CONTENTMENT

I know what it is to be in need, and I know what it is to have plenty. I have learned the secret of being content in any and every situation, whether well fed or hungry, whether living in plenty or in want.

PHILIPPIANS 4:12 NIV

Modern advertisers and marketers have tapped into something about our fallen human nature that makes too many of us easy marks as customers who buy what we don't need and oftentimes can't afford.

The world around us does all it can to make us believe that we don't have everything we need, and if we're not careful, we can find ourselves falling into attitudes of discontent because we don't have the newest and best things.

The apostle Paul learned that contentment had less to do with his setting in life (he was in a Roman prison when he wrote to the Philippian church), with his possessions (he had few), or with physical provision (he had apparently experienced real hunger) and everything to do with the fact that he was doing what God had called him to do.

Paul is an amazing example of what true contentment looks like. While we too often feel the pangs of discontent because we don't have the latest and best (fill in the blank), Paul knew how to feel content when he didn't even have a place to stay, enough to eat, or safe travels.

THE IMPORTANCE OF PLANNING

The plans of the diligent lead to profit
as surely as haste leads to poverty.
PROVERBS 21:5 NIV

The word *planning* sometimes gets a bad rap among certain segments of the Christian world. Some don't think it's important to make a plan; instead, they would rather keep their options open and let the Holy Spirit guide their every step on the fly.

Other believers, when God gives them a vision for something, want to plan everything out to the smallest detail so that they don't head out in the wrong direction.

Is either approach necessarily wrong? Like many things in the Word of God, there is usually a point of balance between moving when God calls you to move and making sure you have a plan of action.

There may be times when God directs you to move immediately (see Abram in Genesis 12:1–4), but in most instances, when He gives you a vision for something He wants to accomplish through you, it's wise to avoid rushing into it before you carefully plan and weigh your options.

So by all means, have a plan. But just make sure that you prayerfully and humbly submit your planning process to God so that He can guide you in every step you take.

GOD HONORS HARD WORK

A sluggard's appetite is never filled, but the desires of the diligent are fully satisfied.
PROVERBS 13:4 NIV

It might be hard at times to believe it (especially when it's time to get up each Monday morning), but from the very beginning, God intended for man to work. His first assignment for Adam was to live in the Garden of Eden and "to work it and take care of it" (Genesis 2:15 NIV). Sadly, when Adam and Eve sinned, work turned into toil—and it has been that way ever since (see Genesis 3).

But the fact still remains that it is God's will that each man work and produce. Not only that, He warns against laziness in today's scripture and encourages us to work hard and with diligence. He tells us that laziness leads to poverty and that those who demonstrate diligence in their work will find that their needs are met.

So work hard. Approach what you do for a living with commitment and passion. And as you work so you can provide well for yourself and your family, don't forget Paul's words: "So whether you eat or drink or whatever you do, do it all for the glory of God" (1 Corinthians 10:31 NIV).

LIVING WITH INTEGRITY

At this, the administrators and the satraps tried to
find grounds for charges against Daniel in his conduct
of government affairs, but they were unable to do so.
They could find no corruption in him, because he was
trustworthy and neither corrupt nor negligent.
DANIEL 6:4 NIV

The famous Christian motivational speaker Zig Ziglar once said, "With integrity, you have nothing to fear, since you have nothing to hide. With integrity, you will do the right thing, so you will have no guilt."

The Old Testament prophet Daniel demonstrated integrity in every part of his life. He honored God—and God honored the prophet in return. . .and also saved him from becoming some hungry lion's lunch (see Daniel 6:10–23).

Daniel had his enemies, but it turns out he had nothing to fear, simply because he had conducted all his affairs in a way that honored and pleased his God.

Bottom line: a real man of God will conduct every part of his life the way the Bible says a man of God should. That's just what integrity looks like.

You honor and please God and establish a good reputation with others when you make sure you live every part of your life—your family life, your work life, and every other aspect—with integrity.

When you do just that, God will honor you in return.

BEING "REAL" WITH GOD

*Immediately the boy's father exclaimed, "I do
believe; help me overcome my unbelief!"*
MARK 9:24 NIV

It's amazing how desperation can often bring out the best
in people. When the chips are down and when our backs
are against the wall (pick your own cliché here), we're
often forced to get real with one another. . .and with God.

The man who spoke the words in today's verse was at
a point where he had no choice but to turn to Jesus for
help. He apparently knew enough about Jesus to know
that He had miraculously healed many people. But it is
equally apparent that he had his doubts as to whether
Jesus could help *him*.

Jesus responded to this man's kernel of faith. . .and to
his honesty. He healed the man's son and then used the
incident to teach His followers some things about real,
mountain-moving, demon-repelling faith.

Jesus repeatedly and consistently taught His followers
that they could do anything if they had faith. Those same
promises hold true for us today. But in those times when
we wonder if we have "enough" faith, when we wonder if
God can reach down and make a difference in our lives,
our best first step might be to confess honestly, "I do
believe, Lord. Help me overcome my unbelief."

Forgive Yourself!

*Therefore, there is now no condemnation
for those who are in Christ Jesus.*
Romans 8:1 niv

Some Christian men haven't quite mastered what it takes to let go of the past. They walk around filled with regret and guilt, believing deep down that even though they've given themselves over to Jesus Christ, God still intends to lower the boom on them for the terrible things they've done.

The Bible calls our spiritual enemy, Satan, the "accuser of our brothers and sisters" (Revelation 12:10 niv) and a "liar" (John 8:44 niv), and he loves few things more than tormenting believers with reminders of their sinful pasts. But the Bible also tells us that there is no condemnation for those of us who belong to Jesus and that our sins are forgiven and buried in a sea of divine forgetfulness (see Micah 7:19).

So no matter what you've done in your past, no matter how awful a sinner you believe you were before Jesus found you, forgave you, and cleansed you, forgive yourself. Let go of your sinful past (God already has) and move on into the wonderful, full life God has given you through the sacrifice of His Son.

BEING PATIENT WITH GOD

Wait for the LORD; be strong and take
heart and wait for the LORD.
PSALM 27:14 NIV

It's so commonly spoken that it's become something of a Christian cliché, but in light of today's verse, it bears repeating here: "God answers prayers in one of three ways—yes, no, and not yet."

Of course we're happy to receive that "Yes" from God, and sometimes we can understand why He says "No." But that "Not yet"—that one can really mess with us. When we pray for something we know is God's will (say, the salvation of a loved one or personal spiritual revival), we're often flummoxed when it doesn't happen right away. So we keep praying—sometimes over a period of years—and waiting.

The scriptural truth of the matter is that God often makes His people wait before He answers their requests. We may not understand why we have to wait, so we must cling to the truth that God's ways and thoughts are different from ours (see Isaiah 55:8).

So be patient and keep seeking God. He has made literally hundreds of promises in scripture, and His track record of keeping them still stands at 100 percent.

Our part of this grand bargain is to wait patiently, knowing that God's very nature keeps Him from letting us down.

ENJOYING INNER PEACE

Great peace have those who love your law,
and nothing can make them stumble.
PSALM 119:165 NIV

One of the great promises of the Gospel message is peace. Somehow, though, many have interpreted that promise as meaning that a new believer's life will be free of troubles and concerns, that God will somehow rid us of all our problems when we commit ourselves to Him.

But nowhere in the Bible will you receive any promise of peace in terms of what life throws your way. The Bible warns that we all have to endure our share of storms and crises. Jesus Himself warned, "In this world you will have trouble" (John 16:33 NIV).

But this same Jesus said, "Peace I leave with you; my peace I give you. I do not give to you as the world gives. Do not let your hearts be troubled and do not be afraid" (John 14:27 NIV).

Jesus wanted His followers to understand that peace isn't about a lack of problems in this world, but about the inner tranquility His followers can and should enjoy even in the most difficult of times.

We enjoy God's inner peace when we do two things: commit to walking with Him daily as His true disciples and focus on Him and not our outer circumstances when we are going through difficult times.

STRENGTH THROUGH TRIBULATIONS

*Not only so, but we also glory in our sufferings,
because we know that suffering produces perseverance.*
ROMANS 5:3 NIV

If we had to guess what words flowed through the pen of the apostle Paul following today's verse, we might try this: "What doesn't kill you makes you stronger."

Of course that's not what Paul wrote, but it might make for a good summary for what he actually jotted down. He wrote that perseverance produces "character; and character, hope. And hope does not put us to shame, because God's love has been poured out into our hearts through the Holy Spirit, who has been given to us" (Romans 5:4–5 NIV).

Right! We might think after reading those words. *What doesn't kill me truly can make me stronger.*

Paul knew as well as anyone that God could and did use his suffering and tribulation (and he endured more than his share of both during his ministry) to strengthen him and to give him the character and drive it took to endure whatever a hostile world threw at him.

Just as an athlete's training regimen (the weight lifting and the cardio work alike) tears his body down but later makes it stronger and more fit for competition, tribulation can make us stronger, more Christlike, and better fit for the work God has given us to do.

Gossip—Stop It!

A gossip betrays a confidence,
but a trustworthy person keeps a secret.
Proverbs 11:13 niv

"Gossip is one of those all-too-common sins that we might think of as a 'little' one". . .certainly not on par with the "biggies" like adultery, murder, or theft.

But when you look at what the Bible has to say about gossip, you'll find that God takes it very, very seriously.

In the first chapter of Paul's letter to the Romans, he writes about God's punishment on sinful humans for their lawlessness. He goes on to provide a list of sinful individuals whose behavior makes them deserving of God's judgment. Right there in verse 29 is the word *gossips*.

Let's get real with ourselves here. God hates gossip, and He hates it because it destroys what He has created and has worked so hard to restore and protect—the name of another person.

So let's be very careful not just in what we say *to* another person, but also what we say *about* him or her. Let's think before we speak about another. Let's ask ourselves first if what we are about to say is true. Then let's ask ourselves if our words are loving and helpful. . .or if they just damage another's reputation.

And if the words we are about to speak don't pass muster, let's keep them to ourselves.

SEEING GOD IN CREATION

*"But ask the animals, and they will teach you, or the birds
in the sky, and they will tell you; or speak to the earth,
and it will teach you, or let the fish in the sea inform
you. Which of all these does not know that the
hand of the LORD has done this?"*
JOB 12:7–9 NIV

There are all kinds of settings in which you can spend time with God and enjoy His presence. Today's verse teaches us that we can see the greatness of God and experience His presence in a setting too few of us get to enjoy these days: in nature.

Ask believers who enjoy spending time outdoors (hiking, camping, fishing, hunting, and other activities) and they'll likely tell you that natural settings are places where they see God's greatness and creativity, where they communicate with Him. . .and where He communicates with them.

Job certainly understood this truth. He had apparently pondered the greatness of God in the natural world around him.

Your time with God in a natural setting should never take the place of time spent in fellowship with other believers, and it should never crowd out "quiet time" spent reading God's Word and praying. But, as Job points out, you can find great blessing in seeing God's handiwork and experience His presence when you spend time enjoying creation and everything in it.

FEELING SMALL?

When I consider your heavens, the work of your fingers,
the moon and the stars, which you have set in place,
what is mankind that you are mindful of them,
human beings that you care for them?
PSALM 8:3–4 NIV

The story is told of a naturalist named William Beebe, who was a good friend of President Theodore Roosevelt. After dinner one night, the two men went for a walk. Roosevelt pointed skyward and observed, "That is the Spiral Galaxy in Andromeda. It is as large as our Milky Way. It is one of a hundred billion galaxies. It consists of one hundred billion stars, each larger than our sun. Now I think we are small enough. Let's go to bed."

King David lived thousands of years before Roosevelt, so he had no real clue as to the vastness of the created universe. Still, what he *could* observe with his naked eye in the skies over Israel way back then still astonished him. But even more amazing to him was the fact that the God who had created it all could look down from His throne in heaven and not just take notice of him, but love him and think about him.

That's a wonderful thought, isn't it? We should never lose our sense of awe and wonder that the all-powerful God who created such a vast cosmos is the same all-loving God who cares so deeply for us as individuals.

KINGDOM WORK—JUST KEEP AT IT!

*Let us not become weary in doing good, for at the proper
time we will reap a harvest if we do not give up.*
GALATIANS 6:9 NIV

Think of some of the great preachers in Christian history.
From the apostles Peter and Paul all the way through the
centuries to men like Billy Graham, certain preachers are
exceptional in our eyes because the results of their work
are both obvious and tremendous.

But it's not like that for every kingdom laborer. Far
from it!

God never promised us that working for Him would
be easy—or that we'd see a huge harvest of souls or large
numbers of lives changed through that work. We don't
always see the results of our hard work for the kingdom
of God in the short run; in fact, we may not see them at
all this side of heaven. But Galatians 6:9 promises us that
if we persevere in our good work for the Lord, we *will*
share with Him in the joy of seeing the furthering of His
eternal kingdom.

So when you begin to wonder whether you're making
a difference in the world around you, don't give up. Just
keep doing what God has laid on your heart to do, and
He'll take care of the rest.

THE FATHER'S DELIGHT

"The LORD your God is with you, the Mighty Warrior
who saves. He will take great delight in you; in his love
he will no longer rebuke you, but will rejoice
over you with singing."
ZEPHANIAH 3:17 NIV

The Old Testament prophet Zephaniah wrote his prophecy during a very difficult time for the nation of Israel. His message is one of coming judgments on God's chosen people. But the book ends with wonderful promises of restoration—restoration of the loving, close relationship between God and His people.

The third chapter of Zephaniah is a series of promises and encouragements, all of which God directs at His people today. It tells us that God isn't just a God who loves His people but also a God who takes delight in us— such delight that His heart breaks out in song.

The promises in today's verse point to a time when God "'will wipe every tear from their eyes. There will be no more death' or mourning or crying or pain, for the old order of things has passed away" (Revelation 21:4 NIV).

This is the beginning of eternal life in the paradise that is heaven, the beginning of an eternity in the presence of the One who will no longer correct or rebuke us—and who will celebrate our presence as much as we do His.

A MOST IMPORTANT COMMAND

Whoever claims to love God yet hates a brother or sister is a liar. For whoever does not love their brother and sister, whom they have seen, cannot love God, whom they have not seen. And he has given us this command: Anyone who loves God must also love their brother and sister.

1 JOHN 4:20–21 NIV

Let's face it: some people are very difficult to love. They're too loud, too opinionated, too overbearing, too unlearned, too. . .you get the point. But the apostle John had some very strong words as to how we as followers of Christ are to relate to even the most unlovable among us.

If you can't love someone who's right in front of you, John taught, *then how can you say you love a God you can't even see?* That's putting John's message rhetorically, for of course the answer is that saying we love God but not the people He's placed in our lives makes us. . .well, liars.

Ouch!

So when you encounter one of the "unlovable"—and there are plenty of them out there!—love them the way Jesus loved, unconditionally and sacrificially. And when your words and acts of love don't change them in the least, love them all the more. It's God's job to change people. . . . It's your job to love them the same way He loves you.

DIVINE FORGETFULNESS

*"I, even I, am he who blots out your transgressions, for my
own sake, and remembers your sins no more."*
ISAIAH 43:25 NIV

If you think about it, part of the message behind
today's verse might seem to contradict the very nature
of God. Sure, we can grasp—and celebrate in—the
fact that God forgives our sins and cleanses us from
all unrighteousness. But how can a God who knows
everything that has happened or will happen in eternity
past and in eternity future forget something?

Let's put this in human perspective for just a moment.
Suppose someone close to you does or says something
to cause you pain or loss. It may be a matter of simple
carelessness, or it could have been something done
intentionally. Either way, you've decided that it is far
better to forgive that person and restore the relationship
than it is to cling to wrongs done and let it die. You can't
literally forget the offense committed, but you can forget
any thought of punishing that person for what he or she
has done to you.

God's "forgetfulness" is a lot like that. He remembers
sins we've committed against Him, but when we come to
Him in humble repentance, He forgives us and casts away
any thought of vengeance against us.

CHOOSING FRIENDS WISELY

*Do not make friends with a hot-tempered person,
do not associate with one easily angered, or you may
learn their ways and get yourself ensnared.*
PROVERBS 22:24–25 NIV

People with bad tempers can be very unpleasant to be around. Sure, they can be good company—as long as other people and life itself are treating them the way they deserve to be treated. But when some offense comes, the ill-tempered can react with unkind words and unkind (or even violent or dangerous) actions.

The Bible includes some simple but very sound wisdom when it comes to dealing with hot-tempered people: stay clear! Sure, we're going to encounter people with bad tempers (and other sinful attitudes and behaviors), but today's passage advises us to avoid socializing too much with these kinds of people.

Our God is all-knowing and all-wise, and He understands far better than we do that we tend to adopt the behaviors of those closest to us. He also knows that a person with a bad temper is headed for disaster, and He will do everything He can to make sure His people don't end up in the same place.

That includes giving us this simple bit of wisdom: don't spend your time with a hothead!

ONE-ON-ONE INTERVENTIONS

Better is open rebuke than hidden love. Wounds from a friend can be trusted, but an enemy multiplies kisses.
PROVERBS 27:5–6 NIV

Confrontation is uncomfortable for most people. We don't like being told that we're harboring sinful or unhealthy attitudes or taking part in actions that displease God or cause others pain. And it can be even harder to be "that guy"—the one who must somehow summon the courage it takes to confront a friend who so desperately needs it.

But the Bible tells us that a true friend is one who is willing to risk the friendship and say what needs to be said to a brother or sister in the Lord who is either living with obvious sin or has some kind of "blind spot" that keeps him or her from living or thinking in a way that pleases God.

It's easy to decide to just mind your own business when your friend strays from God's standards of living and thinking. But today's verse teaches us that part of being a real friend is being willing, no matter how uncomfortable it may be, to speak difficult truth to those you love—and to do it gently and firmly.

Do you have that kind of friend? And can you *be* that kind of friend?

"I'll Pray for You"

*"My intercessor is my friend as my eyes pour out
tears to God; on behalf of a man he pleads
with God as one pleads for a friend."*
Job 16:20–21 niv

The Bible has a lot to teach us about how to pray, when to pray, and what to pray for. One type of prayer the Word tells us to engage in regularly is called "intercession," which is a type of prayer in which we "stand in the gap" before God on behalf of another person.

But just how important is it to God that His people intercede in prayer for others? So important that Jesus, His very own Son, spends His time in heaven interceding for us this very moment (see Hebrews 7:23–28).

When a friend, a family member, or a brother or sister in Christ is hurting and in need of a touch from the hand of God, it's always good to offer comfort by promising to pray for that person. But as you spend time with the Lord, be sure to make good on that promise. God loves to answer His people's prayers, and He is absolutely delighted to answer prayers of loving concern when we offer them up to Him.

So don't forget to make intercession for others a regular part of your prayer life. Someone may very well be counting on you.

FRIENDS WITH GOD

"I no longer call you servants, because a servant
does not know his master's business. Instead,
I have called you friends, for everything that
I learned from my Father I have
made known to you."
JOHN 15:15 NIV

When we approach the work we do for a living in the right way, we can take great joy in that work. But there is something extra special about the work we do in helping our friends. There's something about getting your hands dirty in simple tasks like helping him move or spending a Saturday helping him paint his home or in more "emotional" ways like offering a listening ear during times of trouble that brings you closer to your friend.

The same is true of the greatest Friend you'll ever know—Jesus, who demonstrated His love for His friends by laying down His own life for us (see John 15:13). When we walk closely with Him, listen to Him, and follow His leading, He calls us His own friends (John 15:14).

Jesus is such a loving Friend that He walked the earth for more than 30 years for us, taught us, died for us, was raised from the grave for us, and now resides in heaven, where He constantly pleads our case before His heavenly Father (see Hebrews 7:25).

As the old hymn says, "What a Friend we have in Jesus!"

THIS IS LIFE

*"Now this is eternal life: that they know you,
the only true God, and Jesus Christ,
whom you have sent."*
JOHN 17:3 NIV

We've all seen those T-shirts bearing the none-too-profound message that "Football Is Life," "Baseball Is Life," or "Basketball Is Life."

There are a lot of easily observable things about American culture, and one of them is that we are absolutely obsessed with sports—youth and high school sports (especially for those of us who have children competing), college sports, and professional sports alike.

There's nothing wrong with enjoying spectator sports—as long as you put them in their proper place in your life. These things are not life, just an enjoyable part of it. When they become an obsession, when they dominate your thinking and the way you live, then they become idols—and we know how God feels about idols!

For the believer, life isn't the work we do, in the recreation we enjoy on the weekends, or in the sports teams we follow. Real life—abundant life and everlasting life—is found in knowing God through Jesus Christ, the One He sent so that we could live eternally.

So feel free to root for your team and to enjoy watching a game. But never forget that these things don't define or make your life.

Your Place in the Big Picture

What, after all, is Apollos? And what is Paul?
Only servants, through whom you came to believe—
as the Lord has assigned to each his task. I planted
the seed, Apollos watered it, but God
has been making it grow.
1 Corinthians 3:5–6 niv

Read most every list of the most important/influential people in the history of Western civilization and you're likely to find the name of the apostle Paul mentioned prominently. Of course, Paul was largely responsible for spreading Christianity throughout the known world, and we can't forget that he wrote most of the New Testament.

But you only need to read today's scripture passage to know that Paul's response to being held in such high esteem in such a list would be along the lines of: "I'm nobody!" Paul understood that God had given him a big assignment, but he also understood that it was God, not him, who was worthy of the glory for the results.

God has given us, His servants, responsibilities that are but small parts in the bigger plan of salvation for others. Our job is to sow the seeds by telling others the truth about salvation through Jesus Christ and to water those seeds through prayer. God's part is to illuminate the message we present (to make the seed grow) and bring people to Him through the work of His Holy Spirit.

Establishing—and Protecting—Your Reputation

A good name is more desirable than great riches;
to be esteemed is better than silver or gold.
Proverbs 22:1 NIV

The great basketball coach John Wooden once said, "Be more concerned with your character than your reputation, because your character is what you really are, while your reputation is merely what others think you are."

Wooden's words point out the simple truth that character and reputation, while they are closely related in many ways, are not the same thing. However, a life defined by godly character—the kind of life committed to treating people well, conducting business with integrity, building a family with true love, and worshipping God in both word and deed—will almost always lead to a good reputation.

There are few things in life that are worth guarding with great passion, and one of those is a good reputation. You can establish and protect a good reputation by making sure that the thoughts you think, the words you speak, and the actions you take are those that please God in every way.

Be Careful What You Look At

*"I made a covenant with my eyes
not to look lustfully at a young woman."*
JOB 31:1 NIV

You probably know this already, but if you were to poll those at your weekly men's Bible study about their top struggle in the Christian walk, it would probably have something to do with sexual lust. They'd likely tell you that their eyes go where they shouldn't, and then it's only a matter of moments before the mind follows.

It probably wouldn't come as news to you if someone were to tell you that it's not easy to avoid seeing lust-inducing images in today's world. We live in an R-rated world, and even movies and television shows containing a PG rating often, if not usually, include scenes that can cause the mind to wander to places God doesn't want it to go.

So how do we win this seemingly overwhelming battle? It's a matter of commitment—or, as Job put it, making a covenant with your eyes not to look at images that cause you to stumble into lustful thinking.

So far as it depends on your personal choices, make a covenant with your eyes not to intentionally view lust-inducing images. And when you make a commitment to focus on the right things—namely your love for your family and your God—you will find yourself winning the battle for your mind.

STOP YOUR GRIPING!

Do everything without grumbling or arguing, so that you may become blameless and pure, "children of God without fault in a warped and crooked generation."
PHILIPPIANS 2:14–15 NIV

Let's face it—life can sometimes feel like one frustrating situation after another. Who among us, when circumstances put the squeeze on us, hasn't felt like just griping and complaining to anyone who will listen?

While the Bible contains some examples of godly men who complained to God (David and Job, for example), it also warns us against grumbling and complaining, and also shows us that having a complaining attitude and mouth can have very negative consequences (see Numbers 14).

When we complain, we separate ourselves from God and His peace and we also ruin our testimony for Christ to a lost and hurting world. After all, who wants to listen to someone offering answers when that person constantly gripes about his own life?

So in those times when you don't think life is being fair to you, remember to do as the apostle Paul instructed and "give thanks in all circumstances; for this is God's will for you in Christ Jesus" (1 Thessalonians 5:18 NIV). Also remember God's promise that "in all things God works for the good of those who love him, who have been called according to his purpose" (Romans 8:28 NIV).

GIVING—WITH THE RIGHT MOTIVES

*"So when you give to the needy, do not announce it
with trumpets, as the hypocrites do in the synagogues
and on the streets, to be honored by others. Truly I tell
you, they have received their reward in full."*
MATTHEW 6:2 NIV

We may not want to admit it, but it can be easy to
wonder, *What's in it for me?* when we think of giving to
others. Jesus understood this part of fallen human nature,
and that's why He told His followers not to seek human
recognition when we give.

When we think of the word *giving*, our minds usually
go to the financial. But God also calls us to give of our
time, of our efforts, of any other of the gifts He's given
us. But no matter what we find ourselves in a position to
give, the principle stands the same. When we give, we're
to do it in a way so that only God—and sometimes the
recipient—knows about it.

So give—give generously. But when you give, make
sure your heart and mind are free of any desire for human
recognition or any other earthly reward. When you give
with a pure heart that is motivated by the desire to glorify
God and bless others, God will honor your giving and
bless you in return.

THANK GOD IT'S MONDAY!

This is the day which the Lord has made;
let us rejoice and be glad in it.
PSALM 118:24 NASB

Many men live for the weekends. They only tolerate their jobs because they pay the bills and it's better than being unemployed. That's not an ideal attitude, but there's definitely value in perseverance. Other men like their work. Still. . .sometimes when the workload is heavy, the pressure intense, or coworkers unpleasant, even normally enjoyable employment becomes drudgery. At times like these, most guys don't look forward to Monday morning. But dreading a new week will guarantee frustration and defeat. That's why men need to pause in the morning to commit the day to God in prayer.

God has made this day, and He supplies the grace to face it. Men don't need to just grit their teeth and bear it. They can be glad in it. One time, Nehemiah's workers were discouraged by steady conflict and worn out by the immensity of their tasks, so Nehemiah encouraged them, saying, "The joy of the Lord is your strength" (Nehemiah 8:10 NKJV). They couldn't rejoice in their troubles, but they *could* rejoice in the Lord. Like them, if we continually remind ourselves that the all-powerful God is with us, we can literally rejoice—even if it's Monday.

BEING BOLD

The wicked flee when no one pursues,
but the righteous are bold as a lion.
PROVERBS 28:1 NKJV

Every February 2, many news commentators take a break from serious reporting to do a special on Groundhog Day. They gather around a drowsy groundhog's burrow as it emerges and watch its reaction. According to an old wives' tale, if it's cloudy and the groundhog can't see its shadow, spring will come early. If it's sunny, the groundhog will be startled by its shadow and retreat back to the safety of its burrow—and there'll be six more weeks of winter. Like that groundhog, believers are sometimes afraid of their own shadows. God warned that if His people disobeyed Him, their courage would depart and be replaced by anxiety: "'The sound of a shaken leaf shall cause them to flee; they shall flee as though fleeing from a sword, and they shall fall when no one pursues'" (Leviticus 26:36 NKJV). You can have this problem if you compromise biblical principles or willfully disobey God. You then lose the conviction that He's with you to protect you, prosper you, and bring you success. As a result, you become afraid to launch out into new ventures. It can get to the point where you don't even want to get out of bed. The solution is to repent of any sin that separates you from God's blessing. He doesn't demand perfection, but He does call you to keep a clean heart and seek Him sincerely. Do that and you'll once again experience power and boldness.

Solid and Steady

Tell the older men to have self-control and to be serious and sensible. Their faith, love, and patience must never fail.
Titus 2:2 cev

As they get older, most men naturally become more serious and sensible. In fact, a common complaint is that old men are overly serious and practical. They've lost their sense of fun and adventure to such an extent that they become *unreasonably* sensible, if such a thing can be. At least that's what many younger men think. But while older Christian men should retain a zest for life and be able to lighten up at times, God intended them to be steady pillars of their families, societies, and churches. Some things—such as serving God—are *meant* to be taken seriously.

Advancing age tends to bring about this change in men, but full maturity still requires effort on their part. They must also have exercised a lifetime of self-control. For many people, sexual purity comes to mind when they think of self-control, and this is an important aspect of it, but self-control must extend to every area of a man's life. He must also govern any tendency toward greed or selfishness; he must constantly exercise control over his temper; he must maintain a daily habit of prayer and devotions. Victory in all these areas doesn't happen overnight. It takes years of faithfulness and self-discipline, but it's worth it in the long haul. If a man does these things and *continues* doing them as he gets older, his patience, his love, and his faith will never fail.

Knowing What You Believe

*Always be prepared to give an answer to everyone who
asks you to give the reason for the hope that you have.
But do this with gentleness and respect.*

1 Peter 3:15 NIV

Men who love baseball usually develop an impressive level
of expertise on the subject. They're self-taught, yes, but
they often know all the players on their favorite teams,
how many home runs each one has made, their batting
averages, etc. And it doesn't take much prompting to
get them to talk enthusiastically about the subject. The
same applies to men who are passionate about politics:
they have strong, well-informed, clearly defined opinions,
and they don't hesitate to share them with people of
opposing viewpoints. The Bible tells believers that
they should be the same way about their faith—with
gentleness and respect, of course. They should always be
prepared to give an answer and explain why they believe.
Many men, however, know surprisingly little about their
faith. But the remedy is simple. They must study their
Bibles daily. This may seem like a daunting task, but it
will be easy if they're as passionate about God as they
are about baseball or politics. Once they're fascinated by
the message of Jesus, they gladly immerse themselves in
it. It's not a chore. It's a joy. And as they read and spend
time praying over it, they discover countless truths. Then,
explaining what they believe comes easy. Even if they're
"only" self-taught, if they're full of their subject, they'll be
prepared to give a reason.

SHIFTING OUT OF WORK MODE

Better to be patient than powerful; better to have self-control than to conquer a city.
PROVERBS 16:32 NLT

Most men are purpose-driven, goal-oriented beings. God designed them this way so that they concentrate on their life's mission. They're literally hardwired to be focused and ambitious, and these traits impel them toward success. But many men focus inordinately on building a career. They're like heat-seeking missiles locked on target and they ignore all distractions. This can be a good thing—except when those "distractions" are their family. That's why a man must learn to consciously shift gears when the day ends and leave his work at the office. Otherwise he'll walk through the door of his home still trying to solve work problems and tune out his family. He'll become impatient when his wife requires his attention or his children make demands on his time. Now, his business may be focused on conquering the city and his job may make serious demands of him, but on the drive home he must exercise self-control and refocus on those dearest to him. He must truly value and be thankful for his wife. He must realize that success is not only defined by a job well done but by his love and care for his children. It often takes effort to focus on the home scene. It takes self-control to keep his mind from drifting to a work issue. But the rewards and joys that come from giving undivided attention to his family make the effort well worth it.

WAIT FOR THE LORD

*Wait for the LORD; be strong and let your heart
take courage; yes, wait for the LORD.*
PSALM 27:14 NASB

It can be maddening when a situation demands
immediate action yet you're not able to do a thing. Things
are out of control, and you have the sickening feeling that
they're *not* going to end well. The roof might be caving
in on an important project at work, or a family situation
is going from bad to worse. On top of it, your boss—or
your wife—demands that you think of *something*, that you
do *something*. But you've already tried everything and
nothing works.

At times like this, the best thing to do is pray. Commit
your problem into God's hands then wait for Him to act.
That's sometimes a very difficult thing to do, because
you've learned by now that God doesn't always have your
sense of priorities or work according to your schedule.
Yet twice in today's one short verse it says, "Wait for
the LORD." And while you're waiting, "be strong." Don't
give up. Don't throw in the towel, but "let your heart
take courage." And the best way to have courage is to
trust that God is going to answer prayer and resolve the
situation.

Things may continue to look hopeless for a while,
but God will come through for you. He will either inspire
you with a solution you hadn't thought of before or He
Himself will do a miracle to solve the problem. So take
courage. Wait for the Lord.

SUPER BOWL SUNDAY

And also if anyone competes in athletics, he is not crowned unless he competes according to the rules.
2 TIMOTHY 2:5 NKJV

Today isn't an official holiday, but to many men, Super Bowl Sunday is one of the most important days on the calendar. It's the annual championship game of the NFL, the most watched show of the year, when millions of men across America sit glued to their TVs, devouring vast quantities of food. It's a loud, raucous time, full of excitement, camaraderie, and fun. But sometimes it ends in groans and disappointment, especially if a winning play is disqualified because a player on your favorite team used excessive force or ran out of bounds. When the outcome of the game is hanging in the balance, you *don't* want to see the referees award a free kick or penalty kick to the opposing team. This holds true for everyday life as well. Too many men bend the rules, fudge the figures on their expense account, make dubious claims in their tax returns, or fail to deliver on their promises. For a time, they seem to get away with it. They break free from the pack, surge ahead, and enjoy great "success." They may even score a touchdown. But then the whistle blows. The foul is called out and replayed in agonizing detail for the world to see as the moment of victory turns into defeat. The Bible says that athletes aren't crowned unless they compete according to the rules. This is true in the NFL, and it's true in everyday life.

SUFFERING CHRISTIANS

We didn't want any of you to be discouraged by all these troubles. You knew we would have to suffer, because when we were with you, we told you this would happen.
1 THESSALONIANS 3:3–4 CEV

Today is the first day of the Chinese New Year, and it's a good time to think about China and the multitudes of Christians who live there. According to a 2010 survey, there are now some 52 million Christians in China. While the West has largely forgotten the church behind the Bamboo Curtain, God has been very busy! But great revival has come with a price tag. Many of these believers are ostracized or oppressed or shut out of good jobs. Many suffer intense persecution, including prison, hard labor, and torture. They take their stand for Christ seriously and are willing to suffer and even die for Him. They're aware that suffering is to be expected. It doesn't surprise them. And persecution isn't unique to China. Paul wrote, "Yes, and all who desire to live godly in Christ Jesus will suffer persecution" (2 Timothy 3:12 NKJV). In North America, persecution usually involves being rejected by friends and enduring mockery and backbiting. For the most part, what Western Christians experience is mild compared to what believers in China and other lands endure. So the Bible tells you to remember persecuted believers in prayer (Hebrews 13:3). Pray that they can lead tranquil and quiet lives (1 Timothy 2:2) and that God will gain victories even through their suffering.

HONEST, SINCERE CHRISTIANITY

*The seeds that fell on the good soil represent honest,
good-hearted people who hear God's word, cling to it,
and patiently produce a huge harvest.*
LUKE 8:15 NLT

Many people are so used to thinking that the Parable of the Sower describes salvation that they miss its other important lessons. Now, it does talk about getting saved, but the moment of salvation is part of a larger picture. Jesus didn't intend for you to simply get a ticket to heaven then shift into cruise mode until you die. Being saved is the beginning of an entirely new lifestyle, where "honest, good-hearted people" who accept the Gospel then set out to live it. You must not only hear God's Word but cling tenaciously to it and, as a result, produce good fruit that stands the test of time. And it comes from hearing and obeying the words of Jesus. Moses told the children of Israel, "Take to heart all the words I have solemnly declared to you this day. . .They are not just idle words for you—they are your life" (Deuteronomy 32:46–47 NIV). And this is true for you today as well. You are to be "nourished in the words of faith and of the good doctrine which you have carefully followed" (1 Timothy 4:6 NKJV). You should not only *hear* God's Word but be spiritually nourished by it, cling to it, and carefully follow its instructions. Have you ever wondered what the secret to a victorious life is? This is it.

LENT

"Repent, and believe in the gospel."
MARK 1:15 NKJV

Ash Wednesday is a day of fasting that marks the first day of the Lent season. It's a traditional observance to help believers purify their hearts before Easter. Jesus fasted for forty days in the desert, so Lent mirrors this, beginning forty days before Jesus' resurrection on Easter Sunday. Ash Wednesday starts this six-week season. During the rest of Lent, Christians pray, repent of their sins, give alms, and practice self-denial. The term "Ash Wednesday" came about because the palm branches used on the previous year's Palm Sunday were burned and blessed, and the following year the priest or minister smeared these ashes on believers' foreheads as crosses while saying, "Repent, and believe in the Gospel" or "Remember that you are dust, and to dust you shall return." This practice is a little too liturgical for some modern Christians, but many believers find beauty and rich meaning in such traditions. They see it as a daily reminder (for forty days) of the need to keep their hearts clean and their lives dedicated to the Lord. Observing Lent while focusing on their need for forgiveness and the power of Christ to forgive also helps them appreciate the sacrifice He made on the cross. And the final day of Lent, Resurrection Sunday, is a joyful reminder of Christ's glorious resurrection and His eternal victory over sin and death.

NATURAL AND SUPERNATURAL TALENTS

*[Huram's] father was. . .a skilled craftsman in bronze.
Huram was filled with wisdom, with understanding
and with knowledge to do all kinds of bronze work.*
1 KINGS 7:14 NIV

When the Israelites were in the desert, God chose Bezalel to create all the items for His worship tent. God said, "I have filled him with the Spirit of God, with wisdom, with understanding, with knowledge and with all kinds of skills" (Exodus 31:3 NIV). One of Bezalel's many skills was bronze work. It sounds like God supernaturally anointed Bezalel to do this. But what about Huram? When King Solomon wanted to build God's temple, there was an even greater need for a skilled bronze worker. But God didn't say that Huram's talents were a supernatural gift. In fact, the Bible points out that Huram's *father* was a skilled bronze worker, indicating that Huram had inherited his abilities. They were a natural talent. Plus, his father trained him. That accounted for his knowledge and understanding. But the thing is, even if he was *born* with this talent, it was still a God-given gift. After all, God was the One who wired his DNA and gave him his aptitudes and abilities. The same applies to you today. You may come from a long line of mechanics and the talent may run in your family, but God is the one who gives such gifts—both to families and to individuals. But it's up to you to work to improve your ability. And when you're praying and seeking to serve God, He gives you an extra anointing to be even more skillful.

SERVING OTHERS

*He sat down, called the twelve disciples over to him,
and said, "Whoever wants to be first must take last
place and be the servant of everyone else."*
MARK 9:35 NLT

Many men are leery of the concept of servanthood.
While they understand the need to love their fellow man
and to live honest, virtuous lives—somehow the idea of
being a servant of everyone makes no sense. They can
understand being helpful, even occasionally going out of
their way to lend a hand, but consistently putting others
first and themselves last is an alien concept. It doesn't
seem practical. Yet Jesus stated this on more than one
occasion. In Mark's Gospel, Jesus said, "Whoever wants
to be first must take last place and be the servant of
everyone else." This needs to be understood in context.
His disciples had been arguing about which of them
would be greatest in His coming kingdom. They all
wanted to be first. Jesus, however, informed them that if
they *truly* wanted to be first, they must put themselves
last in their lives. It depended on how badly they wanted
exalted positions in heaven. If they served others,
God would see to it that they were rewarded beyond
measure. But if they didn't want to pay such a price,
they'd still go to heaven; they just wouldn't be as greatly
rewarded. There was no compulsion. It was up to them.
Christ commanded, "Store up for yourselves treasures in
heaven" (Matthew 6:20 NIV), and then told them a surefire
way to obtain that treasure. The question is: How badly
do you want eternal rewards?

REFUSING TO COMPLAIN

Do not say, "Why were the old days better than these?"
For it is not wise to ask such questions.
ECCLESIASTES 7:10 NIV

Many older men can remember when the economy was in a steady upward climb and financial stability was the norm. Middle-aged men miss the years before the Great Recession when they could take job security for granted. Young men were just entering the labor pool when the global downturn hit and all the rules changed. And everyone has the tendency to ask, "Why were the old days better than these?" While this may be a natural question, the Bible says it's not wise to look at life that way, because basically it's just a complaint. People don't like the way things are and don't feel they can stay on top of things. It's a lack of trusting God. Now, this is not to make light of the situation you face. Times *are* difficult, and for you they may be *very* difficult. But complaining won't make things better. It will only contribute to defeat. Instead, you must "gird up the loins of your mind" (1 Peter 1:13 NKJV) and refuse to give in to despair. If beans and rice are the new normal, you must learn to make the most of them, knowing that hard times won't last forever. In the meantime, you can say with Paul, "I have learned the secret of being content in any and every situation. . .whether living in plenty or in want" (Philippians 4:12 NIV). Having a satisfied mind and refusing to give up leads to victory.

ENDURING LOVE

Many waters cannot quench love; rivers cannot sweep it away. If one were to give all the wealth of one's house for love, it would be utterly scorned.
SONG OF SONGS 8:7 NIV

St. Valentine's Day began as a feast day for a Christian martyr named Valentinus—in English, Valentine. According to one legend, while Valentine was in prison, he healed the daughter of his jailer. Then, just before his execution, he wrote her a letter and closed with the words, "Your Valentine."

Many people are enthralled with the idea of romantic love, and it's the theme of the majority of pop songs. They think that the euphoric feeling of "being in love" is the ultimate human experience. It is pleasant, but it's only the effect of a few cents' worth of the love chemical serotonin coursing through their brains. Serotonin is responsible for feelings of infatuation and obsessing over someone. After this initial "in love" stage, however, a chemical called oxytocin is responsible for a desire for long-term attachment. Many people go through life constantly falling in and out of "love," pursuing emotional rushes from new serotonin fixes. But marriages need unselfish love if they are to survive. Only then will love be strong enough so that waters of emotional storms cannot quench it and rivers of hard times cannot sweep it away.

PRAY FOR LEADERS (GOOD AND BAD)

*I urge that entreaties and prayers, petitions and
thanksgivings, be made. . .for kings and all who
are in authority, so that we may lead a tranquil
and quiet life in all godliness and dignity.*

1 TIMOTHY 2:1–2 NASB

In 1879, Congress declared George Washington's birthday, February 22, a federal holiday. These days, it usually goes by the name "Presidents' Day" and is celebrated on the third Monday of February. It's very scriptural to honor a nation's leaders. Peter commanded the early Christians, "Honor the king" (1 Peter 2:17 NKJV), referring to Caesar, king of the Roman Empire. It's easy to respect great leaders who rule wisely, bring peace and prosperity, and demonstrate strong leadership during times of crisis. However, at the time that Peter wrote "Honor the king," Nero was going insane and persecuting Christians. So you are even to honor rulers who aren't that godly or wise. One of the best ways to do that is to pray for them. Paul told Christians to pray "for kings and all who are in authority" (1 Timothy 2:2 NASB), and that includes rulers you don't like and didn't vote for. It's in your own interest to do so. After all, poor decisions and government mismanagement causes emergencies and shortages, so if you desire to live a quiet, prosperous life, you must pray that God gives your leaders wisdom. It's not enough to vote in national and local elections; you must also continually pray for anyone who is elected.

SHAMELESS PERSISTENCE

"But I tell you this—though he won't do it for friendship's sake, if you keep knocking long enough, he will get up and give you whatever you need because of your shameless persistence."

LUKE 11:8 NLT

Jesus told a story about a man whose friend arrived at his house at midnight. The friend was famished, but the man had nothing to feed him. But he remembered that his neighbor had some bread. So he ran to his neighbor's house, beat on his door, and shouted till he woke him up. His neighbor crossly replied that the door was locked and he was in bed, so he wasn't about to get up and give him anything. The fact that they were friends made no difference. But Jesus pointed out that if the man refused to take "no" for an answer and continued pounding and calling, the neighbor *would* finally get up and give him bread. This was shameless audacity at its finest. Jesus then applied this lesson to prayer: "And so I tell you, keep on asking, and you will receive what you ask for" (verse 9). Now, don't miss the point: God isn't a grumpy neighbor who must be pestered before He begrudgingly answers. Jesus was emphasizing the importance of persistence. State your request and state it again—and again and again, until the answer comes. Some people think that repeating a request shows a lack of faith, but you can be sure that the man *knew* that if he kept knocking long enough, he'd be given what he was asking for. So be shamelessly persistent.

Uncertain Wealth

Will you set your eyes on that which is not?
For riches certainly make themselves wings;
they fly away like an eagle toward heaven.

Proverbs 23:5 NKJV

Riches are "that which is not." They appear to be solid but can quickly come to nothing. In other words, as solid and enduring as a gold Krugerrand might seem, it's actually more like a drop of water dancing in a hot frying pan, getting smaller and smaller until it finally sizzles into nothingness. Those who work in the stock market see this often. Most men, in fact, have experienced enough jolts and setbacks to testify to the truth of this principle. And even if you manage to frugally sock away vast riches in a secure savings account where they steadily increase, you will *still* be separated from your wealth. . .guaranteed! "The hot sun rises and the grass withers; the little flower droops and falls, and its beauty fades away. In the same way, the rich will fade away" (James 1:11 NLT). You yourself will fly away toward heaven, an eternal realm where temporal riches mean nothing at all. So Paul advises believers not to trust in their money "which is so unreliable," and adds, "Their trust should be in God, who richly gives us all we need" (1 Timothy 6:17 NLT). Certainly you should set aside funds for emergencies and retirement, but ultimately your trust must be in God.

REGULAR SPIRITUAL CHECKUPS

*But exhort one another daily, while it is called
"Today," lest any of you be hardened
through the deceitfulness of sin.*
HEBREWS 3:13 NKJV

Some men stubbornly refuse to go see a doctor even when they're in pain or have had symptoms for some time. They persuade themselves that it's nothing and that it will eventually go away of its own accord. Whatever their reasons, many men put off getting a checkup long after they know something's not right. They often act this way toward their spiritual health as well. God knows the way men reason. He also knows that sin is deceitful. It often begins as an innocent thought, which leads to a not-so-harmless thought, which leads to temptation, which leads to sin. Being tricked into sinning once is bad enough, but when a man frequently gives in to the same vice, over time it hardens into an entrenched habit, not easily rooted out. That's why God counsels men to "exhort one another daily. . . .lest any of you be hardened through the deceitfulness of sin." If you're struggling with a stubborn sin, make yourself accountable to a solid, trusted Christian friend. Then follow up. Go for your spiritual checkup faithfully. You'll be glad you did.

POWER OVER ENEMIES

Though they plot evil against you and devise wicked schemes, they cannot succeed.
PSALM 21:11 NIV

Paul asks, "If God is for us, who can be against us?" (Romans 8:31 NIV). In a glum moment, you might answer, "*Lots* of people." And that's true. Lots of people could set themselves against you. When you read the Psalms you see that David was constantly praying for God to deliver him from new enemies. But the question is: Who can *effectively* oppose you? Who can prevail over you? Isaiah wrote, "'Those who contend with you will be as nothing and will perish. You will seek those who quarrel with you, but will not find them, those who war with you will be as nothing and non-existent'" (Isaiah 41:11–12 NASB). If you're God's child, doing His will and seeking to please Him, your enemies can't succeed. They may utter fearful threats and seem to succeed for a time, but God is on your side. You will prevail. As Romans 8:32–35 says, if God didn't keep back His own Son but sent Him to die for you, won't He also freely give you all things, including protection? So what if your enemies bring charges against you? God is the One who justifies, and He's on your side. So what if men condemn you? Jesus Christ is at God's right hand. He loves you and is interceding for you. And who can separate you from this great love? No one. Trust God, stay close to Him in the Secret Place of the Most High, and He will protect you.

GENTLE MEN OF GOD

*But we were gentle among you, just as a nursing
mother cherishes her own children. . . . We exhorted,
and comforted, and charged every one of you,
as a father does his own children.*
1 THESSALONIANS 2:7, 11 NKJV

There could hardly be a more perfect picture of
gentleness than a nursing mother tenderly cradling a
newborn infant in her arms as she nurses him, lovingly
cherishing him. No sudden movements, no loud sounds.
Only soft words and tender care. The apostle Paul
said this is how he acted toward the Christians of
Thessalonica. He went on to say that he had comforted
and taught them like a loving father does his own
children. Picture a father hugging and reassuring a small
child, wiping away her tears. You may say, "Fine. That
was the apostle Paul. What does it have to do with me?"
It has much to do with you. Elsewhere Paul wrote that
"a servant of the Lord must not quarrel but be gentle to
all" (2 Timothy 2:24 NKJV). You are to be gentle to others,
even when correcting them. Men are commonly called
"gentlemen," and you may think a gentleman is simply
an old-fashioned title. But a gentleman is exactly that—a
gentle man. God is gentle, and you should be, too. If
you want to be truly great, remember that greatness
doesn't come from bossing people around or snapping
your fingers and expecting them to jump, but by gently
instructing them. David said to God, "Your gentleness
makes me great" (Psalm 18:35 NASB).

NO BAD LOANS

One who is gracious to a poor man lends to the LORD,
and He will repay him for his good deed.
PROVERBS 19:17 NASB

While the concept of God borrowing money may seem odd, it's actually scriptural. When you give to the poor, the Bible says you're lending to the Lord. Now, God sometimes does outright miracles to provide money, but often He wants to involve His children. He wants you to experience the joy of giving. So frequently God chooses to borrow cash from people like you. He will then see to it that you're repaid. And the good news is that God always comes through with His repayments. He never forgets. There's never "insufficient funds" in His bank account, so it's no risk to make Him a loan. You don't need to give begrudgingly, wondering if that's the last you'll see of your hard-earned cash. God says, "Give generously to them and do so without a grudging heart; then because of this the LORD your God will bless you in all your work and in everything you put your hand to" (Deuteronomy 15:10 NIV). That's something else: God doesn't always repay in the same currency He borrows. Many times He's very creative. But He will never shortchange you. He will always repay with interest—whether in this life or in the next. So be glad when God comes along looking for a loan. And yes, while it's true that you must also exercise wisdom and not simply give to everyone looking for a handout, God calls His children to be generous.

THE SOURCE OF POWER

The LORD is the everlasting God, the Creator of all the earth.
He never grows weak or weary. . . . He gives power to
the weak and strength to the powerless.
ISAIAH 40:28–29 NLT

God has absolutely unlimited power. He created the
earth and the entire universe full of billions and trillions
of stars, but this astonishing feat didn't tucker Him out. It
didn't leave Him weak and weary. He has unlimited power
to this day and still delights in doing the miraculous.
Human beings, however, have definite limitations to their
strength. A hard day's work wipes them out. A ten-minute
run wearies them. Even a stressful day can leave them
mentally exhausted. But Isaiah went on to explain, "Those
who trust in the LORD will find new strength" (verse 31).
God can empower you when your batteries are running
low. In fact, even if you suffer from permanent disabilities
and limitations, God can infuse you with His strength
and help you accomplish things that you could never
accomplish even if you had full health and strength. Once
when the apostle Paul was asking God to heal a medical
condition, God told him, "My grace is all you need. My
power works best in weakness" (2 Corinthians 12:9 NLT).
This totally changed Paul's thinking, and he concluded, "I
take pleasure in my weaknesses. . .For when I am weak,
then I am strong" (verse 10). You don't necessarily *feel*
strong when you have God's strength working through
you, but you *are* strong.

CLOTHED WITH HUMILITY

*Likewise you younger people, submit yourselves to
your elders. Yes, all of you be submissive to one
another, and be clothed with humility.*
1 PETER 5:5 NKJV

It's a sign of a good upbringing to respect your elders.
For Peter, it was a reasonable request to ask young men
to submit to their elders. But Christianity goes further.
Jesus wants you to respect others, regardless of their
age. That means that old men must also honor young
men, listen to them, and follow their advice. . .if it's sound.
To do that takes great humility. You have to be secure
in your manhood to submit to someone much younger
than yourself. It takes a self-effacing attitude to let others
have their way when you could demand to be considered
first. The expression "be clothed with humility" brings this
out. When you get dressed in the morning, you choose
your clothes according to what you'll be doing. If you'll
be lounging around the house, you wear casual clothes. If
you'll be attending a formal event, you dress up. If you'll
be changing the oil in your car, you pick your grubbiest
work clothes. To clothe yourself with humility means
to make a conscious decision that you're not going to
insist on *your* way but are determined to put others first.
Elsewhere Paul advised, "Let nothing be done through
selfish ambition or conceit, but in lowliness of mind let
each esteem others better than himself" (Philippians 2:3
NKJV). He wasn't suggesting that you nurture an inferiority
complex. He was talking about having humility.

LEARNING WHAT WORKS

Paul and his friends went through Phrygia and Galatia,
but the Holy Spirit would not let them preach in Asia.
After they arrived in Mysia, they tried to go into Bithynia,
but the Spirit of Jesus would not let them.
ACTS 16:6–7 CEV

It takes a tremendous amount of faith and courage to try
to start a new business, because according to studies,
eight out of ten entrepreneurs crash within eighteen
months. Fully 80 percent of new businesses are doomed
to fail. You know what that's like if you've ever attempted
it. You start out with high hopes, certain that you're going
to beat the odds because you have such a good idea,
such a great product, and such a catchy business name.
Plus, you reason, God is on your side, so you're *sure* to
succeed. But in the Bible, even godly men trying their
best to be about God's business had a hard time figuring
out where to go and when to go there. Paul and his team
went through Phrygia and Galatia seeking an opportunity,
but God blocked them. Perplexed and perhaps frustrated,
they tried to launch into Bithynia. Again they were
blocked. And they couldn't blame it on a dip in the
economy, poor financing, or a bad business location. God
Himself was preventing them from succeeding. So they
just kept trying and kept seeking God, until He opened
a door in Greece. So don't give up! Sometimes you just
have to persevere and keep praying for God to open the
door *He* wants you to go through.

Patient in Everything

In everything we do, we show that we are true ministers
of God. We patiently endure troubles and hardships
and calamities of every kind.
2 Corinthians 6:4 nlt

Any man can cheerfully follow God when everything is going fine. But the true measure of a man is how you hold up when troubles and problems arise, especially troubles that last for prolonged periods of time. It takes patience not to complain, trusting that if you give it a little more time, God will work things out. But the ultimate test is how you react when calamities strike. It's a calamity when an economic downturn hits, wiping out months of carefully managed savings. It's a calamity when once-reliable markets dry up, causing business losses, layoffs, and financial insecurity. It's a calamity when a traffic collision or a workplace accident leaves you injured and unable to work. When calamities strike, you can—and should—pray to God to alleviate your circumstances. But in the meantime, you must bear up patiently in painful and stressful situations. Men often get a bad rap for being uncommunicative, but there *are* times when it's good to be the strong, silent type. If you must give voice to your troubles, share your woes with those who can give you wise counsel. And pour out your complaints to God, and then praise Him because you trust He will help you.

ROAD RAGE

The chariots rage in the streets, they jostle one
another in the broad roads; they seem like
torches, they run like lightning.
NAHUM 2:4 NKJV

The Assyrians were cruel warriors, and their chariot corps
was a fearsome weapon. They were highly effective on the
battlefield in high-speed shock attacks, breaking enemy
ranks, running infantry underfoot, and creating chaos. In
this passage, Nahum describes the last dying hours of
great Nineveh when enemy armies broke through the city's
defenses and the Assyrians were rushing about in fear and
anger like a stirred-up hornet's nest. Made for the open
plains, their chariots were careening through the streets of
Nineveh, colliding, running over friend and foe alike.

Sound like your commute to work? Normally cour-
teous people undergo Jekyll and Hyde transformations,
laying on their horn if someone cuts in front of them, or
exploding in fury if someone jostles them. But the Bible
warns, "Do not be quickly provoked in your spirit, for
anger resides in the lap of fools" (Ecclesiastes 7:9 NIV).
Rather than giving in to it, pray for God to keep you cour-
teous. Better to arrive at your job a few minutes late and
calm, than shaking with anger and barely able to focus.
So relax. Pray ahead of time that God will help you to "be
gentle to all. . .patient" (2 Timothy 2:24 NKJV).

REASONABLE EXPECTATIONS

*"Some of the children are very young, and the flocks
and herds have their young, too. If they are driven too
hard, even for one day, all the animals could die. . . .
We will follow slowly, at a pace that is comfortable for
the livestock and the children."*
GENESIS 33:13–14 NLT

When Jacob and his family and all his flocks and herds
arrived in Canaan, Esau and four hundred men came
galloping up from Edom to meet them. Esau was then
bound and determined that his brother move to Edom
with him—and right now. After all, his four hundred men
were eager to get back to their own flocks. But Jacob
explained that it would be detrimental to drive too hard.
He needed to move at a reasonable, easy pace. Even
today, fathers have the right to expect certain behavior
from their children, but they need to guard against
unreasonable expectations. These will either anger their
children or discourage them. Paul cautioned, "Fathers, do
not exasperate your children, so that they will not lose
heart" (Colossians 3:21 NASB). Yes, at times children need
to be motivated to do better, but know what they can and
cannot do, and set the bar accordingly. They'll be happy if
they're able to please you, and you'll be happy, too.

RESTING IN GOD

"Be still, and know that I am God; I will be exalted among the nations, I will be exalted in the earth."
PSALM 46:10 NIV

Whether you celebrate Saturday or Sunday as the Sabbath, it's important to take one day of rest a week. It's a commandment: "Six days you shall labor and do all your work, but the seventh day is a sabbath to the LORD your God. On it you shall not do any work" (Exodus 20:9–10 NIV). God knew—and science has since discovered—that your body needs to take a break once a week. So take a day to relax and recharge your batteries. But the purpose of the Sabbath is not merely to rest physically. By ceasing your own efforts, deliberately slowing down and focusing on God, you show that you trust Him with your entire life. In that sense, you should enter a Sabbath rest every day. That's why the Lord says, "Be still, and know that I am God." Or as the New American Standard Bible puts it, "Cease striving and know that I am God." Certainly God expects you to work hard throughout the week to provide for your family. But He also wants you to realize that "it is *He* who gives you power to get wealth" (Deuteronomy 8:18 NKJV, emphasis added). It is also God who protects you, blesses you and yours with health, and cares for you in every way. So throughout the week—and especially on the Sabbath—have a trusting attitude, spend time in the Word and in prayer, and remind yourself that God is in charge.

FOLLOWING GODLY MENTORS

*Remember those who led you, who spoke the word
of God to you; and considering the result of
their conduct, imitate their faith.*
HEBREWS 13:7 NASB

Western society puts great emphasis on being an
independent, self-made man—being one's own boss—and
it's true that you must be able to stand on your own two
feet to make your own way in this world. But there's also
tremendous value in recognizing the authority of pastors
and spiritual leaders. There's great wisdom in seeking the
counsel of senior saints who have walked the walk for
many years and have much to teach. Consider "the result
of their conduct"—the good fruit of a sincere Christian
lifestyle and the wisdom that comes with years of serving
the Lord and studying His Word. It's no shame to admit
that you don't have all the answers. It doesn't show that
you're weak if you submit to spiritual leadership. Some
men are afraid to let others teach them how to live their
lives. They think that following others' instructions means
checking their brain at the door. But that's not the case.
Paul said, "Let all who are spiritually mature agree on
these things. If you disagree on some point, I believe God
will make it plain to you" (Philippians 3:15 NLT). So don't
be afraid to follow the counsel of spiritual leaders and
emulate the lifestyle of godly mentors. It's wise to seek
out good role models, and it's wise to be teachable.

PUT YOUR TRUST IN GOD

*Trust in the LORD with all your heart and lean not
on your own understanding; in all your ways submit
to him, and he will make your paths straight.*
PROVERBS 3:5–6 NIV

No matter your level of education, you don't have all the
answers to whatever life throws at you. Whether it's a
difficult predicament, an unexpected turn of events, or
a tragic loss, you may find yourself struggling to solve a
problem and unable to explain why something negative
has happened. Friend, God has all the answers. You don't
need to look any further or seek comfort from anyone
else. He has your best interest at heart. He knows what
you need. All you have to do is submit to Him, praise Him
for the successes in your life, and turn to Him at times of
hardship. The Lord will guide you through every situation
no matter the circumstances. But you must ask Him to
direct you and you must seek God's will in everything you
do. Turn every area of your life over to Him. There's no
halfway with God. You can't choose to follow Him some
of the time and ignore Him other times. If you make Him
a vital part of everything you do, He will lead you because
you will be working to accomplish His will. God knows
what is best for you. He is a better judge of what you
need than you are, so you must trust Him completely in
every choice you make.

It's All Good

And we know that in all things God works for the good of those who love him, who have been called according to his purpose.

ROMANS 8:28 NIV

God works in everything for your good. He doesn't pick and choose situations. He doesn't care about you only on certain days. He loves you every second of every minute of every hour of every day. You may face hardships. You may have people speaking ill about you. You may endure unbearable physical or emotional suffering. But even when something bad happens to you, God can turn any circumstance around for your long-term betterment. Remember, He is always working for your benefit and He is always trying to accomplish His will through you. It's not your will, however. It's His will for you that He wants to help you fulfill. God makes this promise not to everyone but to those who are filled by the Holy Spirit, those who love Him, those who put Him first in their life, those who don't care about worldly treasures, and those who determine heaven is their first priority. If you love God with all your heart, soul, and mind and live your daily life acting out this unconditional love through your interactions with others, He will take care of the rest for you. All you have to do is believe in Him, exercise your faith, and work toward building His kingdom.

To God Be the Glory

*Humble yourselves, therefore, under God's mighty
hand, that he may lift you up in due time.*
1 Peter 5:6 NIV

It's easy to take credit for your success and
accomplishments when you did all the hard work. You
put in long hours studying when you were in school and
made many sacrifices along the way to earn that diploma.
You worked tirelessly at your job and spent countless
nights working overtime shifts to prove yourself worthy
of that promotion. So it's no wonder you soak in all the
praise when everything pays off. But what about God?
Remember Him? He created you. He blessed you with
the gifts you needed to get excellent grades, to work
diligently, and to achieve great things. He put you in
position to be right where you are at this moment. Have
you thanked Him today? Have you given Him the credit?
Humble yourself, exalt Him, and tell others about the
wonders He has done in your life. Stop worrying about
your social standing, your position on the corporate
ladder, and your status. God doesn't care about such
trivial things. His recognition is more important than what
anyone else thinks of you. He will bless you far greater
than you can imagine. He will give you an abundance of
blessings. Now, humbly obey Him, and He will honor you
either in this lifetime or in the next—or both.

HELP ONE ANOTHER

"The King will reply, 'Truly I tell you, whatever you did for one of the least of these brothers and sisters of mine, you did for me.'"
MATTHEW 25:40 NIV

How often do you pass the homeless person on the street corner and look away, avoiding eye contact and continuing on your way instead of offering help—food, drink, clothing, shelter, or money? Would you ignore that person if it were Jesus Himself standing right before you? Certainly you wouldn't. So look for opportunities to extend a hand to someone in need. Jesus specifically says that whatever you do for someone else, you do for Him. Whether you give a drink to someone thirsty, food to someone hungry, clothing to someone who needs it, or you visit someone in prison or in a shelter or look after someone who is sick, you are giving to the Lord. He's watching you. Friend—be thankful for all your blessings and be mindful that others may not be so fortunate. Don't take what you have for granted. Share what God has given you with someone who has less than you. Perhaps you don't have much to give in the way of food or money or clothing. But it doesn't cost anything to go see an elderly person and lend a listening ear. It's free to visit someone in prison and offer a word of encouragement. Consider doing something selfless today.

Focus Your Heart on Him

"What good is it for someone to gain the whole world, yet forfeit their soul?"
MARK 8:36 NIV

Reality television has become very popular over the past decade because viewers can identify with everyday people who live out their daily routine in front of the bright lights, cameras, and microphones. But sometimes reality stars are asked to say or do things that may compromise their integrity. They have to decide whether their pursuit of fame and glory is more important than their reputation. You don't have to be an actor or reality television personality to face similar decisions. Are power, wealth, fame, social status, and material possessions worth more to you than your soul? You may want a bigger house, a fancier car, or an exclusive membership at an elite country club, but consider the ramifications of your actions before you do whatever it takes to get to the top. God wants you to pursue Him more aggressively than anything else. He wants you to follow the path of His Son, Jesus, on your way to the top. Higher than any corporate ladder, the greatest position you can ever achieve is in heaven. Focus all your energy on His kingdom, and He promises that you will live abundantly now and also for eternity.

CAREFUL WHAT YOU SAY

*"But I say, if you are even angry with someone,
you are subject to judgment! If you call someone an idiot,
you are in danger of being brought before the court.
And if you curse someone, you are in
danger of the fires of hell."*

MATTHEW 5:22 NLT

You know that you should not commit murder. It's against the law and breaks the sixth commandment. But anger is a great sin, too. It's a dangerous emotion that can lead to violence and even murder. Even to a lesser degree, anger is an awful sin because it causes bitterness, emotional pain, mental anguish, and spiritual damage. Simply being angry with someone goes against God's law to love one another. It prevents you from developing a closer relationship with God. When you express anger, you aren't acting in a Christlike manner. Instead, you are moving away from the example He set for you in the way He lived His life. Jesus didn't fight back when the soldiers crucified Him. He didn't curse at them or raise His voice in anger. When someone makes you mad, rather than retaliating with hurtful words or physical violence, remember how Jesus responded to His critics and the men who put Him on the cross. Exercise self-control and try to respond in a manner that would please God. He will hold you accountable for your attitude, so train yourself to control your thoughts and that will make it easier for you to show restraint and avoid anger.

WALK YOUR TALK

*"Prove by the way you live that you have
repented of your sins and turned to God."*
MATTHEW 3:8 NLT

Some Jewish leaders followed the Old Testament laws
and oral traditions passed down for generations. John the
Baptist criticized these leaders, calling them hypocrites
for being too legalistic, and he accused them of using
religion to advance their political power. John the Baptist
challenged them to change their behavior and prove
through their actions and by the way they lived their
lives—not through words or rituals—that they had turned
to God.

Friend, you've heard these sayings: "Practice what you
preach" and "Actions speak louder than words." You may
say that you're a Christian. You read the Bible. You go to
church. You offer tithes. You follow the rigid rules in your
particular denomination. But do you truly practice what
you preach? Do you walk your Christian talk? Do others
see Christ in you in your daily life and activities? Only you
and God know the answer to that important question.
God knows your true heart. He knows your intentions. He
looks beyond your words and your religious practices and
ultimately will judge you based on your behavior. Your
actions speak louder than your words. Today, make sure
that you put your Christian faith into practice.

GIVE ME STRENGTH

I can do all things through Christ who strengthens me.
PHILIPPIANS 4:13 NKJV

The apostle Paul turned to Christianity after condemning and even murdering Christians. He eventually dedicated his life to serving Christ, and his journey led him to abundant wealth, extreme poverty, and everything in between. He was imprisoned for several years but still wrote this joyful letter from prison. When Paul says he "can do all things through Christ," he's not talking about superhuman ability to accomplish goals that satisfy his selfish purpose. Paul learned to get by with whatever he had, whether it was little or nothing. He focused on what he should do—serve the Lord—instead of what he should have. Paul set his priorities in order and was grateful for all that God gave him. Paul faced many trials and tribulations, but he found joy in spreading God's Word and was not deterred by any trouble he encountered along the way.

You also "can do all things through Christ." You can accomplish any task, overcome any adversity, and survive any trouble if you come to the Lord and ask Him to strengthen you. He will not grant you the power to accomplish anything that does not serve His interests, but He will help you every step of the way as you build your faith and develop a relationship with Him.

FORGIVE ME, FATHER

Restore to me the joy of your salvation, and make me
willing to obey you. Then I will teach your ways
to rebels, and they will return to you.
PSALM 51:12–13 NLT

Have you ever felt disconnected from God because of your sin? Perhaps you are so embarrassed by your actions that you feel unworthy of being in the Lord's presence at church. David felt this way when he sinned with Bathsheba. He cries out to God: "Restore to me the joy of your salvation." David truly repented of his sin and asked for forgiveness.

God wants you to be close to Him, but sin drives a wedge between you and Him. Unconfessed sin pushes you further away from God, and it can separate you entirely from Him if you don't confront it, beg Him for forgiveness, and learn to obey Him. You may end up suffering earthly consequences for your sin. For example, adultery may lead to divorce. Fraud may lead to imprisonment. But God's forgiveness gives you the joy of a relationship with Him.

Once you experience that joy, like David, you will want to share it with others. David wanted to teach "rebels" and help them "return" to the Lord. You can help your friends and relatives by telling them about the joy of God's forgiveness and your fellowship with Him.

A SHINING LIGHT

Jesus replied, "My light will shine for you just a little longer. Walk in the light while you can, so the darkness will not overtake you. Those who walk in the darkness cannot see where they are going. Put your trust in the light while there is still time; then you will become children of the light." After saying these things, Jesus went away and was hidden from them.

JOHN 12:35–36 NLT

Jesus was speaking to a crowd of people in Jerusalem when they asked Him how the Son of God could possibly die. He explained to them that He would only be with them in person for a short time and urged them to take advantage of His presence on earth. He was the Light of the world, trying to show them how to walk out of darkness. If they followed Him, they would enjoy eternal salvation with His Father in heaven.

As a Christian, God wants you to bear Christ's light to the world. He wants you to let your light shine for others to see. Can those around you see Christ in you? Is your light shining brightly? Or has it dimmed? Today, get up and go out there and spread the Word of the Lord. Be a shining light for someone else to see. Be a blessing to someone. Inspire someone to come to the Lord by illuminating your light to the world around you.

CRITICAL SELF-ANALYSIS

*I realize how kind God has been to me, and so I tell
each of you not to think you are better than you really
are. Use good sense and measure yourself by the
amount of faith that God has given you.*
ROMANS 12:3 CEV

It's important to have self-esteem and healthy confidence
in the talents, skills, and abilities God has given you.
However, you should not overestimate your worth by
basing your evaluation of yourself on worldly standards.
The true measure of your worth to the Lord isn't found
in your bank statements, your job title, the size of your
house, or the cost of your luxury vehicle. You must be
honest and accurate in your self-evaluation, ignoring the
world's standards of success and achievement. Your true
value to God is demonstrated in the amount of faith that
you have, not the total sum of your material possessions.
All that you have is a gift from God. Recognizing,
acknowledging, and being grateful for His blessings
will keep you from becoming too prideful, arrogant,
or conceited. It will lead you to true humility because
whatever you are, God made you so. He wants you to use
the gifts He's given you rather than waste them, but He
wants you to understand and appreciate why you have
those skills.

DEFEATING TEMPTATION

Don't blame God when you are tempted! God cannot be tempted by evil, and he doesn't use evil to tempt others. We are tempted by our own desires that drag us off and trap us. Our desires make us sin, and when sin is finished with us, it leaves us dead.
JAMES 1:13–15 CEV

Often you hear people say: "God is tempting me." Nothing could be further from the truth. It is not God who is tempting you. It's Satan who is tempting you. Temptation comes from the evil desires within you. It begins with a simple thought and can escalate into a wrong action if you allow it. God tests you, but He does not tempt you. He allows you to be tempted because He wants you to strengthen your faith and rely on Christ for help. You can resist temptation by praying for God's guidance and direction in those situations and obeying His word.

People often blame others for their sins. You hear sayings like: "The devil made me do it." No, you made yourself do it. You allowed yourself to succumb to the evil one's temptation. Don't make excuses and shift the blame to someone else. A Christian will accept responsibility for his sins, confess them to God, and ask for forgiveness. You can defeat temptation by stopping it in its evil tracks before it becomes too strong and you lose self-control.

THE WANDERING EYE

Do not lust in your heart after her beauty
or let her captivate you with her eyes.
PROVERBS 6:25 NIV

Lusting after another woman is dangerous and can lead to sin. Therefore, consider lust a warning sign. If you find yourself attracted to a woman who is married or in a relationship, stay away from her. Ask God to change your desires before you submit to temptation and commit sin. Even if the woman is single, lusting after her is sinful. God doesn't want your mind preoccupied with thoughts of sex. If an attractive woman walks past you, it's human nature to appreciate her beauty. However, if you turn your head for a second look, stare at her, and have lustful thoughts, you are sinning. It may be difficult to avoid these temptations when sex is all around you. Don't fall for society's trappings. You can train yourself to have self-control by focusing on controlling your thoughts. Avoid television programming that promotes sex. Stay away from bars or nightclubs that may lead you to sin. Never watch pornographic movies or look at pornographic material. Take small steps and put yourself in a position where you won't fail. Lust can destroy marriages, ruin relationships, and create separation between you and God.

CHOOSE WORDS CAREFULLY

"No weapon formed against you shall prosper,
and every tongue which rises against you in judgment
you shall condemn. This is the heritage of the servants
of the LORD, and their righteousness is
from Me," says the LORD.
ISAIAH 54:17 NKJV

You may face a situation when someone is talking bad about you, perhaps even slandering your name. Your first inclination is to defend yourself and retaliate against that person. But Isaiah tells you that no one can injure you with words and accusations. You must be firm in your beliefs and stand up for righteousness. Words can be weapons. They can hurt you deeply. But God will protect you. There is nothing that anyone can say about you that will damage your relationship with the Lord. He has a special place prepared for His Christian servants and no person and no weapon can destroy it. People have mocked, ridiculed, and harassed Christians for thousands of years, and they will continue to do so. Have no fear, however. God will punish the wicked according to His will. You don't have to take matters into your own hands and seek vengeance. Simply pray that the attacks, lies, and harassment stop and God renounces the evildoers.

ROOTED IN CHRIST

*And now, just as you accepted Christ Jesus as your Lord,
you must continue to follow him. Let your roots grow
down into him, and let your lives be built on him.
Then your faith will grow strong in the truth you were
taught, and you will overflow with thankfulness.*
COLOSSIANS 2:6–7 NLT

Once you receive Christ as your Lord and Savior, it's the
beginning of your new life with Him. But you can't stop
there. Rather, you must build your relationship with Jesus
by following His leadership, studying His Word, learning
from His example, and obeying His teachings. Christ
wants to help you and guide you through problems that
arise in your daily life, and He asks that you commit to
Him and submit yourself to His will. Be rooted in Him
by drawing on His Word and putting the lessons you've
learned into action. You will be protected from those who
try to take you away from your Christian faith and tempt
you with false answers if you call on Christ for strength.
You need constant nourishment to build your faith. You
can feed your soul by reading daily scripture and studying
and meditating on the Word. Let Christ be your strength
and be free from human regulations.

SPREAD THE WORD

For I am not ashamed of the gospel, because it is the power of God that brings salvation to everyone who believes: first to the Jew, then to the Gentile.
ROMANS 1:16 NIV

If you have a favorite pizza place, you tell your friends. You don't hesitate to tell someone about a great experience you had at a restaurant, a hotel, a vacation resort, and so much more. So why do many Christians keep quiet about Christ? You know the Savior of the universe. You know the greatest man who ever lived. Don't be shy about sharing the Good News. Don't feel embarrassed to embrace your Christian faith and share it with others.

Paul was not ashamed to preach the Gospel. He withstood strong opposition and even went to prison for his beliefs, but he boldly and consistently found ways to preach the Word of the Lord.

If the people closest to you don't know you are a Christian, you aren't doing your job. You have the best news anyone should ever want to hear. Jesus changes lives and saves souls. Tell them. Give them an opportunity to hear how the Lord has worked wonders in your life. They may be ready to hear it and accept Him if only you would speak up.

TROUBLED WATERS

*"When you pass through the waters, I will be with you;
and when you pass through the rivers, they will not sweep
over you. When you walk through the fire, you will not be
burned; the flames will not set you ablaze."*
ISAIAH 43:2 NIV

Life is full of good moments. . .and unpleasant ones.
There are days that feel like a breath of fresh air and life
is great, and there are days that feel as if the seconds
and minutes take forever. It could be that you received
bad news about someone dear to you or news about
something you expected to happen that did not go the
way you had hoped.

Many people go through life thinking days are endless
and bad moments will carry on for a while, but you
need to remember that God is in control and that He is
always right by your side. The Lord is not just someone
who can be counted on when things go wrong but also
when things go right. He longs for a relationship with
His children. He wants a relationship with you just like
a relationship you have with a best friend. He wants His
children to run to Him first with good news and first with
bad news. When you have a bad moment, count on Him
to comfort you, solve the problem, and be the first one
there for you. Likewise, when you have a good moment,
run to Him and thank Him for it. Friend, through deep
waters, hills, and floods, He will carry you. Just rely on
Him with all your understanding, and He will see you
through.

A LOVING HEART

We love each other because he loved us first.
1 JOHN 4:19 NLT

One of the most difficult things human beings face is to love the way God loves His children. Many people go through life with so much anger, hurt, resentment, and hate in their hearts. It's easy to hate, but so much harder to love.

Take time today to reflect on how God loves His children; how He has blessed everyone with many gifts, talents, and abilities to suit their own need; how He protects you and keeps you safe from harm. God's love is pure. It is the source for all human love. It has no boundaries and needs no explanation, and it can spread like a wildfire. Friend, have you ever thought about why God loves you the way He does? Have you ever tried to be as loving as He is? It is truly wonderful to be able to love the way God loves. There's something uniquely special about a loving heart that cures sadness, melts any hurt, and mends broken hearts. Next time someone treats you as less than you would like, remember that God loves you and cares about you. So try to live like Christ in love.

OPEN DOORS

*"I know all the things you do, and I have opened a door
for you that no one can close. You have little strength,
yet you obeyed my word and did not deny me."*
REVELATION 3:8 NLT

Many Christians in the world today seek many opportunities, whether it's for a career change or marriage or something new and different. Doors open and close all the time. But how do you know which door to choose? How do you know which one God intended for you to walk through? Many Christians forget the simplest rules of following Christ because they are so intent on getting ahead. They lie and even deny God to advance in their careers or lives in general. Not every open door in front of you is from God. You must remember that if you open a door that takes you away from Him, then it isn't from Him. If it made you disobey Him or break any of His laws, you must close that door immediately. You may wonder, *What can I do? Why didn't that door come my way?* The devil is deceiving. He comes to you when you're at your worst, at your lowest point, and presents a key to your solution. Friend, be aware of his conniving presence when you're going through difficult times. Pray to the Lord to direct you, and ask the Holy Spirit to guide you to the door that God has for you. He will always provide for you, and He will never leave you or forsake you. He has a door for you that will come open just at the right time, a door that no man can ever close. All you have to do is believe that simple truth and walk through it.

Palm Sunday
First Day of Spring

PRAY FOR EVERYTHING

"Ask and it will be given to you; seek and you will find;
knock and the door will be opened to you."
MATTHEW 7:7 NIV

Many believers pray every day for different things. Some pray for more money, a new job, a new place to live. Some pray for health, happiness, and success. Some pray for it all. There's no limit on what you can pray about or ask the Lord to provide. Often people misinterpret today's verse and focus their prayers on material things because God says He will give you whatever you ask. But Jesus is telling you to shift your attention from your daily wants and desires. Instead, ask God to show you more about Him, ask Him for wisdom, ask for His patience and His understanding. The Lord wants His children to have a relationship with Him just like a father has with his son or daughter. As a father tries to give his children whatever they ask for, our Father in heaven wants to give us more. Our Father is more generous and more gracious than any father on earth; He gives us much more than what we can ask for or imagine.

Jesus tells you to be persistent in your prayer and your pursuit of a relationship with God. Don't give up if He doesn't answer your prayer requests immediately. God knows what you need most, and He will provide when the time is right.

BAD COMPANY

Do not be misled: "Bad company corrupts good character."
1 CORINTHIANS 15:33 NIV

When you were a child, your parents probably told you to stay away from the troublemakers at school because they didn't want you to go down the wrong path with them. As an adult, you are careful to avoid people who don't do the right things. Even your girlfriend or wife may not want you to hang out with certain friends, especially single guys who enjoy partying a little too much and are often preoccupied with chasing women.

As a Christian, you certainly should be mindful of the people you surround yourself with on a daily basis. Be careful not to associate too closely with unbelievers, for those who deny the resurrection of Christ can take you away from Him and cause your faith to waver. Also, be wary of friends who don't know the Lord and speak out against Him. Their influence can be greater than you may think. They could fill your mind with doubt and force you to question what you stand for in Christianity. Unbelievers live for today, for the moment, for instant gratification and satisfaction. They don't believe they will one day answer to God, so they do whatever pleases them on any given day. Avoid this type of person. Don't sacrifice eternal salvation for happiness today.

SEEING ISN'T BELIEVING

For we live by faith, not by sight.
2 CORINTHIANS 5:7 NIV

Sight is a beautiful thing. Many of God's wonderful creations are admired visually. Everything from the sun to the moon to the mountains to the oceans was created by God. Many people rely on what they see to make decisions, to take the next step in life, so they know exactly where they are headed. Although the ability to see everything around you is one of God's amazing gifts to His children, He asks you to rely more on faith. Friend, faith is knowing that God is your eyes. He sees what you don't see and He knows what you don't know. Your future is His past. He has a plan for your life and He knows which way is better for you. Trust in Him to guide you, to hold your hand and take you to places you never considered going or imagined you could go. Faith is a powerful thing. It is hope and light in the midst of darkness. Facing the unknown can cause fear and anxiety because you don't know what will happen. Fear of death is natural, for you don't want to leave loved ones behind. But if you believe in Jesus Christ and eternal life with Him, you will have hope and confidence in the most important thing you cannot see.

Don't Worry, Be Happy

Don't worry about anything; instead,
pray about everything. Tell God what you need,
and thank him for all he has done.
Philippians 4:6 NLT

Worry can sometimes consume your mind to the point of frustration. Perhaps you are worried about tomorrow, worried about your children, worried about paying your bills or rent, worried about your health, worried about a loved one, worried about a relationship, worried about what to do when faced with a difficult decision. Your brain plays tricks on you, makes your thoughts race round and round to help you find an answer, and you become obsessed with the problem instead of the solution. Next time you worry, stop thinking. Hit the Pause button in your mind. God asks His children to come to Him for counsel. He asks that you run to Him first before you even consult your best friend. Worrying does nothing to make tomorrow better. It is wasted energy. It's wasted time. Worrying doesn't allow you to appreciate what God does for you. He takes care of your tomorrow. Come to Him with all your burdens; open your heart and mind and believe that He will resolve all your problems and will provide for your tomorrow. He will take your worries away and give you peace and happiness for today and every day. So worry less, pray more.

HE WILL FIND YOU

"For the Son of Man has come to seek
and to save that which was lost."
LUKE 19:10 NKJV

Many believers go through life with no known destination, no direction, and no purpose. You may be questioning what you are intended to do with your life. You may feel that you have no clue where you are and where you are going. Perhaps you have been searching for years and can't seem to find any answers. Friend, have you tried to search for God in your life? Has He taken precedence in your life? Is He involved in every decision you make and every step you take? God searches for you. No matter how far you go and how badly you mess up, He longs for you. He searches for His lost sheep until He finds them, but He wants the ones looking for a relationship with Him. Seek Him today, and He will answer all the questions you were searching to find answers for. Simply sit down and talk to Him about your life, and He will direct you. He will tell you what your purpose is. Life has a greater meaning when you and God meet at the perfect place and the perfect time. That time is when you are ready to find Him. Don't waste any more days wandering aimlessly. Make that time now.

HARD WORK PAYS OFF

*Do your work willingly, as though you were serving
the Lord himself, and not just your earthly master.*
COLOSSIANS 3:23 CEV

You work hard day and night to provide for your family.
You try your best and put in long hours at your job to
impress your boss. Some days you feel valuable. . .and
some days you wonder why you work so hard. Your job
doesn't pay that well, or your boss doesn't appreciate
you. You sometimes feel as if you are invisible. No one
notices what you do or the long hours you put in. The one
who does notice is your Father in heaven. He watches
over you; He sees your dedication, your hard work, and
your loyalty. Sometimes your work doesn't pay off, but
God sees how much effort you are putting in so you can
get that promotion or that new job, so you can fulfill your
duties as a husband and a father. Remember, you are
called to be the priest, protector, and provider of your
household. Friend, always remember that the Lord will
reward all your hard work. He will promote you in the
midst of a market crash. He will take you higher and open
doors for you even if you are underqualified. Trust Him
and always be faithful. He sees your work and He'll give
you what you deserve at the right time.

BE A VOICE FOR THE VOICELESS

*Speak up for those who cannot speak for
themselves; ensure justice for those being crushed.
Yes, speak up for the poor and helpless,
and see that they get justice.*
PROVERBS 31:8–9 NLT

There are instances when you find yourself with
information about a situation that can help or hurt
someone's character or career. Perhaps you overheard
a story or someone shared something with you that you
didn't even want to know. It is important to remember
that you always have to speak the truth. God doesn't
want His children taking sides. You have to stand up
for what is right no matter the repercussions. Speak
up for those who can't speak up for themselves. If you
see someone being bullied, help them. Make it clear
to the bully that their behavior is wrong. Children are
another example. They can't defend themselves, and they
often seek help from their parents. You should always
remember to ask your children about their day—ask
about what happened at school and how people treated
them. You have to look out for them and always put their
best interest first. Always remind your children that you
are there for them and you will protect them just like your
heavenly Father does for you.

Easter Sunday

WE'RE ALL SINNERS

*But he said to me, "My grace is sufficient for you, for my
power is made perfect in weakness." Therefore I will
boast all the more gladly about my weaknesses,
so that Christ's power may rest on me.*
2 CORINTHIANS 12:9 NIV

In the Bible, many of God's followers had faults. Jacob
was a cheater. Peter had a volatile temper. Paul was a
murderer. God didn't choose His disciples because they
were perfect. He chose them as they were, imperfect and
unworthy sinners. The grace of God covers all faults and
impurities, but many believers still shy away from God
because they think they are too much of a sinner for God
to forgive them. His hands are always wide open waiting
for you. What is taking you away from Him?

When you pray tonight, remember all the disciples
and the terrible sins they committed. Then remember
how Jesus forgave their sins and made them new. The
Lord wants to forgive you and wash away your sins. He
gave His disciples a new life and new identity and allowed
them to follow Him. Don't miss out on His grace today.
Take the first step and pray for His forgiveness and grace
to cover you.

LEAD BY EXAMPLE

*Direct your children onto the right path,
and when they are older, they will not leave it.*
PROVERBS 22:6 NLT

Children are a precious gift from God, a blessing greater than any other. It's your responsibility as a parent to raise your children to know God, to love Him, and to fear Him. Teach them to glorify His name in their words, in their thoughts, and in their actions. But you must do it yourself. You can't be a hypocrite. Show them by your example and they will learn to follow your path.

Parents often want to make important decisions for their children, but that won't help them in the future. They need to stand on their own, recognize right from wrong, and make smart decisions for themselves. By raising them in the Church, teaching them the ways of the Lord, and impressing upon them the importance of a relationship with Christ, you will allow your children to grow up knowing this is the best path to take, and they will not take a detour away from it, away from God. Don't worry about the distractions in the world or the negative influences that impact others. If your children are grounded in faith, they won't go wrong.

TRAIN YOUR SOUL

*Have nothing to do with godless myths and old wives'
tales; rather, train yourself to be godly. For physical
training is of some value, but godliness has value for
all things, holding promise for both the present
life and the life to come.*
1 TIMOTHY 4:7–8 NIV

You spend a lot of time working on your outward
appearance—eating healthy food, exercising, and doing
whatever you can to ensure you look your best. There's so
much emphasis placed on outer beauty, and you have to
work hard to keep up. But are you in shape spiritually as
well as physically? Your spiritual health is more important.
Your physical health can fail you whether it's sickness,
disease, and ultimately, death. But your spiritual health
will sustain you. It will carry you through the difficult
times. It will help you endure tragedy and anything that
goes wrong. You have to focus more on your spiritual
well-being because it will benefit you the most in the
long run. It will always be with you, guiding you along.
So, before you go to the gym, make sure to train your
spiritual muscles today. Use the abilities God has given
you to help others around you and be a serviceable
member of the Church.

NEVER TOO LATE

Then he said, "Jesus, remember me when you come into your Kingdom." And Jesus replied, "I assure you, today you will be with me in paradise."
LUKE 23:42–43 NLT

When Jesus was hanging on the cross, two criminals were crucified along with Him. One of them mocked Jesus, telling Him if He is the Messiah, He should save Himself and them. But the other criminal defended Jesus, admitted his own sin, and asked for mercy. This man showed unwavering faith, so Jesus assured him he would join Him in the kingdom of heaven.

Friend, it's never too late to turn to the Lord. Even on your dying day, God is ready to welcome you home. If you accept His Son, Jesus Christ, as your Lord and Savior, your place in heaven is assured, just like how Jesus assured this criminal that he was accepted. But how much more fulfilling would your life be if you made the decision right now rather than waiting until you were on your deathbed. God doesn't care what you have done in the past. You are already forgiven. Turn to Him, accept Him, and reap the rewards of His blessings. You don't know when you will take your last breath. Be prepared. Eternal salvation can be yours this moment if you're ready.

BE STRONG IN SUFFERING

That is why we never give up. Though our bodies are dying,
our spirits are being renewed every day. For our present
troubles are small and won't last very long. Yet they
produce for us a glory that vastly outweighs
them and will last forever!
2 CORINTHIANS 4:16–17 NLT

Whenever you face problems at work, at home, or in your
relationships, it's easy to want to quit. Paul faced daily
struggles and persecution that wore him down. But even
when he was sent to prison, Paul never gave up on his
goal to spread the Good News. No matter the hardships
you face, the pain or anger, the fatigue or criticism, focus
on your inner strength from the Holy Spirit and continue
to push forward. You have an eternal reward waiting for
you, so don't give it up because you are feeling too much
pressure today. Commit yourself to serving the Lord,
and He will empower you, turning your weakness into
strength. Don't allow your troubles to diminish your faith.
There is purpose in your suffering, even though you may
never understand it. God can show His power through
you. Your problems are opportunities for Him to work
through you and for you to witness for Him.

WHOSE FOOL ARE YOU?

The fool says in his heart, "There is no God."
PSALM 53:1 ESV

April Fools' Day is a time for innocent pranks, harmless deceptions, and entertaining practical jokes. But being foolish in our lives and decisions isn't a laughing matter. Most of the misery we experience in life is the result of the foolish choices we or others make.

The Bible is clear. Those who reject God and the truth of His Word are foolish. But the world regards those who love God and live by His Word as foolish (1 Corinthians 1:27). It seems the real question isn't whether someone will think we are foolish, but whose judgment we value.

Those who reject God and His wisdom are certain they are wise and believers are foolish. They point to the fun we miss and think we are naive and gullible. We give our time and money away. We put God and family before career and pleasure. We are like fish swimming upstream against the strong currents of our culture and times.

But Proverbs 16:25 tells us that way of thinking ends in death and destruction. The fear of the Lord is the beginning of knowledge, so those who reject God despise wisdom and instruction (Proverbs 1:7).

A godly life may seem foolish to many but it is the route to true happiness and fulfillment, a shield from the consequences of foolish choices, healing to our broken hearts, and the path to true freedom and eternal joy. So, whose fool are you?

LEAVING A LASTING LEGACY

A good man leaves an inheritance to his children's children,
but the sinner's wealth is laid up for the righteous.
PROVERBS 13:22 ESV

Most people think of their legacy as the money, property, or possessions they pass on after death. That's the clear context of Proverbs 13:22. Of course we want to leave that kind of legacy and care for our wives, children, and grandchildren. It's one way we show our love for them and keep our promises—something every godly man should do.

Our legacy is much more than the material things we leave. Our legacy is spiritual, moral, and relational. It's the influence of our lives on those we love, those we know, our communities, and our world. Our true legacy is our impact in the world. Everyone leaves that kind of legacy— the good and godly person and the sinner alike. They just leave very different legacies.

So, what should we do? We should live with our legacy in mind and ask—at every decision point, at every moment of temptation, and at every opportunity to serve God and His kingdom—what do we want to leave behind. Which choice will make us, our wives, children, grandchildren, and most importantly, God proud of us? We should do that!

Throughout this month we'll look at factors that can add up to a legacy to be proud of in terms of our personal core, our character, our commitments, and our conduct.

AT THE CORE: IDENTITY

*Therefore, if anyone is in Christ, the new creation
has come: The old has gone, the new is here!*
2 CORINTHIANS 5:17 NIV

Who are you?

Men answer that question in many ways. We can answer
it in terms of our relationships as sons, husbands, and
fathers or in terms of our work or the sports we love and
play. We can answer it in terms of our nationality, ethnicity,
personal history, family, or generation. In fact, we are all of
these and much, much more. Who we are is not one thing
but the combination of many things that make each of us
unique individuals.

But at the core of every man is one thing that defines
how he sees himself. This fundamental identity shapes
the person we become, defines all our relationships, and
guides all our decisions. That core identity can come to us
by virtue our birth. Sometimes it's forced on us by society
because of the color of our skin, our last name, or the
circumstances we grew up in.

But the true core of our lives, the single most
important thing about us is always chosen. As Christians,
we chose Christ. That fact should be the most important
thing anyone knows about us. It's the choice out of which
all other choices flow, that impacts everything else in
life. It effects how we see ourselves, those around us, our
purpose in the world, and our sense of right and wrong.

So, who are you? Is your identity in Christ the most
important truth about your life?

AT THE CORE: VALUES

*What is more, I consider everything a loss because of
the surpassing worth of knowing Christ Jesus my Lord,
for whose sake I have lost all things. I consider
them garbage, that I may gain Christ.*
PHILIPPIANS 3:8 NIV

A man's values are those things most important to him.

Every day we are confronted with choices that rest on and often reveal what we truly value. Often the greatest challenge is sorting out competing values and choosing between good things. Is advancing our career more valuable than time with our children? Is work more important than worship? Are our hobbies more valuable than our wives' happiness? Do we value that purchase more than staying out of debt and the financial well-being of our family? Do we value momentary pleasure more than our purpose?

In today's verse, Paul expresses his greatest value. Nothing, absolutely nothing was more valuable to him than knowing Jesus. He willingly let go of everything else and considered it little more than garbage compared to the insurmountable value of Christ in his life. Paul's core value echoed Christ's statement that loving God is the greatest commandment.

Are we like Paul, ready to value our relationship with God more than our ambition, pride, pleasure, and our desire for success, money, and status? Can we give them up? The answer to that question has a profound impact on each man, his family, and his future.

AT THE CORE: PRIORITY

*Therefore, since we are surrounded by so great a cloud
of witnesses, let us also lay aside every weight,
and sin which clings so closely, and let us run
with endurance the race that is set before us,
looking to Jesus, the founder and
perfecter of our faith.*
HEBREWS 12:1–2 ESV

Living out our values means establishing priorities.

Some things are important and worthy of our time, investment, and energy. Other things are great if we get to them. But there are things that we shouldn't do, not because they are sinful but because they distract us from what is more important.

These verses give us a way to think about our priorities. First, we should eliminate sin and everything that hinders a godly life. Things that interfere with our life in Christ or distract us from our calling should never end up on our to-do lists. Second, we should live the life God has called us to with perseverance. Staying spiritually, emotionally, relationally, and physically healthy and happy is a priority. Fulfilling our responsibility as God's ambassadors, sons, husbands, and fathers in ways that honor God and further His kingdom isn't optional. Those responsibilities must be our priority. Finally, we should do all that while staying focused on Jesus and delighting in the joy of a life well lived.

Achieving what's most important in life is always challenging and always worth it!

AT THE CORE: PRINCIPLES

*Trust in the Lord with all your heart and lean not on your
own understanding; in all your ways submit to him,
and he will make your paths straight.*
PROVERBS 3:5–6 NIV

Lofty ideals are fine. But a man's life is full of difficult choices, and we are often tempted to compromise our values and priorities. How can we live out our values and priorities in the challenging reality of everyday life?

First, trust God completely! The pressure we feel and the fears we face are very real. Christ's followers can and do experience very painful consequences for their faith. But we can trust God to make all things right and to reward those who serve Him.

Second, don't trust yourself! All of us have spent our lives immersed in cultures and societies that don't honor God. We learned how this world works. God's ways are so counterintuitive that our instinct is to think and act like those around us. Don't do it!

Third, submit every action and decision to God, His will, and His ways. This kind of submission isn't weak—it's incredibly strong. Submitting to God means we don't give in to the world around us or its temptations and pressures. That takes real strength and courage.

Finally, we do it God's way and walk His paths. The temptation is to wrest control over our lives from God and follow a path that makes sense to us. Adam and Eve tried that. It's never a good idea. His ways are always the best ways.

AT THE CORE: WISDOM

Be very careful, then, how you live—not as unwise
but as wise, making the most of every opportunity,
because the days are evil.
EPHESIANS 5:15–16 NIV

No man wants to live with the consequences of an unwise or foolish decision. But many do. Looking back we can't believe we were that foolish and shortsighted. In these few verses, Paul outlines guidelines for acting wisely.

First, recognize the reality of our times. Paul encouraged his readers to act wisely "because the days are evil." We, too, live in evil times when honoring God is disparaged as intolerant and bigoted while sinful behavior and lifestyles are celebrated. Wisdom sees our world for what it is, dangerous and destructive.

Second, be careful how you live! We can't risk acting recklessly or carelessly. Our marriages, children, the cause of Christ, and our own futures are at stake. It's all too easy to be tempted by the pleasures of a sinful world. We may enjoy it for a time, but in the end that life destroys what we value most.

Finally, we should make the most of every opportunity. Paul's instruction is crystal clear in the context of the rest of the letter. The truly wise man seizes every circumstance, every choice, and every challenge as an opportunity to make the most out of doing God's will. It's the surest way to a wise and noble life.

AT THE CORE: LOVE

"A new command I give you: Love one another. As I have loved you, so you must love one another. By this everyone will know that you are my disciples, if you love one another."
JOHN 13:34–35 NIV

Love is a word with so many meanings and shades of meaning that it's hard to know what a person means when they use the word. But in these verses, what Christ means is clear.

First, love isn't optional. It's a command!

Second, love is mutual. We are to love each other.

Third, the standard of our love for others is Christ's love for us. That's a tall order!

Fourth, Christian love is our surest witness. Our words don't mean much if we don't love each other.

But what does it mean to love like Christ? That isn't an easy question to answer. While there are many definitions, one practical way to think about love is "always acting in the other person's best interest." Isn't that what Christ did for us?

This kind of love isn't selfish. It's focused on the other person. It's not passive; it's active. It's not emotional; it's biblical. It doesn't cower in fear of the consequences; it's courageous.

But what is in the other person's best interest? Here are some litmus tests. When you pray, ask for godly wisdom and the leading of the Holy Spirit. What does the Bible teach? If the Bible isn't clear, ask for wise, mature Christian counsel.

AT THE CORE: SPIRITUAL VITALITY

*And he answered, "You shall love the Lord your God with all
your heart and with all your soul and with all your strength
and with all your mind, and your neighbor as yourself."*
LUKE 10:27 ESV

There is no relationship more important to any man than
his relationship with God because every other relationship
depends on it. When a man loses his connection to God,
his relationship with his wife, his children, his friends, and
everyone else in his life suffers.

We are called to love God with all our heart, soul,
mind, and strength. The question is, how? Maintaining
and developing a deeper, more vital relationship with
God requires what every other successful relationship
demands—time, intention, practice, and service.

Great relationships take time. The problem isn't God. He'll
give us all the time we want. The problem is we don't take
time to pray, worship, study His Word, and listen to His voice.

Great relationships aren't accidental. They are
intentional. We have to want spiritual vitality and
intentionally do what must be done to experience a
greater degree of God's presence.

Great relationships require practice. We have
to actively and consistently do what builds up our
relationship with God. Wanting it isn't enough.

Finally, great relationships mean we serve. We invest our
time, creativity, and energy into those things that benefit the
other person. Serving brings us close to the heart of God.

CHARACTER THAT MATTERS: COURAGE

*"Have I not commanded you? Be strong and courageous.
Do not be afraid; do not be discouraged, for the LORD
your God will be with you wherever you go."*

JOSHUA 1:9 NIV

Winston Churchill, lion of the British Empire, once famously remarked, "Courage is rightly esteemed the first of human qualities. . .because it is the quality that guarantees all the others." Our values don't matter if we don't have the courage to act on them when faced with a great challenge.

After years in Robbins Prison, Nelson Mandela said, "I learned that courage was not the absence of fear, but the triumph over it. The brave man is not he who does not feel afraid, but he who conquers that fear."

Standing on the edge of the Promised Land and years of war, God encouraged Joshua to "be strong and courageous" and banish fear and discouragement. But it wasn't up to Joshua to triumph over his fear. His courage rested on a solid foundation, and so does ours.

We can have courage when we follow God's command. If we do what He calls us to, obey His word and honor Him, God fights for us. He will be our ally in the battle.

We can have courage because God is with us wherever our obedience takes us and in whatever battles we face. God is with us! So be strong and courageous. We have no reason to be afraid or discouraged when we are on God's side.

CHARACTER THAT MATTERS: PASSION

Whatever you do, work at it with all your heart,
as working for the Lord, not for human masters,
since you know that you will receive an inheritance from
the Lord as a reward. It is the Lord Christ you are serving.
COLOSSIANS 3:23–24 NIV

We all pursue our passions, and our passions inevitably drive our lives in their direction. That's not the question. The real question is—what are those passions?

Sadly many men settle "for grime when [they] could reach for glory" (Carl F. H. Henry). Their passions burn for power, possessions, pleasures, and pride. They settle for paths that give temporary pleasure but are ultimately unfulfilling and destructive.

Paul made it clear that the only passion worth living and dying for is an all-consuming passion for God and His work in the world. Nothing can take its place. Nothing is as satisfying or rewarding. Most Christian men wouldn't disagree. But most of us don't pursue that passion. We are distracted by the shiny baubles of the world, dig for fool's gold, and end up empty and exhausted.

William Borden, heir to the great Borden Dairy fortune, was a student at Yale when he found his passion for Christ. He followed that passion and led the great Christian student movement of the early twentieth century. He turned his back on his family's business and fortune and pursued his call to serve God in China. He died on the way and is buried in Cairo, Egypt.

In his journal Borden wrote, "No reserves. No retreats. No regrets." Passion!

CHARACTER THAT MATTERS: GENEROSITY

Remember this: Whoever sows sparingly will also reap sparingly, and whoever sows generously will also reap generously.

2 CORINTHIANS 9:6 NIV

Generosity is long remembered. So is stingy selfishness!

Scrooge, the main character in Dickens's *A Christmas Carol*, has become the epitome of stingy selfishness, of a man so concerned with himself he ignored the needs of all those around him, including his family, his employees, and his neighbors. But after his dramatic encounter with the ghosts of Christmas past, present, and future, he becomes so generous that "it was always said of him, that he knew how to keep Christmas well, if any man alive possessed the knowledge."

Like Scrooge, we would do well to consider generosity in light of our past, present, and future. God is generous with His children in giving us far more than we need and treating us far better than we deserve. His generosity is best expressed in His most generous gift, His own Son, Jesus. It's impossible to imagine a more generous gift to any less deserving.

Today's verse reminds us that both stingy selfishness and joyous generosity have consequences in the future. A large measure of our future joy, in this world and the next, depends on generosity today. True generosity isn't about how much; it's possible to give a great deal and not be truly generous. Generosity is a matter of the heart attuned to a generous God. It is the result of gratitude for what He has done and trusting in what He will do.

CHARACTER THAT MATTERS: PERSISTENCE

To those who by persistence in doing good seek glory,
honor and immortality, he will give eternal life.

ROMANS 2:7 NIV

"Nothing in the world can take the place of persistence. Talent will not; nothing is more common than unsuccessful men with talent. Genius will not; unrewarded genius is almost a proverb. Education will not; the world is full of educated derelicts. Persistence and determination alone are omnipotent. The slogan 'Press On' has solved and always will solve the problems of the human race" (Calvin Coolidge).

Not everyone agrees with the "omnipotence" of persistence. In fact, all of us can think of times when we foolishly and stubbornly persisted in things that were bad for us, bad for our family, and contrary to God's will. That kind of persistence only leads to disaster.

It's only persistence in the right direction that has the power to change our lives and the world. Paul points to persistence in four directions—in doing good, in seeking what brings glory to God, in what is honorable, and in what matters in light of eternity.

Persistence in things that don't accomplish these goals isn't persistence at all. It's just stubbornness.

CHARACTER THAT MATTERS: HUMILITY

Be completely humble and gentle; be patient,
bearing with one another in love. Make every effort to
keep the unity of the Spirit through the bond of peace.
EPHESIANS 4:2–3 NIV

One hundred and four years ago, the British passenger liner RMS *Titanic* struck an iceberg in the North Atlantic and sank. Since that time, much has been made of the statement by her builders that she was "unsinkable." That arrogance and pride led her captain to take reckless and tragic risks.

It's better to live with humility than be humiliated!

Humility doesn't mean thinking less of ourselves than we should. Humility recognizes that each man has strengths and weaknesses, and acts accordingly. Paul makes it clear that such humility can result in great good:

Humility comes with gentleness. Since we have all failed, we don't have the right to be harsh with those who struggle.

Humility comes with patience. We need others to be patient with our shortcomings and others need us to be patient with theirs.

Humility comes with tolerance born from God's love for us and others despite our failures.

Humility brings unity and peace in the church, the family, and all our relationships.

Finally, a truly humble man avoids the disasters of arrogance and pride.

CHARACTER THAT MATTERS: HONESTY

An honest answer is like a kiss on the lips.
PROVERBS 24:26 NIV

Very few would disagree with the old maxim coined by Benjamin Franklin that "Honesty is the best policy." But there are times when honesty seems like the worst possible "policy"!

We aren't always as honest as we could or should be. We shade the truth to avoid embarrassment, save money, or stay out of trouble. Sometimes we exaggerate or downplay the truth so others will think better of us than they would if they knew the whole truth. Some men are pretty clever in the ways they are less than honest. They may not be lying, but they certainly aren't "truthing" either!

The problem with being less than honest is that the truth always and inevitably comes out. Then we are not only guilty for whatever we tried to hide but guilty of not being honest about it. Often the dishonesty ends up hurting us more than whatever we tried to hide.

Honesty can be painful and costly for us and sometimes for others. But in the end, honesty always costs less.

CHARACTER THAT MATTERS: GROWING

For this reason, since the day we heard about you,
we have not stopped praying for you. We continually ask
God to fill you with the knowledge of his will through all
the wisdom and understanding that the Spirit gives,
so that you may live a life worthy of the Lord and please
him in every way: bearing fruit in every good work,
growing in the knowledge of God.
COLOSSIANS 1:9–10 NIV

Great men know there is always more to learn and they are ready to learn it. In fact, all of us want the people we deal with—our physicians, attorneys, financial advisors, and others—to be learners. We want the best they can give us now, not what they learned years ago. We expect them to keep up!

But we all know men who aren't learners. Sometimes it's pride. They don't believe others have anything to teach them. Sometimes it's insecurity. They don't believe they can master new things. But most of the time, it's just neglect and laziness. We're comfortable without the hard work of learning, so why put out the effort?

People can get away with that in some things but never in their spiritual lives. Today's verses make it clear that "a life worthy of the Lord" is a life that is growing in the knowledge of God through the wisdom and understanding of the Spirit. The truth is that no matter how much we know of God and His wisdom there is always more to know.

COMMITMENTS THAT MATTER: GOD

*Now all has been heard; here is the conclusion of
the matter: Fear God and keep his commandments,
for this is the duty of all mankind.*
ECCLESIASTES 12:13 NIV

We all make commitments. And we all know some commitments matter more than others. If we can't keep our commitment to have coffee with a friend, it's not a big deal. If we don't keep our commitments to our wives and children, it's a very big deal!

What we are committed to shapes and makes up much of our lives. There are some things to which we must make unwavering, permanent commitments if we expect to leave a legacy that matters.

The first and most fundamental commitment any Christian man must make is his commitment to God and the Christian life. It has to be a non-negotiable. No matter what comes, no matter what challenges we face, no matter how great our successes or failures, our commitment to God is the anchor that holds in the storm and the compass that guides our days.

There are plenty of examples of men who have given up on their commitment to God and following Him. All of them have some things in common. First, in a moment of trial and temptation they wavered and broke their commitment. Second, their grip on God gradually loosened. Finally, in the end they and those they loved suffered, and they left a woeful legacy.

How committed to God are you today? Are you wavering? Are you losing your grip?

Commitments That Matter: Family

But if a widow has children or grandchildren, these should learn first of all to put their religion into practice by caring for their own family and so repaying their parents and grandparents, for this is pleasing to God.
1 Timothy 5:4 niv

Next to a man's commitment to God, there is no commitment more important than his commitment to be a godly son, brother, husband, and father. Nothing will leave a more lasting impact on the generations to come, and nothing will matter more to him in the end.

Sadly, it seems that many men have abandoned their critical role in the family to pursue their own wants, needs, and desires. They seem to care little for the impact of their choices on their wives, children, and future generations. Being a godly husband and father just doesn't seem important. Nothing could be further from the truth!

We are called to lead our families in faithfully following God, to willingly sacrifice, to love our spouses like Christ loved the church, and to guide our children to a life devoted to God and His service. We are called to be protectors, providers, and examples of godly living.

It's true: there is no such thing as a perfect man, husband, or father. We all make mistakes, have regrets, and wish we had done some things differently. But perfection isn't required. A commitment to live for God and lead and love our family is.

COMMITMENTS THAT MATTER: GOD'S PEOPLE

Do nothing out of selfish ambition or vain conceit. Rather, in humility value others above yourselves, not looking to your own interests but each of you to the interests of the others.

PHILIPPIANS 2:3–4 NIV

"To live above with the saints we love, oh that will be glory! To live below with the saints we know, that's another story!"

To leave a godly legacy we must not only be committed to God and our family but to the people of God, His church. That's not always easy. All too often pain and conflict erupt in the church. It's easy to be disappointed, discouraged, and disillusioned. But that doesn't mean we should walk away from God's people.

Today's verses challenge us in several ways. First, we are not to act out of selfish ambition or vain conceit. Our commitment to the church must go beyond our wants and needs and rest on a deep loyalty to the family of God.

Second, we are to value others. Even those who hurt and disappoint us are valuable and worthy of our grace and forgiveness.

Finally, we should care about and do what is good for others. It's God's church and they are God's people. Perhaps the most powerful question we can ask is, "What can I do for you?" We are all guilty of asking, "What can the church do for me?"

COMMITMENTS THAT MATTER:
GOD'S WORK IN THE WORLD

*"Therefore go and make disciples of all nations,
baptizing them in the name of the Father and of
the Son and of the Holy Spirit, and teaching them
to obey everything I have commanded you."*
MATTHEW 28:19–20 NIV

God is at work in the world! Many doubt it or ignore it
but it's still true. Also, God will accomplish His plans and
purposes. . .with or without us!

The only real issue is whether or not we will be part of
what God is doing. In the end, the best life is one fully devoted to the greatest cause. Nothing can match the gran-
deur, significance, or value of being on a mission with God.

Sadly, there are many myths and misunderstandings.
Serving God isn't a profession. It's a lifestyle. Serving God
doesn't mean giving up everything we enjoy. God isn't a
killjoy! Nor does it mean leaving the life we have and love
and going to some faraway place. We can serve God right
where we are. We think we're too busy. A man's day is
crowded with responsibilities and obligations, and many
think they don't have time. But we all know we make time
for what is most important to us.

Every man is gifted and called to serve God, and each
of us is uniquely equipped and positioned to make a
difference in the world right where we are. . .if we'll do it.

That's the real question, isn't it? Will we?

COMMITMENTS THAT MATTER: PRESENCE

*"And surely I am with you always,
to the very end of the age."*
MATTHEW 28:20 NIV

It's one of the most comforting promises in the entire Bible. Jesus is God Emmanuel, God with us who never leaves or forsakes us.

Presence matters. Being with those we love matters to our wives, children, and friends. Sometimes just being there, just being with those we love, is the very best thing we can do. But being there for those we love only happens if we make it a priority. But it's not always easy.

There are times when being away from family isn't a man's choice. Work and other obligations can demand long absences or that we miss important moments. That's not the point. Our wives and children understand that.

Here are some suggestions. First, make your presence a priority. Family events go on your calendar first! Build the rest of your life around them. Second, find a way to be with your wife and kids every day. Give them your time no matter how tired or stressed you are. When you are with them, be *with* them. Leave the briefcase, the hassles, and the worries at work and focus on them. When you can't be there, find a way to be there. Skype, telephone, e-mail, write notes and cards, Facebook message or Twitter, send flowers or gifts. Do something that shows your thoughts and your heart are with them. You'll never regret it.

Finally, make sure that when your kids and grandchildren leaf through the family photo albums, they'll find pictures of you!

Passover Begins at Sundown

Commitments That Matter: Future

*I consider that our present sufferings are not worth
comparing with the glory that will be revealed in us.*
Romans 8:18 niv

Some men live in the past. Others live only in the present.
All of us should live with an eye on the future.

The future is life's great, undiscovered territory. We
know the past. At least we think we do. We can see the
present, at least most of it. But no one accurately and
truly knows the future. All we can do is make our best
guess. There are too many unknown factors that are
completely out of our control for us to predict the future.
We just wish we could.

But this is a world of cause and effect, of action and
reaction. What we choose today always and inevitably
matters in the future. Sometimes what we think is a trivial
decision has the greatest impact. And we know that God
has revealed great truths and magnificent wisdom. So
how do we live with an eye on the future?

First, don't let the past determine the future.
Whatever happened in the past need not control our
present decisions or future lives. Second, act ethically
not expediently. Make wise long-term decisions not easy
short-term choices. Third, trust God, His will and His ways,
not what you see around you. Remember God, not our
present circumstances, controls the future.

Finally ask yourself, "Do I want this choice to be part
of the story of my life I tell my children or grandchildren?"

COMMITMENTS THAT MATTER: REPUTATION

*Here is a trustworthy saying: Whoever aspires to be
an overseer desires a noble task. Now the
overseer is to be above reproach.*

1 TIMOTHY 3:1–2 NIV

Reputation matters to your legacy.

A man's reputation is what others think of him and what kind of man they think he is. Some men build false reputations. They are good at pretending to be what they are not. They are like Dr. Jekyll who kept his Mr. Hyde carefully hidden. But no man is clever enough or careful enough to keep the truth about himself secret all his life. And when the truth comes out, his carefully constructed reputation is shattered. Building a good reputation can take a lifetime. Destroying it only takes one act or one failure.

Our family, our friends, the church, and the cause of Christ suffer or benefit from our reputation. Rightly or wrongly, others draw conclusions about them from what they know of us.

The surest and best way to build a reputation is to follow the admonition in today's verse, to live "above reproach." First, don't lead a double life. If you have a "Mr. Hyde" lurking somewhere, kill him! Second, pay attention to biblical standards and live well within those margins. Third, ask yourself what others, especially those outside the faith, will think if you act in a certain way. If it dishonors the Gospel in their minds, don't do it.

Finally, leave a reputation worth living up to, not one the church or your wife, children, and grandchildren will have to live down.

CONDUCT THAT MATTERS:
LIVE ABOVE THE LINE

But you, man of God, flee from all this, and pursue
righteousness, godliness, faith, love, endurance and
gentleness. Fight the good fight of the faith. Take hold of
the eternal life to which you were called when you made
your good confession in the presence of many witnesses.
1 TIMOTHY 6:11–12 NIV

On this day in 1990, the Hubble Space Telescope was
launched from the space shuttle *Discovery*. Not long
after, it was discovered that the images coming from the
Hubble were blurred and out of focus. Hubble needed
corrective lenses!

When it comes to living the Christian life, it's easy
for things to get out of focus. Sometimes it's hard to see
the line that separates godly conduct from culturally
acceptable conduct. We need the corrective lens of the
Holy Spirit to help us see clearly and live life above the line.

Living above the line is a matter of what we flee. To
begin, 1 Timothy 6:1–10 contains a long list of things the
man of God should run away from. Second, Paul tells
Timothy to pursue righteousness, godliness, faith, love,
endurance, and gentleness. Finally, Paul reminds Timothy
that living above the line is a fight, but it's a good fight.

Men who leave a great and godly legacy see clearly
what must be left behind and what must be sought, and
are willing to pay the price. They don't live below the line,
below the minimum standard. They don't live at the line,
just barely scraping by. They strive to live above the line!

CONDUCT THAT MATTERS: LISTEN

*"Now then, my children, listen to me; blessed are those
who keep my ways. Listen to my instruction
and be wise; do not disregard it."*

PROVERBS 8:32–33 NIV

Listening is always harder than talking. We all want others to know how we feel, to understand why we act and see things as we do. When people don't listen to us, we feel insignificant and disrespected.

It's easy to forget other people need the same thing from us. When we don't listen to our wives, children, friends, and coworkers, they feel ignored, uncared for, and mistreated. But when we listen well, we open the door to greater intimacy and understanding; we build trust and strengthen the bonds of our relationships. That's why listening is so important.

Before anyone else, we need to listen to God and His Spirit in our lives. All too often when we pray we talk too much and listen too little. Our family comes next. We need to listen to our wives. How else can we know their hopes, dreams, and fears? We need to listen to our children. It's the best way to earn our place in their lives for the rest of our lives. Our wives don't always need to know what we think. Our children don't always need correction or a lecture. Sometimes they just need us to love them enough to let them talk, listen carefully, empathize with their feelings, and show them the dignity and respect every person longs for.

Isn't that what God does for us when we pray?

CONDUCT THAT MATTERS: LAUGH

Our mouths were filled with laughter, our tongues with songs of joy. Then it was said among the nations, "The Lord has done great things for them."

PSALM 126:2 NIV

Oh, lighten up!

Life is serious business. But that doesn't mean we can't find joy and laughter in each day if we look for it. All too often men who feel the weight of their responsibilities wear that burden on their faces. Here's the question: Why would our children follow us into the Christian life if we are constantly joyless and unhappy? No one wants that kind of life.

Enjoying life is largely a matter of perspective. For us, a snowy day may mean shoveling the driveway, a slow commute to work, and the frustration of other drivers on slippery streets. To our children, a snowy day is filled with the boundless potential for fun. There's no school! The snow is beautiful. Sledding is great fun, and there's nothing better than pelting your sister with snowballs. It's all a matter of perspective.

We need to learn how to rejoice in the great things God has done and is doing even in the hard times. Let's learn to laugh at ourselves. We all do some amazingly funny things—we don't mean to but we do! Learn to laugh with others and enjoy being with them. Smile at the silly but annoying things other people do every day. Throw yourself into life and enjoy the trip!

So lighten up! Have some fun. The Lord has done great things!

CONDUCT THAT MATTERS: APOLOGIZE

*Godly sorrow brings repentance that leads to salvation
and leaves no regret, but worldly sorrow brings death.*
2 CORINTHIANS 7:10 NIV

Everyone has done things they regret. Not everyone is
man enough to apologize.

In *Love Story*, the famous book and movie of another
time, a dying young woman looks at her lover and says,
"Love means never having to say you're sorry." Nothing
could be further from the truth! There is little that
damages relationships more than the prideful refusal to
admit we were wrong, take responsibility for our actions,
and apologize to those we injured. That refusal denies
us the forgiveness we need and denies them the healing
they need.

At the core of our faith is the notion of repentance.
In a very real sense, when we confess our sins and
repent we apologize to God for the harm we've done to
Him and others. That act opens the door to His grace,
forgiveness, and new beginnings. All who choose the path
of repentance are welcomed. Those who refuse to repent
lock themselves away from God's love and care.

When we apologize we also set a standard and an
example others can follow to heal broken relationships
and grow in grace and humility.

CONDUCT THAT MATTERS: WORK HARD

And then I will be able to boast on the day
of Christ that I did not run or labor in vain.
PHILIPPIANS 2:16 NIV

There is little to admire in a lazy man. No employer wants to hire one. No woman wants to be married to one, and no child is proud of a lazy father.

We shouldn't be surprised. When God created Adam, He "put him in the garden of Eden to work it and keep it" (Genesis 2:15 ESV). Before God created Eve and gave Adam the responsibilities of a husband and father, God gave him work to do. Work isn't the result of the fall. It just got harder after the fall (Genesis 3:17–19).

Work isn't part of the curse but was meant as an expression of our nature as beings created in the image of God and in partnership with God's creative work in the world. Successfully completing a task and doing a good job brings a sense of satisfaction and self-esteem to a man that little else can bring. No wonder work is so important to us!

In his admonition to the Philippians, Paul pointed out that his work wasn't in vain and he could boast in the day of Christ. Paul put in the effort and worked hard at what mattered most. Paul did his work so well that he could boast not only in his accomplishment but also in the way he worked. So should we.

CONDUCT THAT MATTERS: BUILD OTHERS

*You then, my son, be strong in the grace that is in Christ
Jesus. And the things you have heard me say in the
presence of many witnesses entrust to reliable people
who will also be qualified to teach others. Join with me
in suffering, like a good soldier of Christ Jesus.*
2 TIMOTHY 2:1–3 NIV

There are plenty of people who are ready to tell our
children, our wives, our friends, and our coworkers what's
wrong with them. They don't need to hear it from us!

What they need to hear is what's right with them—why
we are proud of them, why we love them, and why they
are a gift to us and the world. There aren't many people in
their lives who can do that for them, but we can.

Paul's adopted son, Timothy, was an outstanding young
man who faced unfair criticism. There were plenty of people
ready to tell Timothy what was wrong with him. But Paul's
place in his life was entirely different. Paul taught Timothy
who Jesus was and who Timothy was in Jesus.

First, Paul encouraged Timothy. "Be strong in the
grace that is in Christ Jesus."

Second, this letter was part of Paul's long-standing
support, instruction, and help. These were things Timothy
had heard before.

Third, Paul's praise for Timothy and his teachings were
public. He said these things in the "presence of many
witnesses."

It's an example worth following.

Conduct That Matters: Sacrifice

*Therefore, I urge you, brothers and sisters, in view of God's
mercy, to offer your bodies as a living sacrifice, holy and
pleasing to God—this is your true and proper worship.*
Romans 12:1 NIV

We don't use the word *sacrifice* much, except in baseball
and for those who serve in the military. Maybe that's
because so few of us ever really sacrifice.

Sacrifice means surrendering something precious for
the good of another. Sacrifice is always costly, painful, and
challenging. But we should remember that the foundation
of our faith is Christ's sacrifice for us. He surrendered
heaven to suffer and die as a sacrifice for our sins.

A sacrificial life pleases God. It is true and proper
worship. But that sacrifice is taken up in "view of God's
mercy." Christ's sacrifice proved His love for us. It
changed the world and it changed the future. It brought
hope and healing, grace and goodness, joy and peace. So
we follow His example.

There is no more powerful demonstration of love and
courage than when a man willingly sacrifices his wants
and desires for his wife, his children, and the cause of
Christ. Sacrifice, not selfishness, is the stuff of heroes.
Such loving sacrifice sends a powerful message and
leaves a lasting legacy well worth whatever it cost.

A COACH'S WORLD

*You have heard me teach things that have been
confirmed by many reliable witnesses. Now teach these
truths to other trustworthy people who will
be able to pass them on to others.*
2 TIMOTHY 2:2 NLT

This is the age of executive coaching. Corporations have discovered that mentoring shouldn't end after a new employee has been on the job for a few months. Individuals are groomed to take advice, take charge, and take risks.

You may be getting some of your own executive coaching today in church. You may not think of church as coaching, but it can be. It should be.

As Christian men we start with learning biblical basics, but we never learn it all. Our entire lives can be spent being coached and coaching others. Barnabas coached Paul. Paul coached Timothy. Timothy coached his own congregation. Great coaching makes great teams.

Jesus never had much good to say about spiritual pretenders. Matthew 23:27 says, "'You're hopeless, you religion scholars and Pharisees! Frauds! You're like manicured grave plots, grass clipped and the flowers bright, but six feet down it's all rotting bones and worm-eaten flesh'" (MSG).

Intense? Yeah!

When we think we've learned all there is to learn, we need to think again. God never wants us to stop learning, stop sharing, or stop growing.

SHARE YOUR GIFT

*Each of you should use whatever gift you have
received to serve others, as faithful stewards
of God's grace in its various forms.*
1 PETER 4:10 NIV

Today, most board meetings follow *Robert's Rules of Order*. In 1876, US Army Colonel Henry Martyn Robert created the rules based on similar laws used by America's House of Representatives in bringing stability to their sessions. Thirteen years earlier, Robert had been asked to lead a business meeting at his church. By his own admission, he couldn't effectively lead that meeting. The issue of slavery caused the meeting to fall into chaos and Robert lost control. Robert determined to reform the rules to fill a need in his own church.

We might think someone else is taking care of all the needs within our church. We just stand by and allow other capable hands do the work. But God might just be asking someone that looks a lot like you to step up and help by using the skills He's given you.

Ephesians 2:10 says, "[God] creates each of us by Christ Jesus to join him in the work he does, the good work he has gotten ready for us to do, work we had better be doing" (MSG).

Whatever gift God has given you, He gave because He wants you to share it.

SUPERHERO SUBSTITUTE

*We have seen and testify that the Father
has seen the Son as Savior of the world.*
1 JOHN 4:14 NKJV

Each month, more than $250,000,000 is spent on the most popular comic books. Worldwide ticket sales for movies that are based on comic books are in the billions. At least three collectible comic books have sold for more than a million dollars each. Comic book heroes are big business.

People love superheroes because they're passionate about identifying with someone with the power to rescue people from bad situations.

First Timothy 1:15 says, "Here's a word you can take to heart and depend on: Jesus Christ came into the world to save sinners"(MSG).

We're born. We sin. We need rescue.

Jesus isn't make-believe. He is more than a compelling story. He's God's champion. He faced the toughest enemy mankind has ever known—and won.

We read comic books because we want a hero. We want to be rescued. We want everything to be all right in the world. Comic books are a fun substitute, but that's all they are. Spend all the money you want on comic books, but colorful pages can never replace God's living rescue plan.

We need a hero. God gave us Jesus—no charge.

THE HOUSE THAT FIFTY-SEVEN CENTS BOUGHT

Honor GOD with everything you own;
give him the first and the best.
PROVERBS 3:9 MSG

The year was 1912. The Reverend Russell Conwell led the congregation of Grace Baptist Church in Philadelphia. He struggled with the lack of space for Sunday school classes.

Unknown to the reverend, there was a little girl named Hattie May Wiatt who also saw the problem. She began to save pennies, nickles, and dimes. She became sick and died before a new church could be built.

Hattie's mother told Reverend Conwell about her daughter's savings. The handful of coins seemed small and insignificant when compared to the need, but Hattie's big idea was much bigger than she realized. The coins were all converted to pennies and the church sold Hattie's *pennies* for nearly $250.

Hattie's example inspired the Wiatt Mite Society. They used the $250 to purchase a nearby house for church use. The first classes of Temple College were held in the house that fifty-seven cents bought.

Our dreams are only the right size if they're bigger than we can manage on our own. If God gets no credit because we do everything ourselves, then all we've done is fulfill a self-achieving dream. God always dreams bigger than we do, shows up when we have nowhere to turn, and makes the impossible possible.

PRAY...AND DON'T STOP

In every situation, by prayer and petition,
with thanksgiving, present your requests to God.
PHILIPPIANS 4:6 NIV

General George S. Patton is known as a gut and gristle military genius. He's often portrayed as a man familiar with scathing words, blistering criticism, and unwholesome language.

Maybe that's why people thought he was mocking God when he asked one of his chaplains to compose a prayer for clear skies and fair weather for the battle his troops faced.

The man who wrote the prayer was James O'Neill. In his memory of the event, O'Neill quotes Patton as saying, "Chaplain, I am a strong believer in Prayer. There are three ways that men get what they want; by planning, by working, and by praying. . . But between the plan and the operation there is always an unknown. That unknown spells defeat or victory, success or failure. . . That's where prayer comes in."

One day stretched to many as the men prayed for better weather. At the most pivotal point of the battle, the weather changed and the direction of the war changed with it.

When it comes to prayer, never give up, never lose heart, and never stop asking.

HOMEWORK NEVER ENDS

Parents rejoice when their children turn out well;
wise children become proud parents.
PROVERBS 23:24 MSG

Being a dad is hard work. Your children look to you as a model. Your behavior can become their behavior. What you accept is what they accept. What you say is, well, you get the idea.

When you're at home, work at being intentional as a parent. When you ask your children to do, be, or say something different than what they see in your life, they can be confused. They may think, *He wants me to be something he isn't?*

Intentional dads understand their legacy comes at a price. Either they pay the price or their kids do. Dads are investors who never gain a return on their investment when they refuse to invest.

The time you spend doing homework is not just an investment in your children but also in your grandchildren. Leaving our kids without our example and encouragement will ultimately yield a generation with little direction or respect for others.

It's never too late to ask God to help you be intentional about helping your children. They need you, you love them, and God supplies the action plan. Find what you need in His Word.

WITHIN THE BOUNDARIES

Keep your minds on whatever is true, pure, right, holy,
friendly, and proper. Don't ever stop thinking about
what is truly worthwhile and worthy of praise.
PHILIPPIANS 4:8 CEV

Gaze at ranch land and you'll find fences. Ranchers will often say they get along better with their neighbors when there's a good fence between their properties. Why? The property lines are defined by boundaries. When boundaries are clear, the rancher has the freedom to improve, grow, and develop the land within the boundaries.

In our own lives, we have the boundaries of truth, purity, righteousness, holiness, friendliness, and propriety.

Breaking down those boundaries will always make purity less pure, truth less true, and holiness less holy. Broken boundaries allow us to accept bad behavior, participate in poor decision making, and treat others with less respect.

God wants us to embrace boundaries. We can use boundaries to keep other people out, but maybe God wants us to use boundaries to keep His ideas *in*.

We can be content within the fence when we realize it's for our good, a part of God's plan, and to remind us we were born with a purpose.

Discover a freedom to improve, grow, and develop the life within the boundaries.

AN IMPERFECT MOTHER'S DAY

*Watch out that no poisonous root of bitterness grows
up to trouble you, corrupting many.*
HEBREWS 12:15 NLT

She hadn't been perfect. She made her son choose between his father and herself.

The boy was twelve and wanted to spend time with his dad. That decision meant his mother would have almost nothing to do with him for more than thirty years.

In her 60s, she underwent a life-threatening operation. Her son showed up determined to forgive even though she had never asked.

In time, the mother said four words that were long overdue, "I love you, son."

Not every Mother's Day story mirrors a greeting card, but the reason we celebrate is that each of us live because our mothers went through the suffering of birth.

Not every parent gets it right. Neither does every child. Forgiveness restores relationships. Love accepts the rejected. Hope brings you back after you heal.

This isn't a day to stay away. It might be a day that you honor your mom simply because God asks you to. You might be surprised what this step of obedience can do for you—for her.

AN UNUSUAL CANVAS

Jesus. . .said, ". . .Everything is possible with God."
MARK 10:27 NLT

Paul Smith was born in the 1920s. While other children attended school, he lived with cerebral palsy. However, inside a body with limited muscle control was an artist.

In the mid-1930s, Paul discovered a typewriter in the neighbor's trash. He rescued the machine and began to create art. Meticulous repositioning of the paper and specific keystrokes allowed Paul to create typewriter art that looked very much like traditional charcoal drawings.

Friend Jim Mitch said, "[Paul] developed a distinct, beautiful way of creating art. . . Paul's technique required that the entire picture must be planned before he started."

Paul passed away in 2007, but his is the story of a marathon. While he could never run physically, he did have a passion to remain steady, determined, and composed. Once he found the typewriter, this man who struggled to speak created masterpieces from his room in an Oregon nursing home.

God has given you something only you can do. Are you trusting God to help you? Yes, it will be hard. Yes, you will have setbacks. It's true, you may not know how you can reach the finish line; but when determination meets God's provision, the result is always possibility.

THE WIND OF GOD

"In this godless world you will continue to experience difficulties. But take heart! I've conquered the world."
JOHN 16:33 MSG

There's an old saying, "Every time the wind blows, someone gets angry." Okay, so there's no actual saying, but it is true.

Researchers suspect that a change in ions on windy days contributes to irritability, and most agree that wind does change the way people feel—and usually that change is negative.

In our own lives we experience difficult situations, and just like wind, they make us irritable. But those difficult situations give us access to resources we may not have at any other time.

Like water drawn from the ground or power accessed through a windmill, we gain strength when we turn to face the wind of adversity and allow it to bring us closer to the One who gives us living water and spiritual strength.

God never promised only sunshine. He never promised trouble-free days. He promised His presence. He promised His love. He promised His provision. Psalm 31:7 says, "I will be glad and rejoice in your unfailing love, for you have seen my troubles, and you care about the anguish of my soul" (NLT).

So let the wind blow. Be encouraged. God is closer than you think.

CONSUMER TESTING

*It is absolutely clear that God has called you to a free life.
Just make sure that you don't use this freedom as an excuse
to do whatever you want to do and destroy your freedom.
Rather, use your freedom to serve one another in love;
that's how freedom grows. For everything we know about
God's Word is summed up in a single sentence: Love others
as you love yourself. That's an act of true freedom.*
GALATIANS 5:13–14 MSG

Marketers are quick to reach out to consumers. No business wants us to feel neglected, let down, or compelled to visit the competition.

We consume food, clothes, automobiles, news, sports, and amusements of all kinds. There is a love affair with choice, and we're frustrated and sometimes angry if the selection doesn't meet our standards.

What does God's Word say? "Keep your lives free from the love of money and be content with what you have, because God has said, 'Never will I leave you; never will I forsake you'" (Hebrews 13:5 NIV).

God isn't so much anti-stuff as He is pro-contentment. Contentment may best be described as being satisfied in God's presence, being thankful for His gifts, and believing God knows what we really need.

Godly contentment desires to be consumed with His goodness and is useful in showing others His love.

THE INTERSECTION OF INTELLIGENCE AND ENERGY

Jesus said, "'. . .love the Lord God with all your passion and prayer and intelligence and energy.'"
MARK 12:30 MSG

Transportation is usually thought of in terms of highways. However, your blood uses veins to travel throughout your body, your brain sends and receives messages via nerve endings, and phone calls use wires and audio waves.

God has always used transportation to move His message. Often the message God sends reaches our brain first, but for some reason it can't quite figure out the map needed to move a few inches from the head to the heart.

Why is it so hard to take a message that you understand to be true and move it to the place where it can change the way you live?

God's message to us often arrives at four different locations. Our heart is the place where passion lives, and it responds to the message in a way that's different than our soul or prayer life. Our mind is the place where intellect lives, while our strength is a place of energy and activity. Each location is a unique transportation hub.

Stop putting up road blocks and allow God access to every part of who you are. He's got a message—let Him through.

Hours: Spending the Leftovers

*How can a young person live a clean life? By carefully
reading the map of your Word. I'm single-minded in
pursuit of you; don't let me miss the road signs you've
posted. I've banked your promises in the vault
of my heart so I won't sin myself bankrupt.*
Psalm 119:9–11 msg

Each week has seven days. In those seven days, 56
hours are dedicated to sleeping. That leaves 112 hours
for everything else. If you spend an hour per meal, that
removes 21. Now there are 91 hours to use.

Remove the workweek and we're down to 51. Sure,
there are commute times and personal hygiene issues,
but we're still left with more time than we think.

We might attend a church service on the weekend
and read a devotional. So of the 168 hours we have
available each week, the grand total of time dedicated
to the one thing we say is most important could be less
than 2 hours a week. That's 104 hours a year or just over
4 days each year.

Should we be discouraged by this news? Should we
feel bad? No. Two hours is a starting point. Add time
whenever you can. Place God firmly on your priority list.
Pray on the commute. Get connected to a small group.
Find a Bible reading plan and consider reading through the
Bible. Use these ideas to improve the quality and quantity
of time you spend with God and the people He loves.

"He who began a good work in you will carry it on to
completion until the day of Christ Jesus" (Philippians 1:6 niv).

PANIC WITHOUT PROOF

Open your mouth and taste, open your eyes and see—
how good GOD is. Blessed are you who run to him.
PSALM 34:8 MSG

In the fall of 2014, America was overwhelmed. News had been released that the entire country was to be inundated with unprecedented snow depths that would cripple the nation, and only seasoned or quick-thinking survivalists would make it to spring.

Within a news cycle or two, the truth was revealed.

The website that originated the story has an ABOUT US tab. One click of that tab and visitors read, "[We are a] satirical and entertainment website. We only use invented names in all our stories."

Believable, *plausible*, and *terrifying* were all words used in connection with the story, but the real intent of the piece was not to inform but entertain. Few checked. Most panicked.

God has always wanted us to test our sources. First John 4:1 says, "Don't believe everything you hear. Carefully weigh and examine what people tell you. Not everyone who talks about God comes from God" (MSG).

How do we weigh and examine what we hear and read about God? Through His Word, the Bible.

People may not have an ABOUT US tab for us to check, but the ideas they present are either confirmed or denied by what God has already told us. God's Word is always enough.

A COMMUNITY ON THE CORNER

*God is love. Whoever lives in love lives in God,
and God in them.*
1 JOHN 4:16 NIV

The barber shop sits at the end of the block. The chairs and decor were installed in 1961, a few years prior to a man landing on the moon. Until recently, the founder of the shop was the first to greet guests. His name was in neon, just to the right of the rotating barber pole.

Inside you'll find men who've made this a regular stop for decades. One conversation with the owner made it clear why they returned.

He was a great barber, but he understood most people just want to be heard. His gentle questions highlighted an unexpected compassion. He remembered what you told him. If a farmer mentioned a struggle, the barber followed up the next visit to see if things had improved. They usually had.

That barber demonstrated what most men look for in friendship. We want friends who are dependable, listen, remember when they need to, and forget when they don't.

Jesus offered that example, but He wants that example to shine through us.

It's easy to get trapped in our own trouble, but other people may need us, and we need them.

We don't need to cut hair to learn this barber's skill. Perhaps he learned from someone far more compassionate.

THE BEST INGREDIENTS

"Go into the world. Go everywhere and announce
the Message of God's good news to one and all."
MARK 16:15 MSG

Who knew you could take dough, some tomato sauce, cheese, and a few favorite ingredients, toss them in the oven and create a masterpiece?

Statistics show there is more than 250 million pounds of pepperoni used in making pizzas each year. Pizzerias average 55 pizza boxes used each day. Ninety-four percent of us eat pizza regularly. Around the world, five billion pizzas are sold each year. And to show the wild popularity of the "pie," there is a pizzeria in Alaska with annual sales of more than six million dollars.

God has given us some impressive ingredients to deliver a message people crave. They include, "love, joy, peace, patience, kindness, goodness, faithfulness, gentleness, and self-control" (Galatians 5:22–23 NLT).

A message delivered in anger is less tasty and far less effective.

God wants our lives to have flavor. He wants our words to have impact. When we share the Good News we've been given, our ingredient list can be used to develop a craving in those who hear it, or it can leave an aftertaste that is memorable for all the wrong reasons.

Remember, God's top ingredient when sharing with others is love.

USING GOD'S APP

I am not ashamed of the gospel, because it is the power of
God that brings salvation to everyone who believes.
ROMANS 1:16 NIV

Our lives seem consumed with rectangular-shaped phones. They buzz and blip to alert us to incoming messages, calendar events, and phone calls.

Relationships are important to God; they should be to us. That's why we love our phones. With these mobile devices we—communicate—right?

Well, sort of. We click *like*. We decide to *share*. We post a picture of our food. Somehow we believe we're communicating.

There are times in our online world we don't even act like we do in real life. We *pretend* and think no one really pays attention.

God is the master of communication. What He has to say has to be shared. God's life app allows you to use your voice, your life, and your generosity to share His love with real people who live with real hurts.

Effective communication with God allows more effective communication with those who need to access His status updates. We can share them face-to-face and from His Book.

LEAVE THE MUSEUM REJOICING

Jesus Christ is the same yesterday, today, and forever.
HEBREWS 13:8 NLT

Walk into most museums and you find collections inspired by past events. The exhibits depict the best and worst of our past. We can be encouraged, entertained, or thoughtful when we leave a museum. The finest examples of museums engage our memories.

We wouldn't want to *live* in a museum because it only represents something that once was. We *visit* because we want knowledge or entertainment. We leave because there is real life existing in the here and now.

The Bible is filled with *history keepers* who explain what God had done for the people who followed Him. Their role was important and served a great purpose.

When the people remembered a faithful God, they always found a reason to praise Him.

If we look back at our own past, we'll discover that even when we made bad choices God was faithful to love and forgive. We shouldn't be surprised when gratitude to God is the result of remembering.

While the faithfulness of God doesn't change, neither do His commands. Nor does His willingness to guide, love, forgive, and provide.

God doesn't want His people to only live in His Faithfulness Museum because, as wonderful as that is, His faithfulness reaches into real life for real people right now.

Let God redeem your past by walking with Him today.

GOD'S SPENDING LIMIT?

"For all the animals of the forest are mine, and I own the cattle on a thousand hills."
PSALM 50:10 NLT

Accountants are valuable when it comes to keeping track of expenses. They know what assets have value and which have become liabilities. Budgets are an accountant's playground, and they're really good at making sure all expenses and payments are noted.

God's economy is a bit different. God cares less about numbers and more about people.

If God owns everything, then He can use anything to do the most amazing things. God doesn't even get upset at the cost it takes to rescue people. He just keeps relentlessly pursuing with incredible compassion.

He's a lavish God who makes sunsets, forests, stars, and oceans for us to enjoy.

God never has to worry about running out of resources. In fact, He never worries at all. He just keeps loving real people with real compassion leading to real change. And when He asks you to share what you have, it's all about experiencing a similar sense of joy that He felt when He gave His all for you.

HERE TO REPRESENT

GOD hates cheating in the marketplace;
he loves it when business is aboveboard.
PROVERBS 11:1 MSG

Today, if we want to weigh something we usually put it on an electronic scale. There's a more ancient method that's still in use. This method allows someone to put a weight on half of a two-sided scale. On the second half, they would place what they were either buying or selling. When the scale was balanced there was an equal amount on both sides. That's how people used to figure a price when buying or selling.

Sometimes business owners altered the weights. If they were selling something, they wanted the weight to weigh less so they didn't have to give as much to the buyer. If they were buying something, they would use a heavier weight so they could get more from the seller.

God calls this cheating and so would a customer. God would be displeased and so would the person who discovered the fraud. God could forgive, but a customer might never forget.

As a Christian, we're asked to bring integrity with us to the workplace. God wants us to represent Him in the way we do business. We should be willing to go farther than we have to in order to make things right.

We're God's ambassadors. We're not selective servants. We're not undercover believers. We're God's representatives to people who are all too familiar with dishonesty. Our story of God's faithfulness will always bear a hint of tarnish when we can't remember where we left our integrity.

THE BLESSING CONSPIRACY

*As God's chosen people, holy and dearly loved,
clothe yourselves with compassion, kindness,
humility, gentleness and patience.*
COLOSSIANS 3:12 NIV

George is a superhero. Those he serves don't know his name and rarely know what he looks like, but they remember what he *does*.

George visits a lot of restaurants. Usually he orders a cup of coffee. He's on a fact-finding mission. He quietly pays attention to what's going on around him. He puts one or two tables on his short list and asks the wait staff for help in his *blessing conspiracy*.

His *blessing conspiracy* has paid for the meals of elderly couples, single parents, and military veterans. The people try to identify their benefactor, but they don't recognize George and never assume it could be the coffee-drinking stranger.

George doesn't do this with every meal, but when he does, people he's never met leave marveling at his kindness; but he simply smiles and wonders how God allows him to be so blessed.

God doesn't ask us to be stingy and self-centered. We're pretty good at that already. He asks us to wear spiritual clothes that encourage us to pay attention to the needs of other people. This is when God does some of His best work—through us.

NEVER SETTLE

*Do your best. Work from the heart for your real Master,
for God, confident that you'll get paid in full when
you come into your inheritance. Keep in mind always
that the ultimate Master you're serving is Christ.*
COLOSSIANS 3:23–24 MSG

This year marks the 100th running of the Indy 500. Things have changed since the Indianapolis Motor Speedway was built. First-class stamps were two cents, a gallon of gas was six cents, and a new home was under $3,000. The *Titanic* was being built, a woman drove across the country for the first time, and car maker Henry Ford offered workers an eight-hour workday and a daily wage of five dollars.

Today, the famed motor race is still 500 miles, 200 laps, and a whole lot of left turns. The cars have changed, but the desire for the pace car to get out of the way has not.

We all want to see a good race. We won't be impressed when someone who's never actually raced takes to the track in a minivan to compete with compact cars and scooters.

We expect the standards and traditions of the sport to shine through every participant.

God has also given us standards of excellence. His *life plan* encourages adventure. What God has in mind for each of us is huge, but we have to be participants. We can't sit in the stands, use anything less than His equipment, or commit to something less than His best.

Get in—let's go.

INSECURE MUCH?

*There is no fear in love. But perfect love drives out
fear, because fear has to do with punishment.
The one who fears is not made perfect in love.*

1 JOHN 4:18 NIV

When it comes to asking a girl out on a date, most guys
either hesitate or refuse to ask. They may not admit it,
but for most guys there is an absolute fear of rejection. It
may be easier to think of what *might have been* instead of
facing the potential that she might say no.

Every guy faces insecurity. The most masculine
among us will have doubts about whether they're doing
life right. A man can be in any decade of life and wonder
if he really understands what it means to be a man.

We feel like pretenders, and no place seems safe to
admit our insecurity.

For those who think that love is a *girly* thing, you
should know that love is God's gift to you. His love offers
acceptance, invites trust, and is always the safest place to
share what's really going on.

God didn't create us without direction. His love for
us should make us comfortable in accepting His plan
for our lives. God created man, so He knows how we're
hardwired.

Real men accept God's love and engage life—fearlessly.

THE MOTIVATION TO FOLLOW

Whom have I in heaven but you? I desire you more than anything on earth. My health may fail, and my spirit may grow weak, but God remains the strength of my heart; he is mine forever.
PSALM 73:25–26 NLT

It's Cookie Monster's birthday. Who doesn't know about the blue-furred creature with a large appetite for circular-shaped tastiness?

In commemoration of his birthday, there are a few lessons we can learn from Cookie Monster. When he's committed to eating a cookie, he doesn't care what people think. When he talks about cookies, he's passionate. His love for cookies is not a short-term interest, because cookies have apparently changed his life.

Now, let's look at this idea with a few word changes.

When we're committed to following Jesus, we don't care what people think. When we talk about Jesus, we're passionate. Our love for Jesus is not a short-term interest, because Jesus has changed our lives.

The motivation to follow Jesus is tied to how we process His Good News. When we understand what Jesus saved us from, what He offers us now, and what He's preparing for our future, we might really begin to see that God's Good News is the best news—ever.

CHANGING THE FIELD OF PLAY

God's loyal love couldn't have run out, his merciful love
couldn't have dried up. They're created new
every morning. How great your faithfulness!
LAMENTATIONS 3:22–23 MSG

It wasn't long before Billy Sunday became a fan favorite and an accomplished center fielder for the Chicago White Stockings.

Sunday was one of the most exciting players of his era, one of the fastest runners, but one of the worst hitters. He was an orphan from an early age, and baseball allowed him to cope with life's frustration.

In 1886, Sunday was in downtown Chicago when he stopped by a street mission and met Jesus.

By 1891, he left baseball to preach at a local YMCA for $83 a month. Soon he would be preaching in towns throughout the United States. Over several decades Sunday would preach in over 300 revivals. More than one hundred million people heard him preach. A million people accepted God's rescue plan.

Billy Sunday was once in an enviable position. Baseball fans loved him. Offers to play were available to him, but the faithfulness of God contained an irresistible grace that drew the baseball player from the playing field to a harvest field.

Sunday found and shared what we all need to discover. God's loyal love is unending. His mercy is refreshing. His faithfulness is beyond awesome.

PRAY FOR THAT PEACE

[Jesus said,] "I am leaving you with a gift—peace of mind and heart. And the peace I give is a gift the world cannot give. So don't be troubled or afraid."
JOHN 14:27 NLT

Adam and Eve, the first man and woman, disobeyed God's singular request, "Don't eat from this tree." Their disobedience changed how we access peace. It was sin that caused Cain to kill Abel. Wars were common in the Old Testament.

A world without war is not the peace God offers. The peace that God supplies is the assurance that He's in control, trustworthy, and faithful.

Peace is an issue of the heart. Wars can be waged on every continent and God's people can still have a peace that can't be explained. Philippians 4:6–7 says, "Don't worry about anything; instead, pray about everything. Tell God what you need, and thank him for all he has done. Then you will experience God's peace, which exceeds anything we can understand. His peace will guard your hearts and minds as you live in Christ Jesus" (NLT).

Sin has invaded our world. Wars begin with arguments, broken promises, and disrespect. When mankind refuses to follow God, war is often the result.

On the other hand, God's peace can quiet individual hearts, provide reassurance, and is compelling enough to encourage individuals to send their fear into exile.

Pray for *that* peace.

HOW TO FOLLOW GOD'S WILL

*[God has] already made it plain how to live, what to do. . .
It's quite simple: Do what is fair and just to your neighbor,
be compassionate and loyal in your love, and don't
take yourself too seriously—take God seriously.*
MICAH 6:8 MSG

Christians want to know God's will because He might have something big for us to do and we don't want to miss it.

We're confronted with an up close glimpse at a single verse that tells us exactly what God wants from us, but we tend to dismiss this as nonessential because it doesn't seem to point to a *personalized* plan God might have for us.

Yet we learn God can only trust us with big things when He can trust us with small things. So God starts small. It's like He's saying, *"You want to know My will for you? Treat your neighbor right. Be compassionate to others and show them My love. Take My Word seriously, and don't be easily offended."*

If you think this is easy, try it sometime. In a world where we don't know our neighbors' names, it can be hard to treat them right. At a time when people don't trust each other, it's hard to show compassion. In a place where God's Word is mocked, it can be difficult to take it seriously. In a world where humans live, it's too easy to be offended.

Therein lies the difficulty of your starting place. God's will starts here. Get to a place of faithfulness with these issues and God will make sure you know what to do next.

THE SUCCESS OF FAILURE

*Commit your actions to the LORD,
and your plans will succeed.*
PROVERBS 16:3 NLT

We are confronted with innovative products every day.
Many show up on infomercials or shopping channels.
Some stores have kiosks dedicated to products we've
seen on television. Did you know there are plenty of
inventions made by mistake?

Penicillin is a remarkable antibiotic, but it wasn't what
Sir Alexander Fleming was trying to invent. He had been
working on a wonder drug that cured disease. When that
failed he threw everything away; but looking down at his
scientific trash, Fleming noticed a petri dish where mold
was consuming bacteria. What he thought was failure
was actually a success with a refined perspective.

God's plans for us are always *on purpose* plans, but
even if we take a wrong turn somewhere, God can still
cause "everything to work together for the good of those
who love God and are called according to his purpose for
them" (Romans 8:28 NLT).

God never does anything by accident. He loves you
intentionally. There's something He planned for you to do. He
has made sure you have everything you need to accomplish
His plan.

Perspective alters how we define success as well as
failure. God can use both.

BURDEN SHARERS

*Share each other's burdens,
and in this way obey the law of Christ.*
GALATIANS 6:2 NLT

Tomorrow is Memorial Day. The original name for the occasion was "Decoration Day." It started after the Civil War to decorate the grave sites in honor of those who died fighting on either side of the war. Today, family, friends, and communities continue to step up and decorate the tombs of the war dead no matter which war they served in. The day is a simple and straightforward demonstration of gratitude that means a lot to the families who *are* remembering.

You may not have someone you will personally remember tomorrow, but extending compassion to others who do will be a gift to those who may feel as if their loved one is being forgotten. It is likely these moms, dads, husbands, and wives have bits of remembered history they would be honored to share. For them the pain never really leaves; it just becomes something they can endure. Some days are better than others.

Romans 12:15 says, "Laugh with your happy friends when they're happy; share tears when they're down" (MSG).

Tomorrow it's likely you will find both kinds of friends. Serve them well with your attitude, actions, and compassion.

UNITED IN FREEDOM

Those who wait upon GOD get fresh strength.
They spread their wings and soar like eagles,
They run and don't get tired, they walk
and don't lag behind.
ISAIAH 40:31 MSG

Grace Seibold had been awaiting information about her son. Her hope dissolved in 1918 when news arrived that George was a casualty of World War I.

Grace eventually reached out to other mothers who had lost a child to war. She volunteered in hospitals. She used her pain to become productive.

Ten years later, what Grace had initiated came to be known as Gold Star Mothers. These women worked to bring comfort to other families facing similar pain. The organization Grace inspired was named for the gold star placed in the window of military families' homes as a visual reminder of the children who had given everything for their country and a cause.

Today we remember family, friends, and those we never knew who saw freedom as something worth defending.

Today we remember a Savior who purchased freedom with His own life. It is the hope that Jesus offers that can inspire those lamenting a loved one lost too early. The strength we need when remembering our lost loved ones is rightfully found in the embracing grace of Jesus.

THINGS WE THINK

You will keep in perfect peace all who trust in you,
all whose thoughts are fixed on you!
ISAIAH 26:3 NLT

The things we think often astonish, embarrass, and torture us. We think about things we know are off-limits, and without our permission the thoughts return.

When we spend time meditating on God's Word, we can have good decisions show up in our lives based on what we *allow* to take up head space.

Hebrews 12:2–3 gives some great advice on redirecting and reconnecting your brain to God's plan. "Keep your eyes on Jesus, who both began and finished this race we're in. Study how he did it. Because he never lost sight of where he was headed—that exhilarating finish in and with God—he could put up with anything along the way: Cross, shame, whatever. And now he's there, in the place of honor, right alongside God. When you find yourselves flagging in your faith, go over that story again, item by item, that long litany of hostility he plowed through. That will shoot adrenaline into your souls!" (MSG).

The story of Jesus is a remedy for bad thinking. We struggle—He helps. We blow it—He forgives. We wander—He encourages focus.

Grow your thought life in God's direction. A full benefits plan is waiting.

STICKS AND STONES: WORDS AND TONES

*Watch the way you talk. . . . Say only what helps,
each word a gift.*
EPHESIANS 4:29 MSG

Imagine a father saying to his daughter, "There's no use planning to go to college. It's your younger sister that will make it. She's the smart one." Or maybe, "Looks like you could use a little more time in the gym."

The old phrase "Sticks and stones may break my bones, but words will never hurt me" just isn't true. Words can do as much, if not more, damage than physical injury. The words we speak to our children will always effect a result. Those words can encourage and bring about an open spirit that thrives under our approval, or it can cause an uncertain spirit within our children that will wilt and close when they sense they will never be good enough for us.

Often what dads say is believed by the young ears that hear them spoken. Children can live up, or down, to our expectations.

With words God spoke this world into being. With words we can inspire hope or exile our children to a kingdom of doubt.

We can build our children up with carefully chosen but truthful words. On the other hand, we can tear down with words driven more by emotion or carelessness than fact. Sometimes those wounds last a lifetime. Often they impact the next generation. Occasionally they will damage the bond between father and child.

A biblical rule of thumb: pay attention to what you say, use words that are helpful, serve each word as a gift that's memorable for all the right reasons.

BE THE BUBBA

If one person falls, the other can reach out and help.
But someone who falls alone is in real trouble.
ECCLESIASTES 4:10 NLT

Today is National Bubba Day. This is a day set aside to honor men who are either named or simply called "Bubba."

Bubba is most often defined as "brother or friend." This is someone you can count on, turn to, and help out.

Proverbs 17:17 might be paraphrased, "Bubbas choose to help no matter what. When you're in trouble, a Bubba sticks close."

Men have always needed good friends. God has always warned us about accepting the wrong kind of Bubba. "Bad company corrupts good character" (1 Corinthians 15:33 NLT).

Jesus chose twelve men to spend time with and became their first-century "Bubba." If this sounds inappropriate, remember that the Bible encourages us to call God, Abba (Daddy).

Jesus had a plan and a purpose for those men, and for all who followed, He made sure they had everything they needed to develop into the right kind of friend that others would need.

We live in a world that is increasingly isolated. We stay behind the doors of our home and fail to learn the names of our neighbors. Follow Jesus' example and be the Bubba that other folks need.

No Secondhand Story

*Do your best to win God's approval as a worker
who doesn't need to be ashamed and who
teaches only the true message.*
2 Timothy 2:15 cev

The apostle Paul refers to the Christian journey as a race, but that's only part of the picture. There are two steps every Christian man should take. The first is to love God enough to serve those He loves. The second is to know enough of God's message that we don't have to be ashamed when someone asks us why we're helping out. It doesn't do much good to lend a hand but then be unable to tell more about what a relationship with Jesus looks like.

The Bible is where we learn, and we have to balance our walk between helping those who need help and learning more about why we offer help.

In the King James Version of the Bible, we are asked to "study to shew thyself approved of God." We don't assume, guess, or even make something up when it comes to answering questions of our faith. We *hold on* to God's hand, we *dig deep* in His Word, and our *spiritual muscles* grow when we really *know* what God said in the Bible.

Study and serve. Learn and give. Memorize and share God's love. He will approve this plan—every time.

HOPE: BEYOND WISHFUL THINKING

*The fundamental fact of existence is that this trust in God,
this faith, is the firm foundation under everything that
makes life worth living. It's our handle on what we
can't see. The act of faith is what distinguished
our ancestors, set them above the crowd.*
HEBREWS 11:1–2 MSG

The Bible uses the word *hope* dozens of times, but did you know that when the Bible uses the word *hope* it rarely means wishful thinking?

When God tells us to put our hope in Him, He is saying we should have *no doubts*. If we think of hope as wishful thinking, then doubt can creep into our thinking, overpowering what should be confident trust.

In our everyday life we can hope an unexpected check comes in the mail, we can hope our boss doubles our salary, and we can hope our car will sell for more than we paid for it. In each case, that is little more than wishful thinking. If we're honest with ourselves we would admit we have very little confidence that these things will actually happen.

God's hope should be unshakable, fully dependable, and rooted in the promises of a loving God.

It is a brave man who hopes in God the way God wants us to hope. We need to have the intestinal fortitude (guts) to, without doubt, believe that the God who promised *will* come through.

NOTHING ESCAPES HIS ATTENTION

"For all that is secret will eventually be brought into the open, and everything that is concealed will be brought to light and made known to all."

LUKE 8:17 NLT

One of the first things you'll notice if you ever have the opportunity to take a hot air balloon ride is how quiet it can be. Because there's no engine, the only noise is the occasional blast of the propane burner to heat the air. Because you're floating on air currents, there's little turbulence.

Equally remarkable are the clear sounds from the earth below. You can hear dogs barking, the excitement of children when they notice you, and the sounds of people calling to you thinking you can't hear them.

While not a perfect picture, this is a bit like God's relationship with us. Nothing escapes His attention. He sees all. He hears all. He knows who we are.

We can't hide from God. Hiding is a lie our adversary asks us to believe is possible, and when we believe it, he comes back to accuse us of being unfaithful to God.

If you've never been in a hot air balloon, it can be hard to imagine what it is like. If you've never really trusted in God, it can be hard to imagine what it's like for God to know all about you while you continue to ignore His presence.

God knows we *will* break His law. He watches, not as a judge, but as one who can compassionately offer forgiveness.

SOME KIND OF PARABLE

*He saved us because of his mercy, and not because
of any good things that we have done. God washed us
by the power of the Holy Spirit. He gave us new
birth and a fresh beginning.*
TITUS 3:5 CEV

Somebody thought that somehow, someway, someday he
would be someone. So Somebody went somewhere to try
something that would make him some kind of wonderful,
inspiring him to do some snazzy somersaults. But
sometimes the something he tried, in order to become
someone he wasn't, led to a somewhat solemn situation.

Each of us longs for acceptance. We want to be
known for something special. As men, we define who we
are by what we do. God defines who we are by what He's
done.

Is it possible our greatest desire for acceptance can
only be fulfilled in the God who created us? Is it possible
our purpose in life is discovered in the God who came to
somebodies and made them sons?

God's Son takes somebodies and creates something
special. So, somewhat in awe, each of us can somehow,
someday, and in God's own someway be known as the
somebodies accepted by the Son.

God did everything for you. All that's left is for you
to accept what He offers—not someday, someway, or
somehow—but today. His way. That's how.

STOOP DOWN—REACH OUT— SHARE BURDENS

Stoop down and reach out to those who are oppressed.
Share their burdens, and so complete Christ's law.
GALATIANS 6:2 MSG

A friend lost his job. A neighbor lost his health. A coworker lost his promotion. What can you do? How should you respond?

Most men aren't especially gifted in emotional encounters. Maybe we're afraid that if we get too close, the problems we see in the lives of others will become our problems. If things are running smoothly in our own lives, we avoid complications.

Following the Golden Rule (see Luke 6:31) will find us doing for others the things they could only hope for. Our actions might involve sweat equity, a listening ear, or perhaps a few dollars.

We give because God gave. We love because He loves. We forgive because we've been forgiven.

When it feels awkward to share the burden of others, just remember God's Son, Jesus, became one of us and saw firsthand how we live. Jesus fed the hungry, healed the sick, and taught those He encountered.

Stoop down. Reach out. Share burdens.

When you do that, you're living in obedience to the God who has never turned His back on you.

LIFE'S POP QUIZZES

I treasure your word above all else;
it keeps me from sinning against you.
PSALM 119:11 CEV

There's good news: life is an open book test and you have access to all the information you need to answer life's most important questions. There's bad news: the only book you really need is often overlooked.

We live in a world where access to information is not only available but expected. If we want the latest news, a few deft moves on a smartphone, tablet, or computer and the world is delivered to our screens.

We have come to believe that we don't have to be an expert in anything. Why? We can make new discoveries online when needed and then forget them just as quickly—or we store up information that isn't especially important.

God has always wanted us to know what He thinks about the issues that affect us most. We can't act in the way we should if we don't have God's wisdom. We have access to His Word, yet we often stand back and guess when life's pop quizzes show up.

When bad days come and the tests seem the hardest, we should consult God's Word, but our usual response is to complain to the Instructor about the existence of tests.

In school, we review textbooks in preparation for exams, but in real life we tend to view the Bible as an optional text rather than our primary source of wisdom.

We should keep the Bible handy—as a *treasure* for consultation, not bookshelf ornamentation.

THE LORD'S ARMY?

No one serving as a soldier gets entangled in civilian affairs,
but rather tries to please his commanding officer.
2 TIMOTHY 2:4 NIV

There's an old hymn that begins, "Onward Christian soldiers, marching as to war, with the cross of Jesus going on before." This has been sung for more than 150 years.

Some wrongly consider the song an anthem for Christians to engage the culture with violence in order to win back peace. Others object to the notion that God would have us engage in war at all.

This hymn is best understood when we consider that it takes dedication, discipleship, and discipline to follow God.

We are God's soldiers when we do what He commands. God's greatest commands are to love God and then everyone else. We only win when we show God's love.

We're to be at peace with people as often as we can (see Romans 12:18), serve others (see Acts 20:35), and give generously (see 2 Corinthians 9:7).

The war Christians wage is for the spiritual health of those we know. We protect our own health, nurture our children's health, and introduce Jesus to those we encounter. We press forward because lives are at stake. We should protect and defend but never attack.

The role of a military soldier and a Christian soldier are unique. Sometimes they overlap, but being a soldier for God means your first choice is love.

WRITE ON HEARTS

Proclaim the Message with intensity; keep on your watch. Challenge, warn, and urge your people. Don't ever quit. Just keep it simple.
2 TIMOTHY 4:2 MSG

The way the Bible was physically written required painstaking accuracy, long hours, and antiquated writing utensils made of ink and bird feathers or chisels and stone.

In the 1880s, John J. Loud wanted something that could be used to mark leather in his shop. He made an effective but crude tool using a ball bearing and ink for his purpose, but early model pens wouldn't be available until the early 1900s. It was postwar 1945 when America finally embraced the new ballpoint pen.

Yet from the first sentence penned in God's Word, there was a deliberate purpose behind every pen stroke that introduced mankind to the heart of God.

If God had waited until technology made it easy to give us His Word, how many generations would have been without knowledge of the One who created life, love, and forgiveness?

On the other hand, it may be reasonable to believe that today God wants us to use every tool we have at our disposal to share His love. Use a pen, a computer, video production, a stage presentation, a poem, a painting, or any other creative way to write His message on hearts, hearts that will never benefit if we're reluctant to share.

THE GREAT TASTE OF FOOLISHNESS

The instructions of the LORD are perfect,
reviving the soul. . . . They are sweeter than honey,
even honey dripping from the comb.
PSALM 19:7, 10 NLT

It's been called butter-pop, pole corn, long maize, and cornstick, but most just call it corn on the cob, and today is its special day.

There's something you have to bring with you when you indulge in corn on the cob—commitment. No matter how goofy you look, how much you squirt corn juice when you bite into the cob, or how much butter stays on your face and hands, you have to be committed to the task of eating corn on the cob.

Most think it's worth it.

Being a godly man also requires commitment. You might think you look foolish. You may worry about what others think. You might be concerned about your reputation. However, 1 Corinthians 1:27 says, "God chose things the world considers foolish in order to shame those who think they are wise" (NLT).

Are you willing to be committed to something others consider foolish? When you eat corn on the cob, the benefit to looking foolish is good taste. Psalm 34:8 says, "Taste and see that the LORD is good" (NLT). When you get a taste of God's love, any feelings of foolishness are more than offset by God's gift of satisfaction.

One taste and you'll agree—godly commitment is worth it.

Beware the Taunting Clicks

The poor will eat and be satisfied. All who seek the Lord will praise him. Their hearts will rejoice with everlasting joy.
Psalm 22:26 nlt

One quick way to ruin your day is to reach your automobile, place the key in the ignition, turn the key, and—nothing (except a few taunting clicks).

A phone battery needs to be recharged, a remote battery needs to be replaced, a car battery needs a good alternator, but even that needs replacement from time to time.

We men have succumbed to the great deception. We believe we're more valuable to our families and even God when we *do* more.

This thinking leads us to a selfish town called Discontent. In this place, no one is satisfied, everyone is envious of others, and all work for trophies.

At the corner of Restless and Unhappy, you're bound to run into a brute named Rebellion. He'll tell you everything you've done wrong and why you'll never amount to much.

If you hang around this depressing place too long, your inner batteries drain. All you hear from your future is taunting clicks.

Our best satisfaction will always be found in walking with Jesus and learning about *real* life. When your spiritual batteries need recharging, this is a great place to start. Contentment may be closer than you think.

SOMETIMES WE FORGET

*They traded the true God for a fake god,
and worshiped the god they made instead
of the God who made them.*
ROMANS 1:25 MSG

Men are made to worship, and we will. Worshipping God is important, but most of us make time, room, and effort to worship other things.

When left with a sense of awe and wonder we can quickly, and far too easily, turn away from God toward whatever inspired the wonder.

This could mean a visit to the mountains finds us thinking more about the mountains than the God who made them. We can watch sports and find ourselves in awe of the player instead of the One who gave the skill.

But the connection doesn't stop there.

We can worship a car, jobs, entertainment, comfort, and even sex. We replace God with something that doesn't have the ability to rescue lives, forgive sin, or change futures. We reevaluate what's most important and move God from first place.

Faith is important in worship. We have to believe that the God we *do not* see can fill us with more awe and wonder than everything we can see.

Sometimes, we forget.

A DESTINATION TO REMEMBER

*We make our own plans,
but the LORD decides where we will go.*
PROVERBS 16:9 CEV

On this date in 1777, the Second Continental Congress officially adopted the American flag as a symbol of the nation's heritage and freedom. Its most current design with fifty stars was adopted for national use in 1960. This flag was designed by seventeen-year-old Robert Heft as a class project in 1958. If you're curious, he received a B- for his creation.

The only original meaning behind the symbolism of the flag was that the thirteen red stripes signified the thirteen original British colonies while the stars in the blue field represented the number of states within the union. Later, however, Charles Thompson, Secretary of the Continental Congress, stated, "White signifies purity and innocence, Red, hardiness & valour, and Blue. . .signifies vigilance, perseverance & justice."

Sometimes good ideas develop into great ideas over time. Ideas can be little more than seedlings waiting to grow. Often we're surprised with how big they become.

God is the only one who knows 100 percent of the time what will actually happen. He asks us to trust Him with our future. Like the flag, we may be changed over time, but when we agree to follow God, the end result will always be remembered and celebrated in the hearts and minds of the grateful.

HE GIVES BETTER GIFTS

*"Give, and you will receive. Your gift will return to you
in full—pressed down, shaken together to make room
for more, running over, and poured into your lap."*
LUKE 6:38 NLT

Some of the wealthiest in our world have signed the
"Giving Pledge." The idea is for individuals to give away
the majority of thier wealth before they die to social
issues they are concerned about.

While God never asked us to sign a pledge He did tell
us the following two things: 1) giving is His idea, and 2)
we will receive when we give.

What happens when you give and you don't feel that
gift is "returned to you in full"? Let's say you give $100
to your church, but you don't receive $100 in return. You
may doubt the accuracy of today's verse.

God always blesses a cheerful giver. He promises to
take care of our needs, which means His return gift often
goes beyond what we need. Is it possible the gifts we
receive from God have never been limited to money?

What if, when we give, we receive a closer relationship
with Him? What if our gift is a softened heart, improved
outlook, or contentment? What if God's blessing to a
generous heart is so much better than mere money that
we might be ashamed we ever thought God intended to
make us wealthy in the one way that is meaningless in
heaven?

God will always give better gifts than He receives.

ANXIETY AWARENESS

[Jesus said,] "Father, if you are willing,
please take this cup of suffering away from me.
Yet I want your will to be done, not mine."
LUKE 22:42 NLT

As the *Son of God*, Jesus knew what things were like on the other side of His personal sacrifice. He knew forgiveness would be available to all who sought it. Love and grace? A free gift. As a *human,* he struggled with the weight of His final human act.

Some may want to bypass the words of Jesus when He asked God to remove the assignment of death from Him. The part of Him that was God knew what needed to be done. The part of Him that was human was overwhelmed by the task.

We should all be in awe of Jesus' next words, "Yet I want your will to be done, not mine."

God's plan for the rescue of humanity was ironclad. It was perfect, near completion, and unexpected. God didn't need a backup plan. He needed an obedient Son. When Jesus said "It is finished" as He hung from the cross, it was clear God's plan was accomplished on a hill of sorrow.

God is aware of the anxiety we feel when things seem out of control. God knows the strength we need to walk through the toughest days—and He walks with us.

He'll even lead if we let Him.

INTERRUPTIONS ENCOURAGED

*So whenever we are in need, we should come bravely
before the throne of our merciful God. There we will be
treated with undeserved kindness, and we will find help.*
HEBREWS 4:16 CEV

When you were in school, the teacher would invite
students to ask questions, but at some point you were no
longer allowed to ask because you had to take a test or
quiz.

Your parents may have been patient and allowed you
to ask questions, but at some point you may have been
told, "You have asked enough questions."

In the workplace, your boss may not mind questions
that help you learn to do your job without needing to ask
so many questions.

Try to think of someone—anyone—who likes being
interrupted. Is it hard to identify this superhuman?

God is the only One who doesn't mind His children
asking as many questions as they want. He never objects
to interruptions. What God actually tells us is to be brave
when we come to Him, expect kindness we don't deserve,
and find the help we need.

Relationships begin with conversation. Interrupt God
whenever you need to. The end result is a closeness that will
never be found trying to do things on your own—without
His help.

BEYOND LIFE HACKS

*"While you are in the world, you will have to suffer.
But cheer up! I have defeated the world."*
JOHN 16:33 CEV

Have you used a *life hack?* These hacks (or tips) give you an opportunity to use items you probably already own to make certain jobs easier.

With the right life hack you can use a waffle maker to complete a panini sandwich, a clothespin to hold a nail when hammering, duct tape to open a difficult jar, or toothpaste to clear up your headlight covers.

There aren't many life hacks for things like a rebellious child, a struggling marriage, a job in jeopardy, or a habit you can't break.

One universal truth to remember is that *life is hard.* Certainly there are enjoyable parts, but there are plenty of things we just seem to endure. Rather than take this knowledge and become pessimistic, we should remember that we can always draw close to the One who has overcome or defeated the world.

When the apostle Paul struggled with a hard life, God said, "My kindness is all you need. My power is strongest when you are weak" (2 Corinthians 12:9 CEV).

Admittedly, men tend to be self-sufficient, action oriented, and often reluctant to ask for help. God wants us to realize we should ask Him for help because He's the only One who is perfectly reliable.

THE JOB OF BEING DAD

They say—again, quite rightly—that there is only one
God the Father, that everything comes from him,
and that he wants us to live for him.

1 CORINTHIANS 8:5 MSG

Bring up the subject of fathers and you discover those who can recall with great fondness the role he had in their lives. There are also those who live with painful memories of an absent or even unknown father.

Not all men take the job of being a dad seriously, yet here we are celebrating the day and some are feeling pretty awkward about it all.

For some men, the idea of viewing God as their Father seems less than ideal. They know what their dad was like, and if God is anything like their memory, then the term "Father" has negative emotional connections.

When you take the time to look at the attributes of God, you find that He is loving, merciful, kind, all-knowing never-changing, faithful, honorable, holy, and forgiving, just to name a few.

If that sounds different than your father, then maybe getting to know God can help change your understanding of what it looks like from God's perspective to be a father.

If you find that list impressive, then you should know that God has given you a list of traits you can rely on, and He still wants you to know Him as Father.

First Day of Summer

ACQUITTED

"Anyone who trusts in [Jesus] is acquitted; anyone who refuses to trust him has long since been under the death sentence without knowing it. And why? Because of that person's failure to believe in the one-of-a-kind Son of God when introduced to him."
JOHN 3:17–18 MSG

Frank R. Stockton's classic short story, "The Lady, or the Tiger," follows a young man who is unworthy to marry the princess but has fallen in love with her, thus breaking the king's law. The king had his own method of determining guilt and innocence. The accused entered an arena facing two doors. If the accused was a man, there would be a beautiful woman that he was to marry behind one door and a savage and hungry tiger behind the other. He alone could make the choice between doors. That choice determined his fate.

Since this was actually little more than a game of chance there was no reliable way to determine innocence or guilt.

With God we enter His proverbial arena where we're simply asked if we're guilty of sin. Our only truthful answer has to be yes. God will need to know how we'll pay for our guilt. In His court there's only one correct answer. *Jesus* paid the guilt price for our sin. We could choose to try to pay the price on our own, but that choice separates us from the love of God and ends in death.

Choose Jesus—discover real life.

SHOW THE GRACE

Be gentle with one another, sensitive. Forgive one another as quickly and thoroughly as God in Christ forgave you.
EPHESIANS 4:32 MSG

To her, he's just the nice man that helps her. To him, it's heartbreaking to see the woman he fell in love with view him as *the help*.

Confusion is her closest companion. She despises her new best friend as mind and body betray her. Personal dignity left no forwarding address.

The care she requires falls almost entirely on his shoulders. Not fair? Absolutely. Not fun? Who would think such a thought?

But in those times when recollections sparkle, or a comment reaches her funny bone and she reacts—he is reminded that his commitment has unexpected and precious rewards.

There are over 5 million American men and women currently suffering from Alzheimer's disease. That's 5 million families struggling to understand and fight through issues of the disease. They are often overlooked, misunderstood, and in a regular state of distress, and this is only one disease on a very long list.

Everyone's going through something more difficult than you can imagine. Make the choice to show the grace, love, and compassion God has shown to you.

GAME PLAN COMMITMENT

*Keep your eyes open, hold tight to your
convictions, give it all you've got, be resolute,
and love without stopping.*
1 CORINTHIANS 16:13–14 MSG

There can be intense anxiety when you believe you're standing alone in your faith. God gave us everything we need to stand for Him, but it can feel like we're in a battle we can't win when loneliness seems to be our only fellow traveler.

The Bible is filled with examples of men who thought they were alone in their stand for God and against evil. Many felt betrayed, exhausted, and broken.

Maybe this describes you. Maybe you've been looking for reinforcements. Maybe you want to be reassigned to something less *front line*.

God never intended you to be a sideline Christian. He doesn't ask you to sit in the stands. He doesn't commend armchair Christians, but He will give seasons of rest.

Take courage in Paul's speech—"Keep your eyes open, hold tight to your convictions, give it all you've got, be resolute, and love without stopping."

There's work to do. Even if you feel like you're the only one working. Remember, when you serve God even the impossible becomes possible.

In Constant Communication

*"The Holy Spirit will come and help you,
because the Father will send the Spirit to
take my place. The Spirit will teach you."*
John 14:26 cev

They don't spend much time exploring nature, but a reality television show offers them the opportunity to spend a couple of days outdoors. They venture off alone but in constant two-way communication with a survival expert.

The survival expert knows how to get the contestants from the starting point to a celebrated ending. All that's really needed is a contestant willing to follow directions— no matter how strange the instructions sound.

Some contestants start strong but refuse to follow instructions. Others seem to struggle with the circumstances they face, but they listen and do exactly what they're told.

Those who finish have an incredible story to share, are more capable when facing future challenges, and are able to encourage others who struggle.

Christians are asked to participate in adventures we can never finish on our own. We need help.

God will send His Holy Spirit to give us the guidance we need to do every hard thing we face. He is with us— from start to finish.

RESTLESS, AND HATING IT

Why am I discouraged? Why am I restless? I trust you!
And I will praise you again because you help me.
PSALM 42:5 CEV

Have you ever had feelings of restlessness? You feel like you should do something, but you don't know what. You can't sleep well and you don't know why. You feel like you have a deadline, but you don't know when.

Feelings of unrest can leave us with plenty of room for self-reflection. Identifying the reasons why we're restless can help us determine where we're headed next, and why.

Restlessness usually means we're not where we should be and suggests the need to relocate our heads, hearts, and hopes.

God can send unrest into our lives when we get too comfortable in circumstances God doesn't want for us or in a place where we've stayed too long.

Restlessness can be God's invitation to a new adventure.

Confusion, *apprehension*, and *depression* are words that could be used to describe that godly unrest that screams, "*Move*."

God's call can be ignored, but the restlessness will not go away until you answer the call.

When you feel restless, and we all will, it's an incredible opportunity to follow God's plan.

SINGED AND STRUCK

Do not throw away this confident trust in the Lord.
Remember the great reward it brings you!
Patient endurance is what you need now, so that you
will continue to do God's will. Then you will
receive all that he has promised.
HEBREWS 10:35–36 NLT

For thirty-five years, Roy Sullivan was a park ranger in Virginia's Shenandoah National Park. Sullivan's nickname was "The Human Lightning Rod." The Guinness World Records recognized him for being struck by lightning more times than any other human.

Sullivan was new to his job when, in the spring of 1942, he was struck for the first time. Between 1969 and 1976, Sullivan was struck five additional times. Each time he was left with burn marks, singed hair, and a growing fear of storms.

On June 25, 1977, Sullivan was fishing when lightning struck the top of his head for the seventh and final time. As Sullivan aged, he found other people considered him bad luck. Most expressed anxiety, believing that just by being close to him they ran the risk of being struck by lightning. He, too, feared he might attract lightning in a crowd.

He was afraid of death.

No matter what you face, no matter how hard, frustrating, or unnerving, be assured of this—a firm trust in God brings eternal rewards you can't even begin to imagine.

Nothing we face here can be compared with what God has waiting for those who trust Him.

THE THREE INVESTMENTS

"Above all and before all, do this: Get Wisdom!
Write this at the top of your list: Get Understanding!"
PROVERBS 4:7 MSG

Everything we do requires an investment of time, energy, or talents.

If you believe that the best use of these three investments is for monetary or personal gain, then it becomes easy to believe that helping others is a waste. However, if you believe that God has given you these three investments to use for His purposes, then helping others is not only a good use but perhaps the best use of your personal resources. To put this in perspective, understand that God invests everything He has in *relationships.*

What you believe about the use of these three investments will inform how you manage—or mismanage—their use.

First Timothy 6:17–19 is a pretty good overview of how God looks at our investments. "Tell those rich in this world's wealth to quit being so full of themselves and so obsessed with money, which is here today and gone tomorrow. Tell them to go after God, who piles on all the riches we could ever manage—to do good, to be rich in helping others, to be extravagantly generous. If they do that, they'll build a treasury that will last, gaining life that is truly life" (MSG).

IN THE PRESENCE OF GREATNESS

*"Show respect to the aged; honor the presence
of an elder; fear your God."*
LEVITICUS 19:32 MSG

Route 66 covers nearly 2,500 miles of byways, hills, and history. Many still consider it the *Mother Road*.

This highway is the tangible memory of the days of large cars and cross-country adventure when travelers were met with hospitality, full service gas stations, drive-in theaters, and diners.

Today, sections of Route 66 are rededicated to the culture of the road. Classic diners have been restored. Many feel an invitation to return to a simpler time in America's history.

On this date in 1985, Route 66 was set aside in favor of faster travel on the Interstate. Some states have made portions of the old highway national historical sites. The legacy of Route 66 lives on.

There's a similar sense of honor that God calls us to offer those who've lived longer than we have. The wisdom learned or obtained by these men and women is often overlooked and underappreciated.

Invite them to share their stories, triumphs, and even struggles. Younger, more eager ambitions may seem to have displaced them, but given enough honor, their legacy can continue to impact others.

Honor the wisdom of the aging because God commanded it. This gift of honor brings long-term blessings.

THE PLAN, GOAL, AND PURPOSE

*Keep your eyes on Jesus, who both began and finished
this race we're in. Study how he did it. Because he never
lost sight of where he was headed—that exhilarating finish
in and with God—he could put up with anything along
the way: Cross, shame, whatever. And now he's there,
in the place of honor, right alongside God.*
HEBREWS 12:2 MSG

Keep your eye on the prize. Get your head into the game.
Press on. Play with purpose.

Every single thing that requires a plan, completes a
goal, or captures the purpose of the heart requires focus.

When a runner is *beyond* tired, it's the finish line that
inspires him to push forward and finish strong. When a
singer has been invited to perform his first solo, it's the
audience that inspires courage. When an entrepreneur
comes up with a brilliant idea, it's the launch of his
product that gives him his first real sense of hope.

There will be days then the Christian life is hard. Our
adversary will distract us and offer the equivalent of a
recliner, detour, or false promise. He won't care if he's able
to totally ruin our lives. All he really wants is to shift our
focus.

Keep the focus on Jesus. Learn who He is, how He
lived, and what He wants.

Feeling weary? Spend time with His story. Regain your
focus, get your second wind, and press on.

DISCRIMINATION ENCOURAGES COMPARISONS

*Faith in Christ Jesus is what makes each of you equal
with each other, whether you are a Jew or a Greek,
a slave or a free person, a man or a woman.*
GALATIANS 3:28 CEV

Sometimes we compare. We tend to judge ourselves by thinking of someone who doesn't seem to have it all together. *The playing field has become level.*

Sometimes we play favorites and chose our own team while leaving others out. *Where you come from no longer matters.*

Sometimes we feel superior because it doesn't seem we need help. *How much money you make is irrelevant.*

Sometimes we think our spouse would never understand. *Men and women are both welcome to accept this message as equals.*

God accepts everyone who accepts His Son. God loves everyone, and some love Him back. God forgives, and some accept forgiveness. God doesn't discriminate. He offers His best gifts to everyone. Some choose to refuse His gifts.

If we're distant from God, we need to remember He keeps the line of communication open. Maybe He's just waiting for our call—no matter who we are.

GOD OF THE TRANSITIONS

"Be strong. Take courage. Don't be intimidated. . .because
GOD, your God, is striding ahead of you. He's right there
with you. He won't let you down; he won't leave you."
DEUTERONOMY 31:6 MSG

Most sports have a shelf life for players. At some point they'll leave the game, but most will continue to work. We may have more in common with our sports heroes than we thought. Why? Most men will have an average of three different careers in their lives.

Bobby Brown was third basemen for the New York Yankees in the late 1940s and early 1950s. During those years, Brown was studying to be a doctor. When he retired from baseball, he became a respected cardiologist. Brown was also a veteran of two wars.

If you find yourself at the end of a career or you're starting something new, take courage. You might have been inspired by the transitions made by sports figures, but you should know that the apostle Paul moved from persecutor to preacher. Abraham went from living in an ungodly atmosphere to becoming the father of many nations. Matthew was a tax collector who transitioned to be a disciple of Jesus.

God can use seasons of change to make us more effective in sharing His story in a new environment.

A PLACE TO SIT

And seeing the multitudes, He went up on a mountain,
and when He was seated His disciples came to Him.
Then He opened His mouth and taught them.
MATTHEW 5:1–2 NKJV

When we think of the Sermon on the Mount, we picture Jesus (as Hollywood has coached us) perched on a high rock up in the hills, teaching the multitudes—or walking through tall grass on the mountainside, reciting the Beatitudes as He maneuvers among the masses congregated there. But scripture says He walked *away* from the crowd, headed into the hills, and found a place to sit. When His closest followers came to Him, He taught them. This is a picture of intimate impartation to a few, not a scene with stage lights, microphones, and a megachurch multitude.

Men too often long for the soap box and the spotlight. We want to hear the applause and the "amen." But Jesus looks for faithfulness in little things (Luke 16:10). He calls us to feed our own households and teach our own children first and foremost (Matthew 24:45; Ephesians 6:4; 1 Timothy 5:8). Whether or not we're called to speak to the many, we must often step away from the crowds and find a place to sit with the few in our lives who matter most.

BE BLESSED

"Blessed are. . ."
MATTHEW 5:3 NKJV

Jesus begins the Sermon on the Mount with a list of proverbs that the Church calls the Beatitudes (a Latin word for "blessings"). "Blessed" means "happy." In the pagan Greek culture of Jesus' day, the word *blessed* meant to be as happy as the gods—to have *their* perks, *their* rights—to be *above* the toils and troubles of earth while enjoying its treasures.

But this isn't Greek mythology we're reading—this is *eternal truth* that Jesus is proclaiming of a joy much fuller than the worldly blessings of health, wealth, pleasure, power, and the pursuit of happiness.

For "mountain men" (those willing to follow Jesus into the mountain to be taught by Him), the Beatitudes are about life in pursuit of a different set of goals. Philippians 2:5–8 tells us to have the same attitude that Jesus had when He gave up heaven's haven to become a man. He humbled Himself, surrendered most of His God-rights, and became obedient to the Father in all things, even death on the cross.

The Beatitudes aren't about houses, clothes, cars, smartphones, or anything else on this planet. The blessings are about laying up treasures in heaven by living like Jesus here.

THE POVERTY OF PRIDE

*"Blessed are the poor in spirit,
for theirs is the kingdom of heaven."*
MATTHEW 5:3 NKJV

The climb up the mountain with Jesus begins with a descent into the heart—and a commitment to humility. To be poor in spirit is to be humble. Only those who take themselves low will be lifted high enough to inherit heaven (Matthew 23:12). God opposes the proud but gives grace to the humble (James 4:6).

It's hard for men to humble themselves. We've been taught to stand tall, to take the lead, to pull ourselves up by our bootstraps, to never let anybody push us around. Even in the Church we are sometimes encouraged to "claim our rights" as sons of the King—as if God owes us something other than the mercy that Jesus bought for us by His blood. In a religious environment focused on winning the blessings of earth, humility gets stuffed in a closet. In a culture focused on worldly prosperity, spiritual poverty can seem almost heretical!

But wait!—doesn't the Bible tell us that no man can muscle his way into heaven? Doesn't Jesus call us to admit that life is too heavy to carry on our own? Doesn't He tell us to link arms with Him and learn about Him? He said that He is "meek and lowly of heart," and only by embracing those qualities can we find rest for our souls (Matthew 11:29). No wonder we are called to be humble and poor in spirit, for this is who Christ Jesus is!

THE PURSUIT OF SADNESS

"Blessed are those who mourn,
for they shall be comforted."
MATTHEW 5:4 NKJV

The Fourth of July—a day for Americans to celebrate the heritage of life, liberty, and the pursuit of happiness. We spend *much* on pursuing happiness—avoiding suffering, sidelining sorrow, trying to beat the blues. What if somebody told us that true happiness comes with the *pursuit of sadness*? That's what Jesus said: "Blessed are those who mourn." Happy are the sad!

C. S. Lewis wrote, "The settled happiness and security which we all desire, God withholds from us by the very nature of the world." So joy must come from something other than its own pursuit. It comes from facing the truth about our brokenness. Only truth can set us free (John 8:32). To turn our backs on suffering is to turn our backs on truth, on God, and on humanity. The joy of the Lord—and the comfort of the Lord—is for those who weep with those who weep (Romans 12:15).

The secret of joy for those who mourn is that God is with us in the mourning—our comfort comes from His presence. He comes alongside us as we come alongside others, just as Paul wrote, "God the Father of our Lord Jesus Christ, the Father of compassion and the God of all comfort. . .comforts us in all our troubles, so that we can comfort those in any trouble with the comfort we ourselves receive from God" (2 Corinthians 1:3–4 NIV).

MEEK AIN'T WEAK

"Blessed are the meek, for they shall inherit the earth."
MATTHEW 5:5 NKJV

History trumpets the names of men who have tried to conquer the world: Genghis Khan, Alexander the Great, Napoleon Bonaparte, Julius Caesar, Attila the Hun, Charlemagne, Adolf Hitler. As you read their names and recall their character, does the word *meek* come to mind? Probably not.

Had they been men of gentle temperament, they would not have so violently tread so much turf and shed so much blood. And to what end? A grave beneath the earth they sought to rule!

Jesus said of Himself, "I am meek and lowly in heart" (Matthew 11:29 KJV). Was He weak? No way! Physically, emotionally, spiritually, intellectually, and relationally, Jesus was a man's man. Scripture notes His growth in wisdom and stature even as a teen (Luke 2:52). Dean Plumptre wrote, "The Boy grew into youth, and the young Man into manhood, and his purity and lowliness. . .drew even then the hearts of all men." As a man, He endured the torture of crucifixion with astounding self-control (see the Gospel accounts). Then He rose from the dead! Meek ain't weak.

One day Jesus will create a new heaven and a new earth (Revelation 21:1–3). Neither the militant Muslim nor the megalomaniac millionaire will have any part of it. It is the inheritance of the meek, the followers of Jesus.

A HUNGRY MAN

"Blessed are those who hunger
and thirst for righteousness, for they shall be filled."
MATTHEW 5:6 NKJV

When Jesus said this, He wasn't peddling burgers and beer to a TV audience munching potato chips. He was addressing men and women who understood hunger and thirst intimately.

In Jesus' day, the daily wage was equivalent to three cents; nobody got fat on that. Israeli working men—never far from the borderline of real hunger or actual starvation—ate meat once a week. And thirst was worse; few besides the Romans had water in their homes.

In reality, this beatitude is a stark challenge: Do you want righteousness as much as a starving man wants food or a parched man needs water? How intense is your desire for God, for His goodness and glory?

To the privileged, hunger and thirst can become idolatrous. Desiring food we don't need, eating when we've had enough (more than enough), we become gluttons. But hunger and thirst for righteousness is a safe appetite, a holy appetite, a right appetite. We were created for righteousness.

Saint Augustine, in his *Confessions*, wrote, "God, you have made us for yourself, and our hearts are restless till they find their rest in you."

Only God and His word can fill us and refuel us to follow Jesus.

Mercy Me

"Blessed are the merciful, for they shall obtain mercy."
Matthew 5:7 nkjv

A criminal is shown mercy when his sentence is shortened. A prisoner of war is shown mercy when he is treated humanely. The fallen gladiator in the Roman Colosseum was shown mercy when the dignitaries in the box seats gave a thumbs-up to let him live.

We extend mercy when we bless those who curse us, pray for those who persecute us, and do good to those who do us wrong (Matthew 5:44). We show our children mercy when we patiently give them another chance at something they've failed (or refused) to do. Mercy, like grace, is undeserved favor, something extended to others who may not merit it but need it.

Though we deserve judgment for our sin, God's great mercy has given us new birth instead and a living hope through the resurrection of Jesus Christ (1 Peter 1:3). Thus we show mercy and forgiveness to others (Ephesians 4:32).

Saint Augustine, an early church father who received the mercy of God through a dramatic conversion experience, wrote: "Two works of mercy set a man free: forgive and you will be forgiven. And give and you will receive." We could call this "the law of divine reciprocity." In other words, "You reap what you sow."

Do you need mercy? Give mercy.

PURE HEART

"Blessed are the pure in heart, for they shall see God."
MATTHEW 5:8 NKJV

In 1966, The Rolling Stones released a single called "Paint It Black," a somber song sung by a young man whose girlfriend has died. With her death, the color went out of his life: "I look inside myself and see my heart is black. . ." Honest introspection.

Jesus said, "If your eye is bad, your whole body will be full of darkness" (Matthew 6:23 NKJV). He said this while talking about what we treasure and whom we serve. If our eyes are on worldly things, if our hearts are set on serving our desires, then we're not looking to the Light and the light that we think is in us is actually darkness!

1 John 1:5-7 says, "God is light and in Him is no darkness. . .If we say that we have fellowship with Him, and walk in darkness, we lie and do not practice the truth. But if we walk in the light as He is in the light, we have fellowship with one another, and the blood of Jesus Christ His Son cleanses us from all sin" (NKJV).

How does a man walk in the light? By being honest about the state of his own heart. "If we say that we have no sin, we deceive ourselves. . .If we confess our sins, He is faithful and just to forgive us our sins and to cleanse us from all unrighteousness" (1 John 1:8-9 NKJV).

Only the blood of Jesus can wash away the dark stain of sin and purify our hearts. Then we enjoy true fellowship with one another. Then we see God!

PEACEMAKERS

"Blessed are the peacemakers,
for they shall be called sons of God."
MATTHEW 5:9 NKJV

Samuel Colt, inventor of the first revolving cylinder handgun once said, "The good people in this world are very far from being satisfied with each other, and my [guns] are the best peacemaker." When Colt died from a sudden illness in 1862, his wife took over the gun business and developed the famous Colt .45, still known today by its nickname, The Peacemaker. Many a frontier sheriff carried this gun in his role as peacekeeper.

When Jesus said "Blessed are the peacemakers," He didn't have guns in mind. His peace doesn't come with gun in hand but with love in heart. The love of God disarms the heart of man. The kindness, forbearance, patience, and goodness of God lead us to repentance (Romans 2:4). Jesus shed His blood to make peace between God and humankind—and between man and man (Colossians 1:20).

As ambassadors of the Prince of Peace, we don't "walk softly and carry a big stick" (as US President Teddy Roosevelt once described his foreign policy). We simply walk softly, for as Solomon wrote: "A soft answer turns away wrath, but a harsh word stirs up anger" (Proverbs 15:1 NKJV). Christ makes His appeal of peace through us as we implore others to make their peace with God (2 Corinthians 5:20). In this way, like the Prince of Peace Himself, we will be called sons of God.

Improbable Joy

*"Blessed are those who are persecuted for righteousness'
sake, for theirs is the kingdom of heaven."*
Matthew 5:10 NKJV

Church statistician David Barrett estimates that around
70 million Christians have died for the faith since the
stoning of Stephen. In our own day, martyrdom and
persecutions are at an unprecedented high. Globally—
even in America—persecution of Christians is rising as
an antichrist mentality seats itself in the boardrooms,
newsrooms, classrooms, war rooms, rest rooms, and
throne rooms of our world's most influential institutions.

It appears (if we have eyes to see) that we are living
in the day that Jesus spoke of when He told His disciples,
"You will be hated by all nations because of me" (Matthew
24:9 NIV).

So what does Jesus command us to do? "Rejoice and
be exceedingly glad" (Matthew 5:12 NKJV).

What?! We'd have to be crazy to get happy about
persecution—but maybe we know something that our
persecutors don't, that no matter what happens to us
down here we've got heaven! The kingdoms of this earth
will all fall, but the kingdom of heaven will last forever. An
incredible reward awaits us there. "Therefore, my beloved
brethren, be steadfast, immovable, always abounding in
the work of the Lord, knowing that your labor is not in
vain in the Lord" (1 Corinthians 15:58 NKJV).

UNDERFOOT

"You are the salt of the earth, but if the salt loses its flavor. . .[i]t is then good for nothing but to be thrown out and trampled underfoot by men."
MATTHEW 5:13 NKJV

Peanut Butter was a lively, loud-barking golden retriever, always poised at her master's feet and ready to jump. Especially excitable when visitors came, her frenetic attentions were over the top. Mark gave her the nickname "Lady Underfoot."

Years later, with Lady Underfoot gone to her reward, Mark got another retriever, a male this time. The polar opposite of his predecessor, Bono hardly budged and never barked. He was salt that had lost its savor.

Christians are the salt of the earth. We give this tepid old planet the flavor of heaven, and we help slow its inevitable decay. But if we lose our saltiness, what good are we?

In Christ's day, salt was sometimes contaminated by various minerals and therefore rendered worthless as a preservative. Such salt was thrown out, not in a field where it might kill the plants but on the road where traffic would grind it into the dirt. Losing our "flavor" isn't the issue (real salt never loses its flavor). The concern is in nullifying our influence as a preservative. A faith defiled by worldly philosophies and contemporary morality is good for nothing. Only the truth can set men free. Everything else ends up underfoot.

CITY ON A HILL

"You are the light of the world.
A city that is set on a hill cannot be hidden."
MATTHEW 5:14 NKJV

Jesus is the Light of the world, and those touched by His torch are set on fire with the same light from heaven. This dark world needs the light of the followers of Christ, but that doesn't mean it wants it. Chrystostom wrote: "Like men with sore eyes, they find the light painful. While darkness, which permits them to see nothing, is restful and agreeable." Jesus put it this way, "Men loved darkness rather than light, because their deeds were evil" (John 3:19 NKJV).

In the Old West, a gunslinger on the run might take to the desert and pray for nightfall to avoid a determined posse. But in the midst of the midnight sandstorm, the welcome light of another man's campfire always drew him in. At that wild and lonely campfire, coffee and hardtack were offered freely, and no man was an enemy.

The Church, if it is doing the good works it is called to (Ephesians 2:10, John 14:10–12) will not hide the light of life from the fugitive in the desert. We will shine like stars in the night sky (Philippians 2:15), showing the way to life. We will be like a city on the mountaintop, a haven for the lost and weary traveler. Our campfire will signal shelter— eternal shelter—from the storm.

As the old ditty goes (sung around many a church retreat campfire): "This little light of mine, I'm gonna let it shine. Let it shine! Let it shine! Let it shine!"

Phatter Than a Pharisee

*"For I say to you, that unless your righteousness exceeds
the righteousness of the scribes and the Pharisees,
you will by no means enter the kingdom of heaven."*
Matthew 5:20 NKJV

Phatter than a Pharisee? Anyone could beat them to heaven! Didn't Jesus say so (Matthew 23)? He called them white-washed tombs. He said they were blind, dirty, greedy, faithless, merciless. He called them fools and prophet-killers. He. . .

But wait!

To think we are better than them is to fall into the same pit with them. Yes, Jesus called them on their hypocrisy, but the shocking reality is that the Pharisees were 100 percent committed to righteousness as they understood it. They dedicated themselves to the honor of God's Word and the fame of God's name. The problem was, they were so sure of themselves they couldn't see that being sure of themselves was their biggest sin. They believed commitment to right made them right. They thought they had a patent on truth, and they were blind to their own falsehood—blind even to God in their midst (John 1:11).

Pride precedes a fall (Proverbs 16:18). Humility precedes wisdom (Proverbs 11:2). Wisdom says (as John Newton once declared), "I am a great sinner. Christ is a great savior."

Righteousness greater than the Pharisees' comes by grace, through faith in the only Righteous One who can save "a wretch like me."

"You Fool!"

"But I say to you that whoever is angry with his brother
without a cause shall be in danger of the judgment."
Matthew 5:22 nkjv

Jerry's mother left him when he was young, and now they were separated by four decades and several hundred miles. When Richard asked if Jerry was still in contact with his mother, Jerry replied, "That fool? I hope I never talk to her again!" She was "guilty" according to the anger and judgment in Jerry's heart, and he had never let her out of his interior prison. "I can't forgive her," he said.

"Yes you can," Richard countered.

"You're right," Jerry admitted, "but I will not!"

Who was really in prison? Jerry was! Locked up with his anger, it had even eaten away at his body. In his fifties, he was crippled by years of degenerative rheumatoid arthritis. Anger can fester. It can kill. Ecclesiastes 7:9 says, "Do not hasten in your spirit to be angry, for anger rests in the bosom of fools" (nkjv). Ephesians 4:26–27 exhorts, "Don't get so angry that you sin. Don't go to bed angry and don't give the devil a chance" (cev).

What do *you* do with your anger? Have you forgiven others as Christ forgave you? "The hour is coming," wrote Dietrich Bonhoeffer, "when we shall meet the Judge face to face, and then it will be too late."

CUT IT OUT!

"If your right eye causes you to sin, pluck it out and cast if from you; for it is more profitable for you that one of your members perish, than for your whole body to be cast into hell."
MATTHEW 5:29 NKJV

In the sci-fi thriller *World War Z*, a zombie pandemic threatens the world. Only one thing stands in the way of the annihilation of humanity: a courageous team led by a United Nations investigator (played by Brad Pitt). When a woman is bitten by a zombie, Pitt cuts off her hand to save her from the infection that will turn her into a mindless, rampaging maniac.

But in the admonition to pluck out the eye that sins, Jesus isn't telling us to dismember ourselves. That would be a deluded and tragic interpretation of His words. He is using such strong, violent imagery to tell us how critical it is that we cut sin off at its root.

If your eye causes you to sin—if you are looking at things you shouldn't look at—deal radically with the situation. Jesus isn't telling us to blind ourselves. That won't deal with the issues of the heart, will it? Even a blind man can lust in his heart, nurse anger in his heart, covet in his heart, hate in his heart.

Only Jesus can cleanse the heart. Confession and accountability to another brother can often cut temptation at the roots. It's hard to come clean—but look at the alternative!

HITCHED

"But I say to you that whoever divorces his wife
for any reason except sexual immorality
causes her to commit adultery."
MATTHEW 5:32 NKJV

The pickup truck rattled to a halt, and a young man got out and came into the office of the county clerk.

"Sir," said the young man. "Make me up a certificate so that Peter Brown can marry Suzanny Summers."

"Are you Peter Brown?" the clerk asked.

"I am Peter Brown," declared the young man.

"Is the young lady of age?"

Peter hesitated. "No. . .she ain't!"

"Oh! Then you have her father's permission to marry her?"

"Well, you can bet I do!" said the young man, moving over to the window. "See thet old man a-settin' in the back of thet pick-up, shotgun 'cross his lap? That's her pa!"

Shotgun weddings are few these days, but once hitched, maybe we need a little buckshot nudge to *stay* hitched. For believers, the nudge is God's Word itself.

"I hate divorce!" God said (Malachi 2:16 NLT). "Therefore what God has joined together, let no one separate," Jesus commanded concerning marriage (Matthew 19:6 NIV).

"Till death do us part" should not be a death wish for our spouse but a lifetime commitment—come hell or high water—to exemplify the everlasting faithfulness of the One who laid down His life for us (His "bride") at Calvary.

CUSSIN' COUSINS

"But let your 'Yes' be 'Yes,' and your 'No' [be] 'No.'"
MATTHEW 5:37 NKJV

"Why, you dad-flustered, ding-dang, daisy-headed son of a drip-dried dervish!" Farmer Jones shouted over the fence at Farmer Smith.

Smith began to answer with his own string of original pejoratives then stopped himself in midsentence. The parson was coming down the road on his big black bay horse. Louder than before, Smith (a deacon at the local church) exclaimed, "Farmer Jones, our Lord said, 'Do not swear at all! Neither by heaven for it is God's throne, nor by earth for it is his footstool, nor by Jerusalem for. . .'"

Is that the kind of swearing Jesus was talking about in the Sermon on the Mount? No, doggone it! He was talking about swearing an *oath*, about making a promise, about giving our word. He meant: "Don't cross your heart and hope to die. Don't swear on a stack of Bibles. Let your 'yes' be 'yes', and your 'no' be 'no.' Put your money where your mouth is. Anything more than that comes from the evil one."

No need for oaths, because we can't implore heaven to make our pledges come true. We dare not ask the earth to assist us, either. We must simply say what we mean and mean what we say.

The devil uses convincing words to assure us that his ways are better than God's ways. We don't need to use his tactics to sway others to our convictions or make them believe in our sincerity. We must be men of our word. Period.

TOOTHLESS

"You have heard that it was said,
'An eye for an eye and a tooth for a tooth.'"
MATTHEW 5:38 NKJV

An eye for an eye and a tooth for a tooth is quite fair. Rather than suing the restaurant for a million dollars if a waiter spills hot coffee in your lap, you spill hot coffee on his lap in return.

But "an eye for an eye and a tooth for a tooth" doesn't work well within the human heart. When we insist on payback for every little loss in life, we live by the law of self instead of the law of love—and "an eye for an eye and a tooth for a tooth" will soon have us all blind and toothless.

The alternative in conflict is to "turn the other cheek." And not just once. When Peter tried to get Jesus to applaud the idea of forgiving his brother a grand total of seven times, Jesus said, "Nope, not seven, but seventy times seven" (see Matthew 18:22). In other words, again and again and again. . .as often as forgiveness is needed.

Payback, retaliation, vengeance: it's not ours to dole out. Not at all. It belongs to the only One who is truly just (Romans 12:19.)

"To sum up," in the words of Peter (who finally got it), "all of you be harmonious, sympathetic, brotherly, kindhearted, and humble in spirit; not returning evil for evil or insult for insult, but giving a blessing instead; for you were called for the very purpose that you might inherit a blessing" (1 Peter 3:8–9 NASB).

LOVE YOUR ENEMIES

*"Love your enemies, bless those who curse you,
do good to those who hate you, and pray for those
who spitefully use you and persecute you."*
MATTHEW 5:44 NKJV

Matthew 5:44 is more than a love portion for our enemies;
it's a remarkable summary of the application of love in all
relationships: to bless, pray, and do good. We bless with
our lips. We pray from our hearts. We do good with our
hands. Let's look at the "bless" commandment first.

In the context Jesus is addressing, someone has
"cursed" you, someone has intentionally said bad and
hurtful things about you. They're mad at you or don't like
you, maybe even hate you—so they express ill will toward
you vocally. They're not poking voodoo dolls and reciting
incantations against you, but they're speaking evil about
you. Maybe it's behind your back, maybe to your face.

When cursed, Jesus says, "Bless!" When someone
says bad things about us, we say good things to (and
about) them. Maybe we'd rather blast than bless. Maybe
we even pride ourselves on how fast we can come back
with a sarcastic one-liner. But scripture says, "Don't repay
evil for evil. Don't retaliate with insults when people
insult you. Instead, pay them back with a blessing. That is
what God has called you to do, and he will grant you his
blessing" (1 Peter 3:9 NLT).

Speak good to others. Bless, and don't curse.

"Inspiteful" Prayer

"Pray for those who spitefully use you and persecute you."
Matthew 5:44 nkjv

David prayed, "Break the teeth in their mouths, O God; Lord, tear out the fangs of those lions! Let them vanish like water that flows away; when they draw the bow, let their arrows fall short. May they be like a slug that melts away as it moves along, like a stillborn child that never sees the sun" (Psalm 58:6–8 niv).

Why can't we pray against our enemies like that? They deserve it, don't they? It's a terribly degrading thing to be bullied, picked on, and singled out for spiteful abuse. It's wrong. It's sin. And we all hate a bully. When we're being abused, we'd like to pay a bit of it back (with interest), but Jesus says, *"Don't. That's my job. Your job is to pray that I don't* have *to pay it back."*

Jesus prayed from the cross for the men who nailed Him there, for the men gambling for His clothes at His feet, for the men who delivered Him to the Romans and stood gloating, cursing, and mocking Him at His crucifixion. He prayed, "Father, forgive them!" (Luke 23:34 niv)

Stephen, the first Christian martyr, prayed for his executioners when their stones knocked him to his knees, "Lord, do not hold this sin against them!"

When we pray for our enemies, at least two things usually happen: 1) our own hearts change as we become more like Christ, and 2) God hears our prayers! Pray that your enemies will see God's goodness and love, repent of their sin, and be brought near to God (Romans 2:4).

DO-GOODERS

"Do good to those who hate you."
MATTHEW 5:44 NKJV

When wicked people lie on their beds and devise evil against us (as Micah 2:1 says they do), we are to lie on our beds thinking of ways to do them good.

"If your enemy is hungry, feed him. If he is thirsty, give him a drink" (Proverbs 25:21 NCV).

Why do that?

Because, "in doing this, you will heap burning coals on his head, and the LORD will reward you" (Proverbs 25:22 NIV).

Reward me for heaping coals on my enemy's head?

Yes, because your good will overcome his evil (Romans 12:20–21).

How so?

The goodness of God works on the heart to soften it (Romans 2:4). It works on the conscience to convict it. Right deeds done for those who do us wrong heap "hot coals" of conviction upon them. The Holy Spirit uses our good deeds to convict them of their own sin.

We are called to Christ in order to do good works, which He has prepared for us long before we saw the light of our first day (Ephesians 2:10). Some of those good works are meant to be practiced on our enemies so that they "take the heat" of the Holy Spirit's conviction, their hearts expand to let Christ in, and their lips open in praise and glory to our Father who is in heaven (Matthew 5:16).

SECRET SAINTS

"And your Father who sees in secret
will Himself reward you openly."
MATTHEW 6:4 NKJV

Millions watch the Academy Awards. They're fascinating, but self-centered, self-absorbed, and self-exalting. It's Hollywood in love with Hollywood, slapping itself on the back, congratulating itself for the God-given gifts it uses to thumb its nose at the Creator and His commandments. The next morning's news is filled with commentary on what the stars wore to the awards. But when the applause of the world has faded and they stand alone before the throne of God, will they hear, "Well done, good and faithful servant"—or not?

God's people are called to be secret saints. Not necessarily hidden saints, but humble saints. It's not about the spotlight, it's about the motive. We need to be careful that we don't do all the right things (giving, praying, fasting; see Matthew 6:1–8, 16–18) for the wrong reasons. "Watch out! Don't do your good deeds publicly, to be admired by others, for you will lose the reward from your Father in heaven" (Matthew 6:1 NLT). If we are "performing" for the world's camera, we will miss the award of being secret saints. A secret saint doesn't even let his left hand know what his right hand is doing. He seeks God's glory, not his own. God rewards that kind of faith.

James 4:6 states: "God opposes the proud" (those who love the praise of men), "but gives grace to the humble" (those who desire the glory of God) (ESV).

Vain Repetitions

"They think that they will be heard for their many words."
Matthew 6:7 nkjv

Buddhists have prayer wheels with mantras written on the outside of a cylindrical spindle. They believe that spinning the wheel will have the same effect as orally reciting the prayers over and over. The more the wheel turns, the greater the effect of the "prayer." They believe their repetitious chants draw them closer to an inner sense of wholeness called nirvana: a state of perfect peace.

We are not to pray like that. Jesus offers the only perfect peace (John 14:27; Isaiah 26:3). Praying over and over again will not conjure the peace that only comes when we consciously cast our cares upon Him. In the words of a treasured hymn: "What a friend we have in Jesus, all our sins and griefs to bear. What a privilege to carry everything to God in prayer."

Though He already knows our needs, God wants to hear from us. He's a Father desiring relationship with His children. Jesus said, "Come to me, all you who are weary and burdened, and I will give you rest. Take my yoke upon you and learn from me, for I am gentle and humble in heart, and you will find rest for your souls" (Matthew 11:28–29 niv).

God hears His children, not because of their many words but because they come to Him to learn from Him, to walk and talk with Him. He cares (1 Peter 5:6–7).

FORGIVE

"But if you do not forgive men their trespasses,
neither will your Father forgive your trespasses."
MATTHEW 6:15 NKJV

On a hard cot in a cold cell in communist Romania, Richard Wurmbrand witnessed a miracle. In a bed to one side of him was a pastor so badly beaten he was near death. On a cot on the other side was the man who had beaten the pastor, a communist who—for some unknown reason—had been tortured by his own comrades and locked up to die.

The communist, waking from a nightmare, cried out, "Please, pastor, pray for me! My crimes are so terrible that I'm afraid to die!"

The pastor painfully arose, stumbled past Wurmbrand, and sat at his enemy's bedside. To the man who had tortured him, he tenderly spoke some astounding words: "I have forgiven you with all of my heart, and I love you. If I who am only a sinner can love and forgive you, more so can Jesus who is the Son of God and who is love incarnate. Return to Him. He longs for you much more than you long for Him. He wishes to forgive you much more than you wish to be forgiven. You must repent."

In that dark cell, the communist jailor confessed to all the torture and the murder he had done. The two men prayed together. They embraced. The pastor found his way back to bed. Both men died that very night.

TWO MASTERS

"You cannot serve God and mammon."
MATTHEW 6:24 NKJV

In 1777, Benedict Arnold won the Battle of Saratoga, a victory that reversed the Continental Army's losing streak and convinced the French to come to the aid of the colonies. But Arnold was a self-seeking man. Accused of corruption, he once faced court-martial for putting military funds in his own pocket. When a battle wound sidelined him to garrison duty, he bitterly brooded on the underappreciation of his martial genius.

Desire for riches and honor moved Arnold to believe he'd do better as an officer in the enemy's army! While commanding West Point, he systematically weakened the fort's defenses and drained its supplies. For switching sides, he asked the British for money and a major general's commission. But no man can serve two masters—for he'll cling to the one while despising the other. In the end, the traitor earned only the disdain of both Americans and Brits—and his true master (money) could not save him from poor health. He died in London at the age of sixty.

We would be wise to learn from Arnold's foolishness. "For the love of money is the root of all kinds of evil. And some people, craving money, have wandered from the true faith and pierced themselves with many sorrows," but "godliness with contentment is itself great wealth" (1 Timothy 6:10, 6 NLT).

WHAT, ME WORRY?

"Do not worry about your life, what you will eat or what you will drink; nor about your body, what you will put on."
MATTHEW 6:25 NKJV

The hunting, trapping pioneer mountain men of America's West knew the privation of a wilderness where food and clothing were scarce. They knew the sure need of shelter in the bitter winter months. Most of them trusted their own hands for their needs, but Jedediah Strong Smith put his faith in God.

Biographer Dale Morgan called Smith "an unlikely sort of hero for the brawling West of his time, that West about which it has been said that God took care to stay on his own side of the Missouri River." Jedediah, a modest man and true Christian, was also a man for the mountains who quickly emerged as leader among the most significant group of continental explorers ever assembled.

As he crisscrossed the wilderness with God as his provider, he in turn provided for his parents back East, sending money earned through the lucrative trapping trade. To his elder brother, Ralph, he wrote, "It is that I may be able to help those who stand in need that I face every danger—it is for this that I traverse the mountains covered with eternal snow. . .[and] pass over the sandy plains in the heat of summer, thirsty for water. . .[and] go for days without eating. . . . Let it be the greatest pleasure that we can enjoy. . .to smooth the pillow of [our parents'] age."

In that letter, Jed sent his family $2,200—no small sum in his day!

SPLINTER INSPECTION

*"Why do you look at the speck in your brother's eye,
but do not consider the plank in your own eye?"*
MATTHEW 7:3 NKJV

The tattoo on his arm read, "Only God can judge me." His lips spouted judgments about everything and everybody else around him. Jesus said, "Don't judge, and you won't be judged." But He also said, "Stop judging by mere appearances, but instead judge correctly" (John 7:24 NIV). So. . .we're allowed to judge if we do it right? Yeah, but we gotta do the *Judge-Right Two-Step* first: 1) take the log out of your own eye, and 2) then help your brother with the splinter in his eye.

Got dust (or an eyelash) in your eye? It hurts, you blink, a tear rolls. You want to rub it! Get a mirror, look close—lift the eyelid to see what you can see. Eyeball to eyeball, that little hair looks (and feels) like a Popsicle stick! It's a matter of perspective—and that's Jesus' point. The man who truly sees his own sin knows it's no small thing and is far better able to help his brother with his troubles.

"If someone is caught in a sin. . .restore that person gently. But watch yourselves"—examine yourselves—"or you also may be tempted" (Galatians 6:1 NIV). The Message words it like this, "If someone falls into sin, forgivingly restore him, saving your critical comments for yourself. *You* might be needing forgiveness before the day's out."

"But if we judged ourselves rightly, we would not be judged" (1 Corinthians 11:31 NASB). Ouch! Where's the mirror?

PEARLS AND PIGS

"Don't throw your pearls to pigs!"
MATTHEW 7:6 NLT

Solomon wrote that beautiful women who lack discretion are like gold rings in a pig's snout (Proverbs 11:22). He had a large harem of beautiful women, so he should know!

Jesus borrowed Solomon's barnyard imagery for His admonition concerning pearls and pigs. Precious things are wasted on the unappreciative. Good words are wasted on those who can't (or won't) listen. "Don't give to dogs what belongs to God," Jesus said, "they will only turn and attack you" (Matthew 7:6 CEV).

Jesus once opened the scriptures for the home folks in Nazareth—but they didn't like His interpretation. When He said, "A prophet is honored everywhere except in his own hometown," they turned on him (Mark 6:4 NLT). No pearls for pigs.

On the night of His betrayal, Jesus was taken to King Herod for interrogation. Herod was elated to meet the famed prophet at last and hoped to see a miracle. He questioned Jesus profusely, but Jesus didn't answer him one word—and no miracle (Luke 23:8–9). No pearls for pigs.

The Church throws its pearls everywhere and wonders why the world doesn't honor the great value of the words of life. We should ask for wisdom to recognize pigs in wolves' clothing, trusting the Spirit of our Father for words only as we need them (Matthew 10:16–20).

THE GOLDEN RULE

"Whatever you want men to do to you, do also to them."
MATTHEW 7:12 NKJV

These words capture the essence of the Christian life—in every situation, treat others as we ourselves want to be treated. This is indeed the Golden Rule of civilized humanity.

Tragically, the human heart is anything but golden. It is, in fact, deceitful above all things (Jeremiah 17:9), and therefore incapable—apart from God—of living by this rule. It rewrites the rule to say: "Do to others *before* they do to you," anticipating the betrayal of other hearts. It says, "Do to others as they *have done* to you," to justify the age-old maxim of retribution: "An eye for an eye, a tooth for a tooth."

But Solomon wrote, "Whoever digs a pit will fall into it; if someone rolls a stone, it will roll back on them" (Proverbs 26:27 NIV). Any act against anyone will have its eventual payback, because "God cannot be mocked. A man reaps what he sows. Whoever sows to please their flesh, from the flesh will reap destruction; whoever sows to please the Spirit, from the Spirit will reap eternal life" (Galatians 6:7–8 NIV).

The Spirit enables us to obey the Golden Rule, so "let us not become weary in doing good, for at the proper time we will reap a harvest if we do not give up" (Galatians 6:9 NIV).

How do we define "good"? Apply the Golden Rule: what we think would be good for us, do the same for others.

NARROW-MINDED

"Enter by the narrow gate."
MATTHEW 7:13 NKJV

The world is webbed with highways and byways, but there are only two roads that ultimately matter—the one that leads to destruction and the one that leads to life. The road to destruction is a superhighway; the road to life is a narrow path. They run parallel, but in opposite directions. The narrow path is harder to find because it runs down the middle of the wide highway in the face of frenzied traffic.

Most maps don't even mark the narrow path. Many a GPS doesn't have it programmed in. It's too narrow—and our world is increasingly opposed to anything narrow. Those who travel the path are often accused of being narrow-minded, but that's okay, because the One who blazed that trail is narrow-minded. He said, "I am the gate" (John 10:9 NIV). And not the gate only, but "I am the way and the truth and the life. No one comes to the Father except through me" (John 14:6 NIV).

Some call such narrowness "hateful," "exclusive," and "bigoted." Maybe it is: it hates hell, excludes sin, and welcomes only those willing to follow Jesus. But it calls *all* to follow, and it leads to eternal life—there's nothing wider (ultimately) than that!

Jesus is the Way. And that's the Truth. And that leads to Life.

ROCK SOLID

"Whoever hears these sayings of Mine, and does them [is like] a wise man who built his house on the rock."
MATTHEW 7:24 NKJV

In 2011, Hurricane Irene poured out her tears on Lancaster County, raising the Conestoga River higher than most folks have ever seen it. In the city of Lancaster, a new biking trail ran along the river, separated from the water by a rugged rail fence. When Irene sent the river running down that trail, its waters carried away most of the rails and fence posts. Only a few hardy posts were still standing when the river receded at last. Those posts had been secured in a concrete section of the path where folks could park to access the trail. The other posts had been installed only in the soil beside the path.

When Jesus finished His Sermon on the Mount, He told a parable about two houses: one with a foundation on rock, the other with a foundation on sand. When Hurricane Irene (or one of her great-grandmothers, anyway) came whistling through, both those houses took a bad beating. The rains fell, the floods came, and the winds blew. When the storm was gone, only one house was still standing—the house built on rock.

"Anyone who listens to my teaching and follows it is wise," said Jesus, "like a person who builds a house on solid rock. . . . But anyone who hears my teaching and doesn't obey it is foolish, like a person who builds a house on sand" (Matthew 24, 26 NLT).

There's always a storm coming, brothers. Build on rock.

WHO ARE YOU ENCOURAGING?

"Martha, Martha," the Lord answered, "you are worried and upset about many things, but few things are needed— or indeed only one. Mary has chosen what is better, and it will not be taken away from her."
LUKE 10:41–42 NIV

When Martha asked Jesus to send her sister to help prepare food for their guests, Jesus had to choose between the expectations of His culture and the gifts of Mary and Martha. Martha fully expected Jesus to take her side. Why else would she risk a public confrontation in front of their guests?

Surprisingly, the best thing for Martha wasn't necessarily what she wanted. While she wanted Jesus to remove Mary from an opportunity to learn with the disciples, she was actually trying to impose her gifts of hospitality on Mary. At the critical moment when Martha's frustration peaked, Jesus offered encouragement to both sisters, even if Martha received it as a rebuke. Jesus encouraged Mary to continue learning, to sit as His feet as a disciple, and to seek "what is better." At the same time, Jesus put Martha's many worries into perspective. She was concerned about a lot, but her gift of hospitality didn't have to leave her aggravated or resentful toward others. At a crucial moment, Jesus offered important insights that pointed both women toward fulfilling their callings. Who do you know who needs encouragement to take risks or to find contentment and peace in their present circumstances?

LOVE THAT BREAKS THE RECORD BOOKS

Love is patient, love is kind. It does not envy, it does not boast, it is not proud. It does not dishonor others, it is not self-seeking, it is not easily angered, it keeps no record of wrongs.
1 CORINTHIANS 13:4–5 NIV

If we believe that God is love, as John assures us (1 John 4:8), and that love keeps no record of wrongs, then we have a staggering revelation on our hands. God's love isn't a conditional, record-keeping kind of love. Our wrongs have been forgiven *and* forgotten. Perhaps our greatest barrier to loving others with this kind of generous abandon is our inability to receive God's love. We may believe that God can only love us if we pray more, live ashamed of our failures, or even hide our faults. This checklist approach to love alienates us from God and robs us of the experience of love that could revolutionize how we interact with our family, friends, and colleagues. Once we understand that God loves us and isn't keeping track of our wrongs, we'll begin to extend that generous love to others. That isn't to say others can't or won't hurt us. They will. But once we experience the depths of God's love and forgiveness for us, we'll have a solid foundation and assurance of our worth that doesn't require the approval of others. When we know that we are loved without condition, we become free to extend the same forgiveness to others—a forgiveness that keeps no record of wrongs.

How Our Journeys Begin

*Then Jesus came from Galilee to the Jordan to be baptized
by John. But John tried to deter him, saying, "I need to
be baptized by you, and do you come to me?"
Jesus replied, "Let it be so now; it is proper for us to
do this to fulfill all righteousness." Then John consented.*
MATTHEW 3:13–15 NIV

At the start of His ministry, Jesus humbly sought baptism
under John in order to fulfill all righteousness, placing
Himself alongside the people among whom He planned to
minister. Just as death precedes resurrection and new life,
the baptism of Jesus was a lowly moment of identifying
with repentant people who had gotten far more wrong
than they had gotten right. The muddy waters of the
Jordan River were no place for a King to begin His reign.
Even a powerful army commander thought these waters
were beneath him. For all that Jesus accomplished in His
ministry, He didn't begin by rising to the top. He began
by descending to the lowest point so that He could reach
all people. It's one thing to read about starting small or at
the bottom and working your way up, but actually taking
a step down at the start of a ministry or new season of
life takes a lot of faith. In fact, Jesus' faith was firmly fixed
in the power of God to raise Him up from both the lowly,
muddy waters of the Jordan River and the darkness of
death so that He could offer new life to all who have faith
to follow Him.

THE END OF PAIN

And I heard a loud voice from the throne saying, "Look!
God's dwelling place is now among the people, and he will
dwell with them. They will be his people, and God himself
will be with them and be their God. 'He will wipe every tear
from their eyes. There will be no more death' or mourning or
crying or pain, for the old order of things has passed away."
REVELATION 21:3-4 NIV

When we hear about tragedy in the news, experience a
personal loss, or pass through a difficult season of life, it's
tempting to think that our grief and sorrow has no end
in sight. It may feel like life is an irredeemable mess that
lacks direction or meaning. However, the final revelation
of God will end all death, crying, and pain. As we consider
the hope that God offers us, we can find peace in this
assurance that our future is leading toward a day when
God dwells among us and brings us the comfort we have
longed for all our lives. The Bible points us consistently
in this direction: God dwelling among us. From the days
of the tabernacle among the Israelites in the wilderness
to the temple in Jerusalem to the coming of the Spirit
at Pentecost, God has consistently moved closer to us,
not farther away. While Revelation assures us that God's
coming will bring justice, we do the story of scripture and
the hope of the Gospel a great disservice if we overlook
the comfort that God will bring to us. In the light of God's
presence, darkness can't help but flee.

ARE WE PASSING RULES OR THE STORY OF GOD'S RULE?

We will not hide them from their descendants; we will tell the next generation the praiseworthy deeds of the LORD, his power, and the wonders he has done.

PSALM 78:4 NIV

It's easy to pass along rules and laws to younger generations and new believers, but the psalmist writes that rules aren't enough. While resolving to pass along the law of the Lord to the next generation, the writer of this psalm points us toward sharing the deeds of the Lord, His power, and the wonders He has done. This isn't just a matter of leading good Bible studies. The most powerful truth we can pass along is the power of God in our own lives. It's not enough to just pass along stories of God's power based on hearsay or legend. We have to live lives of faith and dependence that result in testimonies of God's presence and power. We need to demonstrate how the words of scripture have come to life in our daily lives. In fact, we are assured by Jesus that His followers can perform the same acts, and the early Church in Acts repeatedly called themselves "witnesses" of God's deeds. If we haven't experienced the power and goodness of God for ourselves, what makes us think the next generation will do any better? If we hope to pass along the stories of God's power and deeds, we should first seek the presence of God so that our stories will be grounded in real-life experiences that we can relate to others.

WHO ARE WE TO TELL GOD WHAT TO DO?

Do not be anxious about anything, but in every situation,
by prayer and petition, with thanksgiving,
present your requests to God.
PHILIPPIANS 4:6 NIV

While talking with a friend who was brand-new to the Christian faith, I learned that her family was experiencing a difficult situation. When I offered to pray for her, she hesitated but then told me to go ahead. After praying for her and her family, she asked me a really, really good question—"I appreciate you praying for me, but who are we to tell God what to do?" I agreed with her that we can make that mistake sometimes in prayer. In fact, some people can use prayer to control and manipulate others, to say nothing of trying to do the same with God. However, Paul offers us a helpful path forward. We begin with gratitude for God's present work, lest we forget all of the ways God is working in our lives and in the lives of those around us. We also let go of anxiety when we pray because anxiety betrays a struggle to control our circumstances. With our hands off future outcomes, we are in a better position to humbly present our requests to God. These are only requests, not commands. In fact, while praying we may get a better sense of what to ask for before presenting another request. Lastly, God welcomes our requests and petitions. We may never overcome our anxiety if we don't invite God to intervene in our lives. Until we tell God what we're really thinking, we may never experience His peace.

RESTORATION AFTER WE FAIL

"Give ear, our God, and hear; open your eyes and see
the desolation of the city that bears your Name.
We do not make requests of you because we are
righteous, but because of your great mercy."
DANIEL 9:18 NIV

We've all failed in some pretty major ways over the years. Perhaps we failed a spouse, child, relative, or close friend. Perhaps we even went so far as betraying someone. After we've confessed our wrongs and tried to make things right with others, it can be daunting to seek out reconciliation with God. How do you begin again with God after a significant failure? Those who have disregarded the commands of God or inflicted others with pain may not even feel worthy of following a holy God.

The book of Daniel was written after the worst national tragedy that ever befell the people of Israel. After years of religious unfaithfulness and systemic injustice against the poor and vulnerable, the majority of Israel was sent into exile by the Babylonians. In the midst of national failure, the prophet Daniel continued to pray because of God's mercy alone. He knew his people had nothing good to show. They couldn't pretend to have it together. The destroyed city stood as a testimony for everyone to see. Nevertheless, they could still approach God. It's not up to us to make ourselves righteous before we approach God. Even at our worst, we can count on God's mercy to begin the long process of restoration.

What Gets in the Way of God?

Then Jesus said to his disciples, "Truly I tell you, it is hard for someone who is rich to enter the kingdom of heaven. Again I tell you, it is easier for a camel to go through the eye of a needle than for someone who is rich to enter the kingdom of God."

MATTHEW 19:23–24 NIV

Jesus' words to the rich young ruler can be jarring, especially to readers in the western part of the world that tends to have more wealth. Perhaps we are joining the Philippian jailor in crying out, "What must I do to be saved?" According to Jesus, wealth is a tremendous obstacle to entering God's kingdom, and so those who want to remove any obstacle to God's kingdom need to ask some hard questions about their attachment to money and physical possessions. Keep in mind that Jesus had wealthy followers. Jesus was supported by women with significant funds who cared for His needs. Wealth itself is not sinful. Rather, wealth can become a substitute for God. The same goes for our possessions. We can rely on our possessions to provide comfort, to define our self-image, and to care for ourselves when we should be caring for the people around us. In other words, wealth can compete with treasuring God's kingdom over anything else. The best way we can remove the obstacle of wealth is to practice regular generosity so that we learn to rely on God alone and minimize the distractions that could keep us from serving God and others.

HOW DO WE REPENT?

But Zacchaeus stood up and said to the Lord,
"Look, Lord! Here and now I give half of my possessions
to the poor, and if I have cheated anybody out of
anything, I will pay back four times the amount."
LUKE 19:8 NIV

We often hear pastors and teachers say that repentance means turning around and changing course. However, we may struggle to imagine what this could look like in our own lives. The story of Zacchaeus provides one of the most powerful pictures of true repentance in action. Zacchaeus didn't just commit to follow Jesus. He recognized that following Jesus meant he had to completely change his life according to the priorities and standards set by Jesus. He saw the invitation from Jesus as an opportunity to pursue a new course for his life. At his moment of conversion, Zacchaeus didn't just stop cheating people. He vowed to right the wrongs he had committed. He also pledged to give generously to the poor from his wealth. Zacchaeus recognized that much of his wealth had been acquired dishonestly, and he rightly recognized that following Jesus called for justice to those he'd wronged and the poor in his community whom he'd exploited as a tax collector for Rome. He signaled his newfound trust in Jesus and allegiance to the kingdom of God by removing the wealth and dishonest tactics that he had relied on for so long. Zacchaeus repented by not only changing his future but by repairing his past.

WE ARE DIRECTED BY OUR DELIGHTS

Blessed is the one who does not walk in step with the wicked or stand in the way that sinners take or sit in the company of mockers, but whose delight is in the law of the LORD, and who meditates on his law day and night. That person is like a tree planted by streams of water, which yields its fruit in season and whose leaf does not wither—whatever they do prospers.

PSALM 1:1–3 NIV

We often speak of being delighted by a visit with friends or by spending time with family, but the sources of our delights can have a far more significant spiritual meaning. Our delights determine the direction of our lives. Perhaps we may be shocked to learn that God isn't interested in shutting down our delights or what gives us joy. Rather, God is interested in redirecting our delights and joys toward the most certain sources of both. In fact, these redirections aren't petty or frivolous. Although it may feel like a sacrifice at first, this is for our benefit. Those who follow the way of mockers and sinners will certainly find their own kinds of delights, but those delights will last only as long as the last punch line. Those who meditate on scripture and delight in communing with God will find a deeper, lasting delight that will carry them through the best and the worst that life has to offer. The delight offered by God takes time and commitment, but it's assured to last us.

WHEN IS GOD AT WORK AMONG US?

*So he replied to the messengers, "Go back and report to
John what you have seen and heard: The blind receive sight,
the lame walk, those who have leprosy are cleansed,
the deaf hear, the dead are raised, and the good news
is proclaimed to the poor. Blessed is anyone who
does not stumble on account of me."*

LUKE 7:22–23 NIV

Perhaps we read the story of Jesus and John the
Baptist, and we can't believe that John dared to harbor
doubts about Jesus. How could John see the miracles
of Jesus and His power over demons and doubt? What
more could John have asked of God? If you know the
backstory of John, he expected quite a lot more. John
expected Jesus at least to destroy the Roman occupiers
of Israel with His "winnowing fork." When Jesus preached
a message of repentance for all people, even the Romans,
and limited His power to healing the sick and demon-
possessed, John was tempted to write Him off. John's
story is a powerful reminder of the ways our own agendas
can cloud our perspective. Perhaps God is working
mightily in our lives or in the lives of those around us, but
we've been missing out because we keep expecting God
to show up in other ways, in other places, and among
different people. Sometimes faith means learning to see
where God is working right now in the moment, rather
than asking God to show up on our terms.

FINDING THE BLESSING OF SABBATH

By the seventh day God had finished the work he had been doing; so on the seventh day he rested from all his work. Then God blessed the seventh day and made it holy, because on it he rested from all the work of creating that he had done.
GENESIS 2:2–3 NIV

With pressure to advance our careers, to own larger homes, and to increase our incomes, rest often becomes optional. If anything, taking a break means that others will pull ahead of us or we could lose out on the possessions that promise us peace and fulfillment. Even if we know in our heads that we don't need larger homes or more possessions, such lines become blurred in the heat of the moment. When the status of a new car or promotion at work beckons us, it's easy to forget what exactly we're striving for. While work can be deeply meaningful and possessions can be useful and constructive, we shouldn't overlook the blessings that come from rest. The creation account in Genesis is intended to shock us—it's entirely unexpected that an all-powerful God would take a break and even bless a day of rest. The rest offered on the Sabbath day can save us from the never-ending cycle of working for yet another raise or promotion. The Sabbath is an opportunity to experience God and to more fully rest in God's provision for us. The Sabbath offers us blessings that we'll never tap into if we fail to stop long enough to discover it.

THE BLESSING OF AN ENDING

*Teach us to number our days,
that we may gain a heart of wisdom.*
PSALM 90:12 NIV

Aging sparks no end of troubling moments and crisis points. There's a quarter-life crisis that hits around twenty-five, the mid-life crisis at forty, and then a crisis that typically hits around the sixties as many look into retirement. If anything, we may find less wisdom and more regret and recklessness as yet another year passes by. Each crisis of aging is rooted in the realization that death is a terrifying reality that we will all face one day. However, the writer of the Psalms assures us that numbering our days with the end in mind can actually lead us to greater wisdom. Perhaps this strikes some as impossible, but consider this—once we view our days as limited, aren't we compelled to consider how to use them best? Doesn't each day become all the more valuable once we see that our days aren't available in an endless supply? The wisdom that the psalmist talks about will help us ask hard questions about how we spend our time. We may be more driven to prioritize time spent in prayer. We may set aside more time to be with our family. We may change our professional goals or at least measure our success by different means. As we number our days with an awareness of their limited supply, we'll have greater clarity when discerning our priorities and will find greater peace in the knowledge of God's presence throughout each day.

THE POWER OF SOLITUDE
FOR TAKING RISKS

*At daybreak, Jesus went out to a solitary place. The people
were looking for him and when they came to where he was,
they tried to keep him from leaving them. But he said,
"I must proclaim the good news of the kingdom of God
to the other towns also, because that is why I was sent."*
LUKE 4:42–43 NIV

Jesus had just preached a powerful sermon in Nazareth
and healed many in the village of Capernaum. His
popularity was at an all-time high in the village where
He had started to make His home, and the people even
begged Him to stick around. Why shouldn't He consolidate
His position and continue to perform miracles among His
friends and neighbors? Jesus had very different plans. He
had a clear mission that called Him beyond the familiarity
of His hometown. Despite the attractiveness of sticking
around where He could be comfortable and popular, Jesus
saw that His ministry required Him to pursue solitude and
to venture beyond His village into many others. While God
may just as likely call others to stay put, this story reminds
us that the calling of God often runs against conventional
wisdom or at least the "popular vote." In fact, we can
assume that Jesus' pursuit of solitude and commitment
to His mission were undoubtedly linked. The power and
clarity He drew from solitude certainly prepared Him to
make the difficult decision to leave what was familiar and
to pursue God's calling for His life.

HOPE FOR DOUBTERS

He said to them, "How foolish you are, and how slow to believe all that the prophets have spoken! Did not the Messiah have to suffer these things and then enter his glory?" And beginning with Moses and all the Prophets, he explained to them what was said in all the Scriptures concerning himself.
LUKE 24:25–27 NIV

At one point or another in our lives, we all struggle through situations that test our faith or cause us to question the goodness of God. Perhaps we can't make sense of a profound loss or our faith just wears down gradually as one hard season gives way to another. In the story of the disciples along the road to Emmaus, we find two "followers" of Jesus who have essentially given up. They're confused and fearful, and they've most certainly left Jerusalem for fear of losing their lives. So far as we can tell, they believe Jesus' movement is finished. If they expected Jesus to rise from the dead, they would have stayed around. Despite their doubts and, as Jesus said, foolishness, Jesus still showed up, explaining the scriptures to them and eventually revealing Himself in the breaking of bread. While it's true that doubt and unbelief can undermine our ability to follow Jesus, this story reminds us that Jesus won't discard His followers who struggle or who pass through a season of doubts. Whether we're looking for Him or just walking along in confusion, all is not lost. He is more than willing to show up and lead us back to faith.

OUR DAILY BREAD VS. OUR ETERNAL BREAD

"Do not work for food that spoils, but for food that endures to eternal life, which the Son of Man will give you. For on him God the Father has placed his seal of approval."
JOHN 6:27 NIV

When Jesus taught His disciples how to pray, He told them to ask God for the provision of their daily bread. Daily bread isn't something that you can store up for the long term, especially back in Jesus' day. He didn't instruct them to pray for storehouses of grain or even reserves of coins that would give them the ability to manage any crisis. They were welcome to ask God for provision, but only daily provision. How often are we tempted to pray for a long-term solution to our problems and needs? It's almost maddening to think that a God with limitless resources would instruct us to ask for so small a provision, but then perhaps Jesus knew something of human ambition and our tendency to rely on our possessions and resources rather than God. Ironically, even our best "long-term" solutions are actually quite limited and fleeting. The presence of Christ in our lives and a long-term faith in Him will never let us down, but our strength, finances, and even relationships may well let us down when we need them the most. The only sure "long-term" bet is the eternal bread of Jesus Himself present in our lives, nourishing us and providing for our needs day by day.

GOD TREATS US AS WE'D TREAT OURSELVES

"If you, then, though you are evil, know how to give good gifts to your children, how much more will your Father in heaven give good gifts to those who ask him! So in everything, do to others what you would have them do to you, for this sums up the Law and the Prophets."
MATTHEW 7:11–12 NIV

At a time when the religious believed that following God required adhering to a long list of laws and avoiding particular people, Jesus cut through the expectations of His audience with a very simple summary of the Law and Prophets. "Caring for others as we would care for ourselves" forced His audience to stop placing barriers between each other and to treat each other with mercy. However, Jesus isn't just talking about the way we treat each other in this passage. His focus is much wider than personal interactions. He assured His listeners that God is far more kind and merciful than anticipated. We shouldn't be surprised to find an assurance of God's goodness followed by a command to be kind and merciful to each other. Jesus is asking us to imitate God's mercy and generosity that we've received. Just as God mercifully gives good gifts to those who ask, we should extend the same kindness to each other. If we're going to be merciful toward anyone, we'll be merciful to ourselves above anyone else. Thank goodness God extends that very same mercy to us when we pray.

WHAT DOES IT MEAN TO LIVE BY FAITH?

Who may ascend the mountain of the LORD? Who may stand in his holy place? The one who has clean hands and a pure heart, who does not trust in an idol or swear by a false god.
PSALM 24:3–4 NIV

Living by faith each day requires more than believing in the saving work of Christ on the cross. That is just the starting point for our life in Christ! The life of faith is manifested in our day-to-day decisions when we have to choose whether we will trust God to provide for us. When the writer of the Psalms says that those who stand in God's holy place will not trust in an idol or swear by a false god, we would do well to remember that idols and false gods weren't just passing fads or sources of personal fulfillment in Old Testament times. Idols and false gods were trusted to provide essentials for life, such as rain for crops or fertility for future children. Some Israelites surely felt tempted to mix prayers to the Lord with prayers to an idol in order to cover all their bases. Those who live by faith in God place their trust in God alone for their daily needs, believing that their obedience will not be in vain. The kind of faith God requires means placing all our hope in God's provision and deliverance rather than wealth, our personal influence, or relationships with people in power.

WILL JESUS RESTORE US AFTER FAILURE?

The third time he said to him, "Simon son of John,
do you love me?" Peter was hurt because Jesus asked
him the third time, "Do you love me?" He said,
"Lord, you know all things; you know that I love you."
Jesus said, "Feed my sheep."
JOHN 21:17 NIV

Perhaps we imagine that Jesus can't do much of anything with us after we've failed. Maybe we believe we've been disqualified or have fallen away because of our misconduct. Maybe we believe that grace only works up to a point and we've gone too far beyond it. However, Peter committed the grave sin of denying Jesus. He essentially chose to cut himself off from Jesus when his life could have been on the line. How did Jesus respond to Peter? First, Jesus went to the heart of the matter, "Do you love me?" Despite his failure, Jesus still offered mercy to Peter because He recognized that Peter still loved Him, even if that love was imperfect and prone to fail at times. Second, Jesus restored Peter immediately, tasking him with caring for His followers. While we can hardly use this as a catchall template for all sins, Jesus was quick to turn Peter from a denier to an affirmer. The point person in teaching others about Jesus was the man who had denied Him. Peter's love for Jesus made the difference when his future hung in the balance, and Jesus restored him even after the most humbling of failures.

How to Stop Anger in Its Tracks

My dear brothers and sisters, take note of this:
Everyone should be quick to listen, slow to speak
and slow to become angry, because human anger does
not produce the righteousness that God desires.
James 1:19–20 niv

When I perceive someone as a threat or believe I've been insulted, it's easy to jump to conclusions and to become angry. It's even easier to meet a situation with a ready-made reply based on a snap judgment I've reached in the moment. The problem with being quick to speak and slow to listen is that once I've spoken, I've typically made up my mind and changed the situation. If I respond with anger, it will become more difficult to slow down to listen again since tensions will rise and arguments can spiral out of control. Once I've spoken, I may never slow down enough to truly listen well. James wisely counsels us to be quick to listen, because listening first is the best defense against unhelpful and unrighteous anger. If we aren't listening, there's a good chance we've already arrived at a judgment, and there's an even better chance that it won't be a helpful one! James doesn't tell us to stop being angry. He tells us to listen first, and then we won't become angry for the wrong reasons and undermine the righteousness that God desires. Perhaps if we prioritize listening first, we'll also begin to hear the still, small voice of God speaking into our lives and guiding us away from anger.

THE COURAGE TO RUN AWAY FROM TEMPTATION

*One day he went into the house to attend to his duties,
and none of the household servants was inside.
She caught him by his cloak and said, "Come to bed
with me!" But he left his cloak in her
hand and ran out of the house.*
GENESIS 39:11–12 NIV

We often think of courage and strength in terms of taking a stand and never backing down. We imagine ourselves in situations where we must hold our ground at all costs. However, there are times when the most courageous thing we can do is run away. In a situation that offered no easy solution, Joseph recognized that his master's wife would continue to pursue him if he remained alone with her. Out of his love for God and loyalty to his master, he had the courage and strength to run away. There are some "battles" that cannot be won by staying put. When temptation threatens to trap us, there are times when our safest move is to retreat by changing our location, seeking help, or starting a new activity. Resisting temptation can be just as much a matter of where we choose to stay or not stay as it can be a mental battle. Whatever Joseph thought or felt in the moment, his resolve to run away made it possible for him to, in a sense, stand strong.

THE JOY OF GROWING STRONGER

*Consider it pure joy, my brothers and sisters,
whenever you face trials of many kinds, because you
know that the testing of your faith
produces perseverance.*
JAMES 1:2–3 NIV

Everyone wants to experience "pure joy," but not many people would think of a trial or test of faith as an opportunity to experience it. What could James be thinking? For starters, James is looking at the big picture for Christians. He sees the whole of life stretched before him and even into eternity where God will reward those who have remained faithful. All believers will face difficulties in the future as well, so trusting God in today's trials will prepare them to remain faithful in future challenges. James didn't see faith as something that you either have or don't have. Faith must be developed and grown over time. We can say that we "have" faith, but our faith becomes stronger the more we use it. Those who see trials and difficulties as opportunities to draw near to God and grow their faith will find greater joy in the most unlikely places. More than anything else, James is eager for his readers, and us, to see that our relationship with Christ is more valuable than our comfort. It is like the pearl of great value that a man sells everything he has to purchase. If our difficulties help us remain close to Christ, then we can trust that seeming setbacks will help our faith leap forward.

WHY WE SHOULD PUT OTHERS FIRST

Do nothing out of selfish ambition or vain conceit.
Rather, in humility value others above yourselves,
not looking to your own interests but each of
you to the interests of the others.
PHILIPPIANS 2:3–4 NIV

Most of the conflict we face in life is rooted in seeking our own interests above those of others. Our ambitions to succeed can be a healthy expression of our talents and gifts, but they can also put us at odds with others if our success becomes linked to prospering at the expense of others. When we place our needs ahead of others, we're bound for conflict, as plenty of other people will also seek their own needs first and foremost. Paul's solution to conflict is stepping back and seeking out the interests of others above our own. Beyond removing potential points of conflict from our lives, this also forces us to trust God in the same way that Christ trusted God with His life on earth. Rather than seeking our own exaltation at the expense of others, we can trust that God will see and reward our selflessness and generosity. Jesus assured us that the first will be last and the last shall be first. We can save ourselves from a lot of anger and conflict by choosing to be last, putting the needs of others first, and making ourselves a servant above all else. While we can strive to use our gifts well, servants never seek their own benefit at the expense of others.

LOVE BEGINS WITH FAITH

We love because he first loved us. Whoever claims to love God yet hates a brother or sister is a liar. For whoever does not love their brother and sister, whom they have seen, cannot love God, whom they have not seen. And he has given us this command: Anyone who loves God must also love their brother and sister.

1 JOHN 4:19–21 NIV

Our image of God will determine how we treat others. Jesus assured us that those who have received mercy will extend the same mercy to others. When John writes about love, it's from the perspective of someone who sees God's love with tremendous clarity. His worth is determined according to God's love for him. Out of that deep reserve of love and acceptance, John found that he was able to extend that love to others. In fact, the best way to gauge our relationship with God is how we treat others. If we are able to love others, then we have experienced the love and acceptance of God. If we are fearful, angry, or uncaring toward others, then we are most likely living out of fear, defensiveness, or judgment. Showing love may require some effort on our part, but it most certainly begins with faith: believing that God loves us. That foundation of love makes it possible to love and accept others regardless of how they have treated us.

THE COURAGE TO SEEK GOD FIRST

The Spirit of God came on Azariah son of Oded. He went out to meet Asa and said to him, "Listen to me, Asa and all Judah and Benjamin. The LORD is with you when you are with him. If you seek him, he will be found by you, but if you forsake him, he will forsake you."

2 CHRONICLES 15:1–2 NIV

In a time of turmoil and confusion, King Asa took courage in the promise from the prophet Azariah that he would certainly find the Lord if he sought Him. He had an enormous task before him. The land was filled with idols and surrounded by threatening armies. While we wouldn't blame him for focusing on military solutions and building better forts, he prioritized his loyalty to the Lord by removing the idols from the land. He had to trust that putting his allegiance to the Lord first would help solve his many other problems. We can imagine critics who may have said that he was wasting his time with all his religious reforms. However, he moved forward in the belief that God can be found by all who earnestly seek Him. By the same token, unfaithfulness brought its own consequences. He couldn't hedge his bets by relying on idols and the Lord. Just as Jesus said we cannot serve two masters when referring to God and money, Asa realized that his best "military strategy" rested in trusting God alone.

DOES GOD HAVE YOUR ATTENTION?

Do not be like the horse or the mule, which have no
understanding but must be controlled by bit and bridle
or they will not come to you. Many are the woes of
the wicked, but the LORD's unfailing love
surrounds the one who trusts in him.
PSALM 32:9–10 NIV

C. S. Lewis wrote, "God whispers to us in our pleasures, speaks in our conscience, but shouts in our pains: it is his megaphone to rouse a deaf world." I suspect that many can relate to this, as God often seems most present when we are suffering or struggling. Perhaps a difficult situation prompts us to rely on God in new ways. The writer of this psalm suggests that those who fail to trust in God must be led like a horse, and sometimes our pain and difficult situations can feel like a bit or bridle that drags us back to God. The solution, according to this psalm, is to understand and to trust God's unfailing love to surround us whether our lives are difficult or pleasant. In fact, those who trust in God's unfailing love will be spared the many struggles and disappointments that the wicked face. While the trusting and untrusting will pass through difficult seasons of life, the difference will be that God's loving presence will carry us through our pain. God's gentle love moves around us. It doesn't drag us or force us to act in a particular way. It is a love that is present and comforting, remaining faithful even when we wander and become stubborn yet again.

SUFFERING MAKES US CONFIDENT

The Spirit himself testifies with our spirit that we are God's children. Now if we are children, then we are heirs—heirs of God and co-heirs with Christ, if indeed we share in his sufferings in order that we may also share in his glory.
ROMANS 8:16–17 NIV

Perhaps our first thought in a season of suffering or persecution is that something is terribly wrong. If we are God's children, shouldn't life get easier? We will no doubt pray that our suffering ends soon and that God will bring us relief. However, Paul encourages us to think of suffering in far different terms. Besides the comforting testimony of the Holy Spirit that we are God's children because we suffer, we also can look to our suffering as an act of solidarity with the sufferings of Christ. If we suffer because of our allegiance to Christ, we'll place ourselves firmly among God's children who can look forward to sharing in glory one day. While we shouldn't hope for our suffering to continue indefinitely, God may give us our greatest confidence and hope of future glory in the midst of our darkest moments today. Jesus assured us that His own sufferings signaled that the same would surely come to His followers one day. If you're going through a season of suffering or isolation because of your faith, that doesn't mean God has abandoned you. Rather, it means that this world has recognized you belong to a different family and your hope is in a different place.

RECEIVING GOD'S GIFT LIKE A CHILD

But Jesus called the children to him and said,
"Let the little children come to me, and do not hinder
them, for the kingdom of God belongs to such as
these. Truly I tell you, anyone who will not receive the
kingdom of God like a little child will never enter it."
LUKE 18:16–17 NIV

We can all recall what it's like to give a gift to a child. She may well cling to it for hours if we let her. Some children may even obsess over keeping the box that the gift came in, re-creating the moment they opened it over and over again. Children offer their complete attention to gifts, receiving them with joy and focus. There is a simplicity and lack of cynicism among children that allows them to be fully present in the moment. They are brimming over with faith, hope, and joy rather than doubts, fears, and arguments. Perhaps Jesus had grown weary of the latter when He embraced a group of children despite His disciples' efforts to keep them away. Their eagerness to learn and to receive His blessing offers the perfect picture for receiving God's kingdom. For a kingdom that is compared to a tiny seed or little flecks of yeast that are worked through the bread, children are the most likely to perceive its value. Rather than coming up with sophisticated explanations for or against Jesus, they demonstrated that coming to Jesus with open arms is the perfect place to begin.

DO WE BELIEVE GOD ABOUNDS IN LOVE?

*But you, Lord, are a compassionate and gracious God,
slow to anger, abounding in love and faithfulness.
Turn to me and have mercy on me; show your strength
in behalf of your servant; save me, because I serve
you just as my mother did.*
PSALM 86:15–16 NIV

While there's no doubt in the Bible that God is just, the psalmist reminds us that God is abounding in love and faithfulness. Perhaps we are slow to confess our sins and weaknesses because we believe that God is actually abounding in judgment and justice rather than love and faithfulness. Are we slow to confess our faults because we fear we've gone too far this time? Do we believe we are the exception to God's patience and mercy? We could share the same fear as the psalmist that God has turned away from us. However, we are assured that, despite our darkest moments and deepest doubts, the Lord is compassionate and gracious, offering forgiveness to those who turn to Him. In fact, the Lord isn't offering mercy in drips and drops. The Lord's very character is love and faithfulness to His people. We can trust that the Lord won't just turn to us but will act in our lives, intervening when we are full of despair. The Lord's people are not cast aside despite failures or seasons of doubt. We can trust that the Lord holds on to us faithfully, not out of duty or obligation but out of abounding love.

THE SOURCE OF TRUE FREEDOM

Now the Lord is the Spirit, and where the Spirit of the Lord is, there is freedom. And we all, who with unveiled faces contemplate the Lord's glory, are being transformed into his image with ever-increasing glory, which comes from the Lord, who is the Spirit.
2 CORINTHIANS 3:17–18 NIV

As Paul compares the Law of Moses to the new covenant under Christ, he is careful to say that both covenants displayed the glory of God, but Christ has brought a deeper level of intimacy with God. We could say that the picture of God painted by one covenant has been filled in with greater color and detail by the new covenant under Christ. For instance, while the glory of the old covenant forced Moses to wear a veil and failed to transform minds and hearts, the new covenant under Christ removes the veil between God and humanity. As we turn to the Lord and receive His Spirit, we are transformed into a new kind of freedom that empowers us to follow the lead of the Spirit. We aren't cut off from God's will or struggling to obey laws on our own. God isn't waiting for us to get our acts together. We are welcome in God's presence through the mediation of the Spirit and are being transformed by the glory of the Lord. While the Law of Moses shared the glory of God with us, the Spirit gives us the freedom to dwell in God's presence and transforms us into the image of Christ.

HOPE IN WHAT GOD HAS SPOKEN

I reach out for your commands, which I love, that I may meditate on your decrees. Remember your word to your servant, for you have given me hope. My comfort in my suffering is this: Your promise preserves my life.
PSALM 119:48–50 NIV

The graduation speaker shuffled forward with the help of his wife. He tapped his stick along the stage with each step. Over the past few years he had gone completely blind, and he made his blindness the topic of his talk. He shared with unseeing eyes clenched shut, "Never doubt in the darkness what God has shown you in the light." In this life of peaks and valleys, it's easy to forget the clarity of a mountaintop experience with God when we're mired in a valley of uncertainty and despair. The psalmist reminds us that we find our hope by meditating on the decrees of God, remembering His promises, and finding hope in what God has revealed to us. Just as the Israelites often set up monuments to the great works of God in their history, we will find great hope by remembering the promises and works of God in the past. We will surely face adversity and discouragement, and the investment we make in remembering God's promises and presence may be the only thing that carries us when we have many reasons to doubt and despair. The light we've been given by God will only guide us in the darkness if we resolve to carry it with us.

BOLD LIKE DAD

. . .according to his eternal purpose that he accomplished in Christ Jesus our Lord. In him and through faith in him we may approach God with freedom and confidence.
EPHESIANS 3:11–12 NIV

God wants His children to share in His personality, to take on His likeness, to live like Him. Boldness is often one of the overlooked traits that He wants us to experience. God is bold, invading history, overturning kingdoms, interrupting our well-crafted plans to have a relationship with us, and by doing so He risks the very opposite— our rejection. His great boldness can only come from His great love. He has not withheld even His own Son (Romans 8:2–3) to bring us into a life-giving relationship with Himself. Writer Francis Chan has coined a name for this kind of relentless pursuit—"Crazy Love." It's the kind of love that makes no excuses for its audacity.

So what does a bold, seeking Father enjoy seeing in His offspring? Reluctance? Hesitance? Or the kind of boldness He Himself demonstrated toward us? What would please Him more than having His children throwing off everything that hinders them (Hebrews 12:1) and approaching Him with freedom and confidence (Ephesians 3:12), knowing He made it possible? In Christ, our boldness pleases the Father, because it tells Him that we are His. Boldness isn't disrespectful as long as we know who made it possible for us to enjoy it. Rather, we are bearing His likeness, showing ourselves to be His children.

A Fool's Game

"A voice came from heaven, saying, 'King Nebuchadnezzar, to you it is declared: sovereignty has been removed from you, and you will be driven away from mankind, and your dwelling place will be with the beasts of the field. . .until you recognize that the Most High is ruler over the realm of mankind and bestows it on whomever He wishes.'"
Daniel 4:30–32 NASB

Success and achievement are great—unless they lead you to forget basic spiritual truths. Truths like "You cannot really accomplish anything apart from God." He is the *Most High,* and no matter how much we may achieve on earth, our "success" is ultimately His gift, for His purposes.

Another spiritual truth that's easily forgotten in the midst of success is that arrogance always invites correction. As the apostle Peter says, "God is opposed to the proud, but gives grace to the humble" (1 Peter 5:5 NASB). He doesn't ignore the proud, or work around them—He actively opposes them. When we are tempted to slap ourselves on the back, we should take note, as Nebuchadnezzar eventually did, that we are playing a fool's game. And you don't have to be some prideful "overachiever" to get God's attention. Anyone who takes credit for what God has done can enjoy His harsh mercy. God rebukes the foolishness of high and low alike, because He is merciful to all.

OPENING YOUR EYES

*For since the creation of the world His invisible attributes,
His eternal power and divine nature, have been clearly seen,
being understood through what has been made,
so that they are without excuse.*
ROMANS 1:20 NASB

Invisibility doesn't mean inaccessibility. Just because a thing cannot be seen doesn't mean it can't be known or understood in some meaningful way. The air we breathe is an example. So are the inner qualities of people: diligence, intelligence, impatience. When we see a beautiful painting, we see clearly the invisible quality called talent. In the same way, God declares that at least two of His invisible qualities have been "clearly *seen*" from the creation itself. First, His eternal power, that He is outside of time, without beginning and without end. We don't have to wonder who came before Him or who will come after Him. The second invisible quality is His divine nature. He is above the created order and not one of us. He was not born and will not die. He is the first and final authority of all things.

The irony of seeing the invisible is resolved in creation itself. The fullest revelation of God in Christ is not required for God to hold mankind accountable for at least the two qualities He has published across time and space. As the psalmist writes: "The heavens are telling of the glory of God; and their expanse is declaring the work of His hands. Day to day pours forth speech, and night to night reveals knowledge" (Psalm 19:1–2 NASB).

OVERFLOWING

*For we wanted to come to you—I, Paul, more than once—
and yet Satan hindered us. For who is our hope or joy or
crown of exultation? Is it not even you, in the presence of
our Lord Jesus at His coming? For you are our glory and joy.*
1 THESSALONIANS 2:18–20 NASB

Paul's enthusiasm for the Thessalonian believers bursts
forth in his words, using language usually reserved for
God Himself. Imagine! Paul's "hope" and "joy" and "glory"
are tied to this small group of people into whom he
has poured his life. When Jesus returns, Paul plans on
showing them off.

When we come to Christ, we begin our experience as
a child of God. We are adopted (Romans 8:15) and begin
rethinking our lives as one of His offspring. Then as we
share our faith and help people grow in Christ, we begin
to see the *other* side of the relationship—the parental
side. God's side. This is what Paul is expressing and why
he speaks so joyfully. He's displaying the same excited
attitude toward the Thessalonians that God has about all
of us—pride and joy!

God rejoices over us, brags about us, dotes on us,
and takes pride in us—and the things He's preparing in
heaven for those who love Him are beyond imagination (1
Corinthians 2:9). When we see Him face-to-face, we will
truly understand what an extravagant parent God is. We
will rejoice in Him, and He will rejoice in us.

THE LIVING AND WORKING WORD

We also constantly thank God that when you received the word of God which you heard from us, you accepted it not as the word of men, but for what it really is, the word of God, which also performs its work in you who believe.

1 THESSALONIANS 2:13 NASB

In the first chapter of the Bible, we see that God's spoken Word was powerful enough to bring all creation into being. John 1 further explains that the "Word of God" is the person of Jesus Christ Himself, through whom all things were created and find their purpose. Throughout the Bible, we see that God's Word continues to work since the beginning—giving life, protecting, enlightening, redeeming, effecting change according to God's will.

"So will My word be which goes forth from My mouth; it will not return to Me empty, without accomplishing what I desire, and without succeeding in the matter for which I sent it" (Isaiah 55:11 NASB).

God's Word works because it is alive. Jesus declares that "the words that I have spoken to you are spirit and are life" (John 6:63 NASB). The writer of Hebrews similarly asserts that "the word of God is living and active" (Hebrews 4:12 NASB). It works because it simply can't sit still!

Paul was delighted with the Thessalonians because they accepted his message as the authoritative, purposeful, and living thing that it was, and by doing so, they opened up its divine power to work in their lives.

DOWN TO THE TOP

*The LORD came down on Mount Sinai, to the top of
the mountain; and the LORD called Moses to the top
of the mountain, and Moses went up.*
EXODUS 19:20 NASB

Moses received the Law from God in a dramatic face-to-face meeting. And He chose an unusual place to do it considering Moses was about eighty years old—the top of a mountain. God had Moses make the arduous climb to the top of Mount Sinai alone to meet with Him. A truly remarkable feat at his age—it was no doubt painful and exhausting, requiring perseverance and commitment. But even at the top of a mountain, there was yet a distance between Moses and God. Even if Moses had ascended the highest peak on earth, God would still have had to close the gap by coming *down* to meet with him. And this is *Moses*—a central figure in Israel's history—who was called by God at the burning bush, who faced Pharaoh and the power of Egypt, who parted the Red Sea! And even Moses could not completely close the distance between man and God.

In this story lives a beautiful metaphor of man's need to have God fill the space that always remains even after we have done everything we can do to reach Him. No amount of human effort will ever connect us to God—only God's effort will bring us face-to-face. Fortunately, we do not have to have Moses' résumé or repeat his grueling trip up a mountain; we have perfect access to God through Christ, who forever closes the gap.

THE ODDS ARE IN YOUR FAVOR

The Spirit of the Lord God is upon me, because the Lord
has anointed me to bring good news to the afflicted;
He has sent me to bind up the brokenhearted,
to proclaim liberty to captives and freedom to prisoners;
to proclaim the favorable year of the Lord
and the day of vengeance of our God.
ISAIAH 61:1–2 NASB

Our God is amazingly generous. He sent His Son to bring the good news of a truly amazing opportunity. Christ was sent to proclaim "the favorable year of the Lord" and "the day" of judgment by God. That's a 365 to 1 ratio in our favor! This propitious arrangement is symbolic of God's great mercy and patience, "not wishing for any to perish but for all to come to repentance" (2 Peter 3:9 NASB). He is interested in us in a way that does not always make sense. Even Jesus' disciples didn't quickly grasp this divine patience, eager to "command fire to come down from heaven and consume" those who rejected Christ (Luke 9:54 NASB). The Lord's response was firm: "But He turned and rebuked them, and said, 'You do not know what kind of spirit you are of; for the Son of Man did not come to destroy men's lives, but to save them'" (Luke 9:55–56 NASB).

God wants all to repent. To confuse this time of favor and opportunity is to be of a different spirit than the Lord; not "regard[ing] the patience of our Lord as salvation" (2 Peter 3:15 NASB) is to miss God's heart and the chance to be part of it.

NOT SO FAST

Now when He was in Jerusalem at the Passover, during the feast, many believed in His name, observing His signs which He was doing. But Jesus, on His part, was not entrusting Himself to them, for He knew all men, and because He did not need anyone to testify concerning man, for He Himself knew what was in man.
JOHN 2:23–25 NASB

We all know from experience how different we can be from one day to the next. Everything from the temperature of the room to our greatest fear can change our moods and influence our decisions. As an old saying goes, "The only thing constant in life is change." Not that change is bad in itself. On the contrary, we would never see revival if change couldn't also be positive. But the very fact that we are creatures prone to extremes means we must be watched closely. Jesus knew this better than anyone. Even though He went through changes while on earth from birth to resurrection, He was stable in His essential nature and purpose—unlike those who surrounded Him. Fickle crowds would follow Him one day, awed by His miracles and teachings, and the next try to throw Him off a cliff (Luke 4:29)! The crowd that sang "Hosanna" as He rode into Jerusalem would be the same crowd that days later cried, "Crucify Him!" This is why Jesus would not be swayed by popularity. He looked beyond earthly success to His eternal Father whom He could trust as the only true unchanging Source.

THE DIVINE PROMISE

God made great and marvelous promises, so that his nature would become part of us. Then we could escape our evil desires and the corrupt influences of this world.
2 PETER 1:4 CEV

God's plan, as incredible as it may sound, is that we should partake in and reflect His own divine nature. He wants children that look and sound and act like their Father, free from corruption inside and out. "Therefore, having these promises, beloved, let us cleanse ourselves from all defilement of flesh and spirit, perfecting holiness in the fear of God" (2 Corinthians 7:1 NASB).

What were God's promises? That He would live among His people and be their God, that they would be set apart from the world, even counted as His sons and daughters (2 Corinthians 6). How are those promises fulfilled? Through His Holy Spirit living in us:

"'I will give them an undivided heart and put a new spirit in them'"(Ezekiel 11:19 NIV).

"When you believed, you were marked in him with a seal, the promised Holy Spirit" (Ephesians 1:13 NIV).

The role of the Holy Spirit is to create a people who could freely and honestly interact with God. Without His working in us, nothing in our experience will ever change and He won't get the children He wants. Only through the Holy Spirit indwelling and empowering us can we live out the full plan of our salvation.

The Flip Side of Faith

But My righteous one shall live by faith; and if he shrinks back, My soul has no pleasure in him.
Hebrews 10:38 NASB

People usually assume that doubt is the opposite of faith. But in the New Testament (NASB) the words *doubt* or *doubting* appear only a handful of times, while *fear* or *afraid* show up over one hundred times. While we can't build theology over a single observation, it's clear that a life of faith is often a battle against fear.

Fear certainly was the synagogue official's test when, in faith, he had begged for Jesus to heal his sick daughter. Then his little girl died. Jesus, knowing the man's heart, comforted him with these words, "Do not be afraid any longer, only believe" (Mark 5:36 NASB).

Later, Jesus, knowing the fear Peter would face after He was arrested, said, "Simon, Simon, behold, Satan has demanded permission to sift you like wheat; but I have prayed for you, that your faith may not fail" (Luke 22:31–32 NASB).

Of course God is not pleased when His people give in to fear because it means we are shrinking back from Him. But the good news is that we have a Father and a Savior who knows our weakness and "has not given us a spirit of timidity, but of power and love and discipline" (2 Timothy 1:7 NASB). We move forward in faith as we keep in step with the Spirit who is our Helper (John 14:16). We may well wrestle with fear, but we are never alone in the struggle.

A GOOD FOUNDATION

See to it that no one takes you captive through philosophy and empty deception, according to the tradition of men, according to the elementary principles of the world, rather than according to Christ.
COLOSSIANS 2:8 NASB

The test of every building is in its foundation. No matter how fine in appearance it is, if the foundation is faulty, the whole structure is at risk. Sadly, this is also the way our lives can be if we build our thinking on faulty reasoning and shifting philosophies. The world offers its perspective and solutions to our problems twenty-four hours a day, over television, radio, in bookstores, newspapers, and around the lunch table. The voice of this world rarely lacks confidence and the advice often seems wise and time tested. The proponents of worldly philosophies may even mean well, but they don't perceive the empty nature of their own beliefs. Why would they? *If it was good enough for Dad*, it's reasoned, *it's good enough for me*. Traditions passed down from one generation to the next carry weight whether they're right or wrong.

But Christ offers truth, reality, and a future that is eternal rather than fleeting. If we build upon His work and His words, we will avoid the captivity of a dying world and the loss of our opportunity for a solid foundation.

JUST DON'T

The LORD God commanded the man, saying, "From any tree
of the garden you may eat freely; but from the tree of
the knowledge of good and evil you shall not eat,
for in the day that you eat from it you will surely die."
GENESIS 2:16–17 NASB

Adam and Eve were designed to enjoy uninterrupted
union with God, and the only "don't" for them was eating
the fruit that would end that joy. But of course they went
directly against that single commandment, passing on
that tendency to all generations that followed. Their
one act of disobedience multiplied into all the things we
call sin today. No wonder the "don'ts" seem to multiply
throughout the Bible. They're just keeping pace with the
ways man has invented to disregard God.

Some people dismiss the Bible as a mere collection of
rules and restrictions. This misses the original purpose of
God to have "a people for His own possession out of all the
peoples who are on the face of the earth" (Deuteronomy
7:6 NASB). The Old Testament Law was a gift to set His
people apart and increase their joy, not end it. It was
ultimately designed to lead people to Christ (Galatians
3:24), people who would fulfill God's original purpose
when He "gave Himself for us to redeem us from every
lawless deed, and to purify for Himself a people for His own
possession" (Titus 2:14 NASB). Now the things we consider
"don'ts" from God do not constitute a law—they provide
real freedom and create a holy experience with our Lord.
Any "don't" from Him means life for us.

SORRY I ASKED

Then the LORD answered Job out of the storm and said,
"Now gird up your loins like a man; I will ask you,
and you instruct Me. Will you really annul My judgment?
Will you condemn Me that you may be justified?"
JOB 40:6–8 NASB

Sometimes people lament that God doesn't answer them in their suffering. They look at Job and say, *"At least God answered Job."* True, but look at the answer! God *rebukes* Job, confronting him with a harshness that seems inappropriate considering his painful circumstances. But God's had enough of being questioned; now it's Job's turn.

Chapter after chapter, Job has complained that he's done nothing to deserve his situation, and he was right. God Himself declared Job "blameless" and "upright" in Job 1:8. Yet Job's friends argued that his suffering was the consequence of sin, though Job knew better. They were rebuked because they condemned him without being able to address his argument. Job's rebuke was different. His error wasn't some hidden sin, or even a faulty argument, but in forgetting whom he was addressing. He was demanding that God justify Himself, explain Himself, even defend Himself.

"Oh, if only someone would give me a hearing! I've signed my name to my defense—let the Almighty One answer! I want to see my indictment in writing" (Job 31:35–36 MSG).

When we suffer, let us "pour out [our] complaint" to God (Psalm 142:2 NASB), always remembering whom we are talking to.

FREEDOM'S PURPOSE

*All things are lawful for me, but not all things are
profitable. All things are lawful for me,
but I will not be mastered by anything.*
1 CORINTHIANS 6:12 NASB

Grace wouldn't be grace if it didn't allow us room to
make mistakes without fear of losing our relationship with
God. Grace is God's determination that our sin will not
stand between Him and us. As believers we have come to
accept Christ's work alone for our reconciliation to God.
In Christ, God fulfills the demands that the Old Testament
Law made upon man and eliminates our need to rely on
any set of laws to make us acceptable to Him.

But there is always the chance that such a wonderful
freedom can be misused. Some Corinthian believers, freed
from the arduous burden of legalism, were using their
new "freedom" as an excuse to indulge in unprofitable
things—a spiritual waste of time. Some had gone further,
becoming addicted to activities that, although technically
allowable, had replaced God as the focus of their lives.
How absurd to think that God's gift of grace would push
aside the One who gave it! The whole point of grace was
to free us to move *toward* our Father, not *away*.

No amount of rationalizing should overrule godly
common sense (Hebrews 5:14). God wants preeminence
in our lives, and even death will be overcome to achieve
this end. So for today, let us use our freedom to become
like Him, not test the limits of His patience.

ALWAYS THE BEST POLICY

Truthful lips will be established forever,
but a lying tongue is only for a moment.
PROVERBS 12:19 NASB

If you've ever looked someone in the eye and wondered if they were telling you the truth, then you understand the uneasy feeling it creates. Sometimes, of course, it's easy to tell when a person is lying, like when a child blurts out, "It wasn't me!" Even if people don't outright lie to you but just "shade the truth," is that any less deceptive? Maybe the consequences are less severe for a child with cookie crumbs on his mouth than a man with blood on his hands, but neither is without deceit. The acorn of deception may not always grow into an oak, but it still has all the same DNA—whether we plan the lie or whether it just pops out when we're caught off guard.

The value God places on truthfulness has always been made plain in the Bible. The power of truth is that it lasts. It's eternal because it comes from the very nature of God. Jesus claimed to be "the truth" itself (John 14:6 NASB), and promised that "the truth will make you free" (John 8:32 NASB). God wants us to live in truth and the Truth to live in us. "Behold, You desire truth in the innermost being" (Psalm 51:6 NASB), and so God sends the Helper who is "the Spirit of truth" (John 15:26 NASB) to indwell believers. We keep pace with the Holy Spirit by living honestly and affirm our connection to God as His children. Truth is our heritage and our birthright as members of God's family.

WELL-SEASONED SPEECH

Conduct yourselves with wisdom toward outsiders,
making the most of the opportunity. Let your speech
always be with grace, as though seasoned with salt.
COLOSSIANS 4:5–6 NASB

Biblical wisdom is less about fortune cookie clichés than about instruction for right living. The prophets and disciples of the scriptures weren't like the hermit sages we sometimes envision living on mountaintops dispensing clever sayings. They spoke wisdom that could change lives and were not concerned with answering every philosophical question people raised. They knew that right living makes a person wise by biblical standards and spoke truth to help people understand their choices in all manner of circumstances.

Like the prophets of the Bible, we are surrounded by people who do not see the kingdom of God and need spiritual truths explained. Thus we will always be surrounded by opportunities to share our hope and our faith if we are prepared—not with clever sayings, or a rehearsed speech, or even theological arguments, but with words that are gracious and practical.

It's true some people will only be interested in engaging us to debate our faith, but no matter what the reasons, any opportunity to speak of Christ is a good one. Let us just remember to speak as He would, graciously treating each person as an individual created in the image of God.

FLATTERY WILL GET YOU NOWHERE

*Now I urge you, brethren, keep your eye on those who
cause dissensions and hindrances contrary to the
teaching which you learned, and turn away from them.
For such men are slaves, not of our Lord Christ but of
their own appetites; and by their smooth and flattering
speech they deceive the hearts of the unsuspecting.*
ROMANS 16:17–18 NASB

Paul was always watchful of his flock. He poured out his
life to build the church of Christ on a solid foundation.
But he knew others would come who worked only for
their own interests and who were slaves "of their own
appetites." You can tell who they are, he warns, because
they create arguments where there shouldn't be any. They
stand out because they teach what is contrary to the
truth found in Christ. Jesus described these same people:
"Beware of false prophets, who come to you in sheep's
clothing, but inwardly are ravenous wolves. You will know
them by their fruits" (Matthew 7:15–16 NASB). What kinds
of "fruits"? For one, their "smooth and flattering speech,"
which never has a place in the body of Christ. Flattery
always comes from an ulterior motive, to manipulate the
listener. It always serves the flesh.

To heed Paul's warning about such people, we need
to be sure we are not one of the "unsuspecting." The
unsuspecting are those who have never made the effort to
mature in Christ. Growing in our understanding of Christ is
the only way to guard against deception.

WHO IS GOD'S WILL?

*"I searched for a man among them who would build up
the wall and stand in the gap before Me for the land,
so that I would not destroy it; but I found no one."*
 EZEKIEL 22:30 NASB

When God wanted to do something on the earth to make Himself known or to teach His people, He always started with a person. Think of the history of the Bible—it's the story of people who demonstrated faith. Hebrews 11 provides a "Hall of Fame" of such faithful people: Abel, Enoch, Noah, Abraham, Isaac, Jacob, Sarah, Joseph, Moses, Gideon, Barak, Samson, Jephthah, David, Samuel, and all the prophets. These are some of the *who* of God's will—men and women who became the fulcrum for God to move the world.

God is still looking for individuals who will stand with Him and answer the call the way Isaiah did: "Then I heard the voice of the Lord, saying, 'Whom shall I send, and who will go for Us?' Then I said, 'Here am I. Send me!'" (Isaiah 6:8 NASB)

Of course, the ultimate Who in God's will is His Son, Jesus of Nazareth—"All things have been created through him and for him. He is before all things, and in him all things hold together" (Colossians 1:16–17 NIV). And He came "to purify for Himself a people for His own possession, *zealous for good deeds*" (Titus 2:14 NASB, emphasis added). Through Christ, we have the privilege of becoming the who God is seeking to "build up the wall and stand in the gap."

THE GREATEST TEACHER

*"Behold, God is exalted in His power;
who is a teacher like Him?"*
JOB 36:22 NASB

God is a gracious and faithful Teacher, and this life is His classroom. Lessons begin with the creation itself: "God's glory is on tour in the skies, God-craft on exhibit across the horizon. Madame Day *holds classes every morning*, Professor Night *lectures each evening*. Their words aren't heard, their voices aren't recorded, but their silence fills the earth: *unspoken truth is spoken everywhere*" (Psalm 19:1–4 MSG, emphasis added).

In addition to creation, God teaches us through His written word: "All Scripture is inspired by God and profitable *for teaching*, for reproof, for correction, for training in righteousness (2 Timothy 3:16 NASB, emphasis added). Jesus was God in the flesh, and who could make God known more clearly than God speaking face-to-face? Peter understood this when he exclaimed, "Lord, to whom shall we go? You have words of eternal life" (John 6:68 NASB).

And as if Christ's earthly appearance wasn't enough, we are given the Spirit of God to be our Teacher forever! "But the Helper, the Holy Spirit, whom the Father will send in My name, He will *teach you all things*, and bring to your remembrance all that I said to you" (John 14:26 NASB, emphasis added).

THE RIGHT KIND OF STUDENT

*I will instruct you and teach you in the way which you
should go; I will counsel you with My eye upon you.
Do not be as the horse or as the mule which have
no understanding, whose trappings include bit
and bridle to hold them in check, otherwise
they will not come near to you.*
PSALM 32:8–9 NASB

As a good Father, God provides opportunity after
opportunity to learn—about Himself, about ourselves,
about the world, and about eternity. He is a faithful
Teacher and promises to "counsel" us as we apply His
teaching to our daily lives.

As an involved, loving Teacher, what kind of student
is God hoping for? Certainly not those who need to be
guided like a senseless animal, pulled along day after day.
Being resistant to learning is a grief to any teacher and
useless to any student. "Obey your leaders and submit
to them, for they keep watch over your souls as those
who will give an account. Let them do this with joy and
not with grief, *for this would be unprofitable for you*"
(Hebrews 13:17 NASB, emphasis added).

The goal of all teaching is to pass along new
information, resulting in a new perspective, which in turn
leads to a new experience. In other words, *growth*. Our
Mentor wants to see us imitating Christ, making our own
choices, and taking risks. He wants us to grow up in our
understanding and see the changes in us, just as any
good dad or coach or counselor would.

SEVEN QUALITIES OF SPIRITUALLY EFFECTIVE PEOPLE

Do your best to improve your faith. You can do this by adding goodness, understanding, self-control, patience, devotion to God, concern for others, and love. If you keep growing in this way, it will show that what you know about our Lord Jesus Christ has made your lives useful and meaningful.
2 PETER 1:5–8 CEV

Most men enjoy being good at something, whether it's a career, a sport, or a hobby. We love the idea of being effective, of pursuing goals and achieving results. It's in us by design. To really stand out at something means acquiring a set of specific skills. Men spend a lot of energy acquiring the right skills for the job.

But in spiritual work—in building the kingdom of God—skills are not the main concern. Certainly they have their place, and God gives each of us spiritual gifts to be used to help others grow (1 Corinthians 12:7). But effectiveness in the kingdom is tied to the character of the worker. Peter points us to seven "qualities" that make up a foundation for being useful and fruitful in God's plan. The promise is pretty clear—we can't fail if we possess these qualities as growing traits because "no grass will grow under your feet, no day will pass without its reward as you mature in your experience of our Master Jesus" (2 Peter 1:8 MSG).

HAPPY ENDINGS

*For I am confident of this very thing, that He who
began a good work in you will perfect it until
the day of Christ Jesus.*
PHILIPPIANS 1:6 NASB

To "perfect" something means to work on it until it's right.
Another way to translate "perfect" is to "carry it on to
completion" (NIV). Christ does not start something in us
only to leave it all in our hands. God already tried that, in
a manner of speaking. The Old Testament Law was that
very opportunity, but it could not make us right with God
(Romans 3:20), and it had no power to make us different
from the inside (Romans 8:3). It takes Christ to do those
two things. That's why Jesus is the "*author* and *finisher* of
our faith" (Hebrews 12:2 KJV, emphasis added).

Our journey with Christ is part of a process called
sanctification. The part we experience in our daily lives
is when we begin to think and choose the way Jesus
would, approving "the things that are excellent, in order
to be sincere and blameless until the day of Christ"
(Philippians 1:10 NASB). This is in stark contrast to the Law
that didn't require an internal change but still required
blamelessness. The Law was a long and burdensome
road, traveled alone. But it was meant to be so we would
welcome the help of a Savior (Galatians 3:24). Now, since
it's His work in us and not our work for Him, we can have
confidence for a lifetime and beyond.

GODLY REBUKE

And they came to Him and woke Him, saying, "Save us, Lord; we are perishing!" He said to them, "Why are you afraid, you men of little faith?" Then He got up and rebuked the winds and the sea, and it became perfectly calm.
MATTHEW 8:25–26 NASB

The disciples were an unlikely mix of educated and uneducated, craftsmen and professionals, strong character and weak. But nothing breaks down barriers like a life-threatening event. When the storm threatened to swamp their boat, the disciples all agreed: wake Jesus up!

Jesus wasn't grumpy for being awakened; He was disappointed in their lack of faith. It's ironic to think that calling on Jesus for help could bring a rebuke. In this case, it would have shown more faith for the disciples not to cry out for Jesus' help. After all, He was right there with them. Peter repeats this watery lesson later: "Peter got out of the boat, and walked on the water and came toward Jesus. But seeing the wind, he became frightened, and beginning to sink, he cried out, 'Lord, save me!' Immediately Jesus stretched out His hand and took hold of him, and said to him, 'You of little faith, why did you doubt?'" (Matthew 14:29–31 NASB).

The lesson they seem to keep reviewing is that fear is the most potent form of doubt. Jesus wants us to be free from fear and live like He is truly with us, even in the storm.

CURSES TO BLESSINGS

Shimei was yelling at David, "Get out of here, you murderer!
You good-for-nothing, the LORD is paying you back for
killing so many in Saul's family. You stole his kingdom,
but now the LORD has given it to your son Absalom.
You're a murderer, and that's why you're in such big
trouble!" Abishai said, "Your Majesty, this man is as useless
as a dead dog! He shouldn't be allowed to curse you.
Let me go over and chop off his head." David replied. . .
". . . . If Shimei is cursing me because the LORD has told
him to, then who are you to tell him to stop?"
2 SAMUEL 16:7–10 CEV

A willingness to hear from God even when it comes
from someone who hates you is the truest form of
humility. King David was running for his life from his
son Absolam, who had usurped his throne. Along the
way, an embittered old man from Saul's family took the
opportunity to ridicule David. "Pay back!" shouted Shimei.
Of course he was wrong, since David was God's anointed,
but David did not even attempt to correct him. He did not
retaliate (though he could have) on the chance that God
was using this moment to speak to him. He simply trusted
in the Lord's judgment of the situation.

It's hard enough not to defend ourselves when
confronted by a friend. But what about someone who
honestly doesn't care about us? When we are rebuked,
are we willing to look for God's message to us even in the
words of those who are ignorant and hurtful? God's voice
would be worth the effort.

BEING THE MAN

*[King David to Solomon] "I am going the way of all the
earth. Be strong, therefore, and show yourself a man.
Keep the charge of the LORD your God, to walk in His ways,
to keep His statutes, His commandments, His ordinances,
and His testimonies, according to what is written in the
Law of Moses, that you may succeed in all that
you do and wherever you turn."*
1 KINGS 2:2–3 NASB

Solomon had the unique though difficult blessing of being
at his father's side as he was dying. Few men get that kind
of farewell, and fewer still get the life-directing exhortation
that would guide Solomon as the next king of Israel.

David was a warrior and a successful king, leaving
Solomon with huge boots to fill—a "man's man," as they
say. But at the end of his life, what did he point to as the
basis for being a *man*? Keeping "the charge of the Lord"—
following wholeheartedly the ways God had revealed. And
that, he well knew, would take courage. So David clarified
things for Solomon so all the other issues he would
potentially wrestle with in life as a man—purpose, success,
legacy, leadership—would fall into place. David did not
want Solomon to be distracted by what the world says a
man is but to be a man in God's eyes first and foremost.

Solomon's defining moment had come, and with it the
weight of a kingdom but also the blessing of being set on
the right course. For all men, in all circumstances, being
on the firm foundation of God's will makes a man succeed
as a man.

LIFTED LOW

The cords of death encompassed me and the terrors
of Sheol came upon me; I found distress and sorrow.
Then I called upon the name of the LORD: "O LORD, I beseech
You, save my life!" Gracious is the LORD, and righteous;
yes, our God is compassionate. The LORD preserves
the simple; I was brought low, and He saved me.
PSALM 116:3–6 NASB

How often we find that being brought low is the only road to rescue! Sometimes it's the only way to see what the psalmist saw: that God is gracious, righteous, and compassionate, that He stands ready to save. We are frequently distracted by our circumstances or by other people or by our own thinking. Sometimes we discover a beseeching heart only when God gets our full attention through difficulty. It's merciful to shake us to the foundations of our faith, to crush our expectations, to allow distress and sorrow to "win" for a while, and thus force from us an earnest cry for God's help. The humbling of hardship and suffering is a kindness. "It is never fun to be corrected. In fact, at the time it is always painful. But if we learn to obey by being corrected, we will do right and live at peace" (Hebrews 12:11 CEV).

Humbling ourselves means we stop looking for solutions, for *how* or *what,* and start looking for *Who.* God gives grace to the humble and answers the earnest prayers of His children with the gift of Himself. Being brought to our knees is to be brought into closer communion with our Father.

THE PAINFUL TRUTH

"And you, Capernaum. . .if the miracles had occurred in
Sodom which occurred in you, it would have remained
to this day. Nevertheless I say to you that it will be
more tolerable for the land of Sodom in
the day of judgment, than for you."
MATTHEW 11:23–24 NASB

Sentimental images depicting Christ carrying a lamb or
gently blessing little children, though well meaning, can
create an imbalanced view of Jesus. While He was indeed
gentle and caring, rcripture records another side, too—a
forceful and confrontational side. Just ask the Pharisees!
Christ decried them in the strongest possible terms because
they were God's spiritual leaders and yet opposed God in the
flesh, and misled the people. But Jesus didn't stop with them.
    Jesus actually denounced entire towns that didn't
repent, though they had witnessed many miracles. Wicked
cities from Israel's history would have changed their ways
had they seen the same miracles, claimed Jesus. Imagine!
Sodom, for all its debauchery, will find it more tolerable on
the day of judgment than the small fishing village where
Jesus called his first disciples, healed Peter's mother-in-
law, and marveled at the faith of the Roman Centurion!
Jesus' warning was appropriately blunt, and His message
to those who should know better perfectly clear:"But
the one who does not know and does things deserving
punishment will be beaten with few blows. From everyone
who has been given much, much will be demanded; and
from the one who has been entrusted with much, much
more will be asked" (Luke 12:48, NIV).

SEVEN THOUSAND REASONS

"Lord, they have killed Your prophets, they have torn down Your altars, and I alone am left, and they are seeking my life." But what is the divine response to him? "I have kept for Myself seven thousand men who have not bowed the knee to Baal."

ROMANS 11:3–4 NASB

In 1 Kings 18, the prophet Elijah challenged 450 priests of Baal to a showdown of epic proportions. With all Israel watching, Elijah calls down fire from heaven, devouring a massive, water-soaked offering in divine fashion. The people fall on their faces, confessing to God, then dispatch the pagan priests. But Queen Jezebel is furious and swears to kill Elijah. He runs away, hides in a cave, and completely discouraged, pours out his complaint to God.

What was God's encouragement to Elijah during his spiritual depression? The anonymous men who had resisted the pressure of their times, ordinary men who were faithful day after day. Elijah may have been the star of this epic, but this remnant of unknown men was the story behind the story. And God used them to encourage one of the most powerful prophets of the Bible.

Few of us will ever know anyone who faced the pressures Elijah did, but we all know someone who feels alone in standing for God. Just remember, in a faithless world, all it takes to be an encouragement to others is to be one of the seven thousand.

GODLY HATE

"If anyone comes to Me, and does not hate his own father and mother and wife and children and brothers and sisters, yes, and even his own life, he cannot be My disciple."
LUKE 14:26 NASB

It's obvious that Jesus is not instructing us to actively hate our families. That would be absurd, since it would contradict just about everything else the Bible says is a man's responsibility to his family. Likewise, despising oneself is not the point since God loves us and has adopted us.

In the verse, Jesus lists the most likely competitors for His rightful place in our hearts, our minds, and our choices. He doesn't list career or success. Those things can be serious distractions, but they aren't what truly compete for the affection of sincere believers. It's relationships that contend with Him the most—other personalities and desires. Other voices. Choosing a godly "hate" of family is an important philosophical position. It needs to be in place so that when following Christ means alienation from those closest to us, our love for Him is the *only* love that matters. He wins, hands down.

Then there's our own desires, our own voices. If we cling to our vision for ourselves, then that will disqualify us from being His disciples. If what we want matters more than growing in the true knowledge of the One who created us (Colossians 3:10), we won't be *able* to follow Christ. He's not the one who rejects our service—we make ourselves unavailable.

EXPERIENCING GOD,
OR THE OTHER WAY AROUND?

Work out your salvation with fear and trembling;
for it is God who is at work in you, both to will
and to work for His good pleasure.
PHILIPPIANS 2:12–13 NASB

Paul consistently connected knowing God with pleasing Him. He prayed that believers, "may be filled with the knowledge of His will in all spiritual wisdom and understanding, so that you will walk in a manner worthy of the Lord, to please Him in all respects, bearing fruit in every good work and increasing in the knowledge of God" (Colossians 1:9–10 NASB). Our growing understanding of God gives us new experiences of Him, but it also gives God new experiences of us. Just as earthly fathers enjoy seeing their children grow, so does our Father in heaven. As we mature spiritually, we gain the opportunity not just to receive from our Father but to give to Him. And the great news is that not only can we bring our Father pleasure (1 Thessalonians 4:1), He Himself is so committed to His own experience of us that He actually works in us to see that it happens. If we want to make Him happy, we have nothing to stop us!

LEARNING WISDOM AND SELF-CONTROL

*Proverbs will teach you wisdom and self-control
and how to understand sayings with deep meanings.*
PROVERBS 1:2 CEV

Do you struggle with self-control? If you have given up hope and given yourself over to one sin or another, Solomon has something to say to you. In today's verse, he says the book of Proverbs will teach you wisdom and self-control. Hope does exist. You just have to access it.

When is the last time you worked your way through the book of Proverbs? There are thirty-one Proverbs, one for each day of the month. Would you be willing to spend some serious time and contemplation in one chapter of Proverbs per day for the next month? Would you be willing to journal about your revelations? How about enlisting another man to go through them with you? Commit to not talking about anything temporal during the month, but instead speak only about the truths you are learning. It might be awkward at first, but awkward is okay. All it will take is one revelation to set you on a new course.

Solomon says that in addition to gaining wisdom and self-control, you will learn how to understand sayings with deep meanings. This doesn't come as a natural gift or even a developed skill. It comes from the Spirit of God as you ingest the wisdom of His Word.

If your soul has been dry during this season of sin, expect a change. Expect deep understanding. Expect deep revelation. Expect victory.

PLEASING THE WEAKER BROTHER

*If our faith is strong, we should be patient with
the Lord's followers whose faith is weak. We should try
to please them instead of ourselves.*

ROMANS 15:1 CEV

If you've ever wondered whether you fall into the "stronger" or "weaker" brother camp as expressed in the scriptures, the truth in Romans 15:1 might help you answer that question.

Generally speaking, stronger brothers have been and continue to be immersed in the Word. They have clarity regarding the precepts of God. They are under authority and accountable. And they treat those who are just starting out in their faith journey with the utmost respect and patience—so much so that they try to please their brother rather than themselves.

When it comes to issues that fall under the banner of Christian liberty, stronger Christians should never attempt to flaunt such liberties but rather be sensitive toward the weaker believer who is still formulating his personal theological understanding of such things.

If that means not ordering a glass of wine at dinner with a weaker brother who might object, then the stronger believer gladly does so out of love and concern for how his actions might be perceived by the weaker brother.

As the weaker brother grows, he will find himself in the presence of newer, weaker brothers, and your witness of loving him right where he was will help him do the same for others.

PUT OFF ANGER, PUT ON CHRIST

Don't make friends with anyone who has a bad temper.
PROVERBS 22:24 CEV

The biblical principle of not befriending people who have a bad temper is meant to keep us from becoming just like those people. We are influenced by the people we hang out with, and vice versa. There is little room for grace in the life of a hot-tempered man, and wisdom is far from him.

But most of us know this. In fact, we nod our head in agreement when we read this verse, believing it to be good common sense, but have you ever considered it from the opposite point of view? Are fellow believers avoiding friendship with you because you have a bad temper? If you know you have a problem with anger and are currently experiencing isolation as a result, now is the time to ask for help.

Approach your pastor, small group leader, or someone who has known you for a long time and allow him to ask you hard questions that examine your motivation(s). Once he finds your triggers, you can begin the work of putting off your spirit of anger and putting on the mercy of Christ.

If anybody ever had a right to be angry, it was Jesus. He was betrayed, falsely accused of blasphemy, beaten beyond recognition, and executed in the most painful of ways. But after conquering death, He was anything but angry. Instead, He was with His apostles for forty more days, speaking about God's kingdom (Acts 1:3)—one that practices love, happiness, peacefulness, patience, kindness, goodness, faithfulness, gentleness, and self-control.

Become a God Pleaser

I am not trying to please people. I want to please God.
Do you think I am trying to please people? If I were
doing that, I would not be a servant of Christ.
Galatians 1:10 cev

The apostle Paul was indeed a people pleaser at one point in his life. As a Pharisee, he studied to show himself approved by men. As a persecutor of those who followed Jesus, he pleased men by holding the coats of the men who stoned Stephen to death (Acts 7:58). He even approached the high priest for permission to persecute Christians (Acts 9:1–2).

Post conversion, Paul became a God pleaser, contending for the Gospel at all cost, no matter what men thought. His letter to the Galatian church was a warning. He heard that they were straying from God and ultimately the Gospel as it had been taught to them by the apostles. His language was sharp, saying, "I pray that God will punish anyone who preaches anything different from our message to you! It doesn't matter if that person is one of us or an angel from heaven" (Galatians 1:8 cev).

As believers, we are called to love one another and our neighbors as ourselves. And we are called to be humble. But when a false gospel is presented, we must speak the truth as lovingly as possible. We cannot afford to be people pleasers when it comes to the Gospel. Souls are at stake. We are not servants of Christ if we compromise in this area.

A LEADER OF HONOR

Every honest leader rules with help from me.
PROVERBS 8:16 CEV

In our modern world in which leaders often try to cover up one scandal or another, it's easy to lose trust in leaders of all stripes—from political to religious to business. But some leaders are indeed honest, and whether they know it or not, they are only able to be so because God governs the affairs of men at every level.

He cares about how our presidents, governors, senators, members of congress, and mayors use their power. He wants to see them use their power for good, not for personal gain. He cares about how pastors, elders, and Sunday school teachers shepherd the flock. He wants to see them use their power to bring His people to a deeper understanding of Him, which helps us draw closer to Him. He cares about how CEOs, COOs, CFOs, and the like run the companies they have been entrusted with. He wants them to use honest weights and measures because trusted companies lead to stable economies.

At some level, you are a leader. You are a leader at work, at church, or at home—maybe all three. Do those who are under your authority trust you? Would they say you are honest? If you have made mistakes or committed sins in your leadership role, ask for forgiveness. And then trust God to help you be the honest leader He spoke about in Proverbs 8:16.

JUST WALK AWAY

Stay away from stupid and senseless arguments.
These only lead to trouble.
2 TIMOTHY 2:23 CEV

Pride is easily engaged in stupid and senseless arguments.

In 2014, a news report surfaced about a twenty-three-year-old who allegedly stabbed and killed his stepfather over a puppy. The stepson brought a puppy into the house without his stepfather knowing about it, and his stepfather asked him to remove it. When the stepson wouldn't comply, it led to a heated argument that ended in trouble for the stepson. He was charged with felony murder and aggravated assault.

Another news report chronicled a fistfight in the parking lot of a Mormon church in 2013 as a result of "seat saving." The fistfight escalated to the point that one of the men allegedly hit the other one with his vehicle.

You may have started or been lured into senseless arguments in your church, workplace, or home only to realize several hours later that your anger over an incidental matter was a huge waste of time at best and hurtful to one or both parties at worst. The apostle Paul knew that such senselessness could get out of hand in a hurry. That's why he advised the young Timothy to avoid such quarrels. They just aren't worth the trouble they cause.

If you are given to such arguments, consider the possible end result before you even begin. Be the bigger man and walk away before it escalates.

OUR BODIES ARE NOT OUR OWN

*The wife does not have authority over her own body
but yields it to her husband. In the same way,
the husband does not have authority over
his own body but yields it to his wife.*

1 CORINTHIANS 7:4 NIV

In theory, as men we understand the principle of leaving and cleaving. And we understand that when we marry, we become one flesh with our wives. More than one of us, however, have used today's verse to point out why a wife shouldn't deny her husband in the marriage bed. And we throw a spiritual fit when she uses the marriage bed as a weapon. She belongs to us, not herself! She has no right.

While all of this is true, we rarely consider the second part of the verse. If our bodies belong to our wives instead of ourselves, that means we do not have the right to abuse it with fornication, adultery, pornography, or any other type of sexual impurity. Doing so unjustly wrenches control of our bodies from our wives. Our bodies do not belong to us, so we do not have the right to pleasure them outside of the marriage bed.

This is a counter-cultural message in a sex-crazed society, but the Holy Spirit resides inside of us and stands at the ready to empower us to live as only the followers of Christ are able. We have the same power in us that raised Christ from the dead. Surely that is ample to empower us to obey and embrace the truth of this verse.

REPORTING FOR DUTY

*But when the week was over, we started on our way
again. All the men, together with their wives and children,
walked with us from the town to the seashore.
We knelt on the beach and prayed.*
ACTS 21:5 CEV

Pastors will tell you that men in America are largely
AWOL in both attendance and in the work of the church.
Women, on the other hand, are plentiful and willing
subjects, anxious to be used by the Lord in any capacity
He sees fit. But that's not the way it is supposed to be.

In Acts 21, Luke chronicles Paul's journey that
ultimately led to Jerusalem, where he faced harsh
persecution. When the ship he was on stopped in the
port of Tyre in Syria for a week to unload its cargo (verse
4), the shipmates went in search of other believers.
When they found them, they grew quite close—staying
with them and listening to their warnings not to go to
Jerusalem. Paul was undeterred, however, deciding to
press on. But before he did, all the men took their wives
and children to the seashore to see him off. They kneeled
and prayed.

Not a single member of this group of believers was
AWOL. Every one of them accompanied Paul all the way
to the seashore, and then they sank to their knees to
implore heaven to keep him safe. Imagine the difference
the modern church could make if every believing man
reported for duty. If you've been AWOL, it's not too late
to change that.

MODELING CONSISTENT SELF-CONTROL

Tell the older men to have self-control and to be serious and sensible. Their faith, love, and patience must never fail.
TITUS 2:2 CEV

The apostle Paul left Titus, one of his charges, behind in Crete to do the difficult work of appointing leaders for the churches in each town (Titus 1:5). Paul gave him instructions about which type of men to choose as leaders, as well as instructing him about the type of people they would be ministering to.

Paul quoted and confirmed what one of the Cretan prophets said, "The people of Crete always tell lies. They are greedy and lazy like wild animals" (Titus 1:12 CEV). He wanted Titus to be hard on such people so they could grow strong in their faith (verse 13). This brings us to today's verse regarding older men in Crete. Ordinarily, older men don't need to be told to have self-control and to be serious and sensible, but apparently the older men in Crete were among those who were greedy and lazy and therefore needed to hear this message.

When young Christian men are unable to look up to older men in the faith in matters of appetite control, a sense of hopelessness can set in. If older Christian men cannot temper the flesh, what hope does a young man have? Regardless of where you find yourself on the age spectrum, self-control is not only possible, but followers of Christ are called to exhibit it.

Columbus Day

STARTING AT HOME

Crispus was the leader of the meeting place.
He and everyone in his family put their faith in the Lord.
Many others in Corinth also heard the message, and all
the people who had faith in the Lord were baptized.
ACTS 18:8 CEV

———

Crispus was the ruler of the synagogue at the time Acts was written. As the ruler, he would have presided over the assemblies, interpreted the law of God, and judged whether actions were lawful, among other duties. As such, the Jews certainly wouldn't have expected to see a mass conversion to Christianity from his household, but that is exactly what happened.

Crispus is believed to have come to the faith after either hearing Paul's preaching or when he was in Justus's house. Either way, once he became a Christian, it changed everything. Under his leadership, Christianity spread even further—that's the mark of a true Christian leader. His love for the Lord was contagious, and he couldn't wait to share it with everybody he loved, beginning in his own household.

In modern America, often mothers are the ones who pass along their faith to their children because men are busy with other pursuits. But nothing is more important than the Gospel. On this day when we celebrate Columbus for discovering America and for bringing the Gospel with him, what better way to celebrate his efforts than to be just as motivated to bring the Gospel to fruition in our families?

WALL BUILDING

*Losing self-control leaves you as helpless
as a city without a wall.*
PROVERBS 25:28 CEV

During biblical times, cities often had walls built all the way around the perimeter for protection from the outside. The walls also probably kept people on the inside from wandering into trouble on the outside. Smaller villages were often unwalled (Ezekiel 38:11, Leviticus 25:29–34), and as a result, they were easier prey for predators.

When we lose self-control, Solomon says we are as helpless as a city without a wall—open, vulnerable to attack, an easy mark for Satan. The converse is also true—a person who has self-control is as safe as a city with a wall. It might sound silly to try to re-create the notion of wall building for the purpose of maintaining self-control, but those who practice it will tell you it helps them stay on track one hour at a time.

The practice is called building hedges, and the process looks different depending on the person. In matters of lust, some use an accountability partner. Some use filters on their computers to keep their eyes from straying. Others resolve to use positive reinforcement— such as writing love letters during times they would otherwise be weak or placing photos of loved ones in places they might otherwise be tempted. What sort of wall can you build to keep yourself from straying?

REPLACING OUR CHILDISH WAYS

When we were children, we thought and reasoned
as children do. But when we grew up,
we quit our childish ways.
1 CORINTHIANS 13:11 CEV

A recent *Christianity Today* article makes this observation about the state of men: "Recently, several articles and statistics have shown that women are making history with career achievements, while men in increasing numbers are seemingly living in a prolonged state of adolescence, sitting back with their buddies and playing video games."

Throw in fantasy football, rampant use of pornography, and a growing disinterest in marriage and you have a near epidemic of men who never grow up.

Our prolonged state of adolescence extends even to our faith. Some of us became Christians at an early age. We were baptized under the direction of our parents. We attended Sunday school. We read our Bibles. But then we graduated from high school, got a job, moved, and quickly fell away. As a result, some of us are in the same place spiritually that we were five, ten, and twenty years ago. Paul didn't approve of this in his day. He certainly wouldn't approve of it in our day.

He spoke of quitting childish ways in today's verse. What sort of childish activities are you engaged in that you need to put away? Replace them with spiritual activities and you'll begin to see spiritual growth that will help you make an impact for the kingdom.

THE BIBLICAL WORK ETHIC

Don't be selfish and eager to get rich—you will end up worse off than you can imagine.
PROVERBS 28:22 CEV

You don't have to look far to find get-rich-quick schemes. They are never presented as such, but if you listen to the pitch for any length of time, it's hard to conclude otherwise. Often those who are at the lower levels of these schemes have the best of intentions. They are just trying to make a little money on the side, but when they hear the promises of greater riches if they can sign up more people, they start to see real dollar signs.

The Bible warns against such selfishness, saying you will end up worse off than you can imagine. Commentators say that such a heart leads to envy, dishonesty, and covetousness—grieving over those who have more. Such wealth is gone as quickly as it comes. In the most extreme cases, freedom is lost as well. To make matters worse, when these schemes topple, those who are involved lose their reputation and even friendships among those they take down with them.

The biblical work ethic has always been about slow and steady growth (Proverbs 6:6, Matthew 20:1–16), accomplished with hard work that is performed with the utmost of integrity, as unto the Lord (Colossians 3:23). If you are weighing a business opportunity that isn't in line with those principles, run from it. It isn't from God.

KNOWING WHEN TO HIDE

*When you see trouble coming, don't be stupid
and walk right into it—be smart and hide.*
PROVERBS 22:3 CEV

Sometimes situations call for us to stand boldy against injustice or in favor of the oppressed. The prophet Nathan stood against King David and his sin of adultery (2 Samuel 12). Peter and John stood against Annas, Caiaphas, and other members of the high priest's family when they were told never to teach anything about the name of Jesus again (Acts 4).

Other times we are called to run and hide, as mentioned in today's verse. The New International Version, New Living Translation, New American Standard Bible, the New King James Version, and The Message describe the person in this verse as "prudent." In other words, they are wise—immersed in the scriptures, able to know the difference about when to stand and when to run. And when trouble is on the way—the type of trouble that doesn't need to be confronted, they run. Noah heard God's voice, saw impending trouble, and hid in the ark. Joseph was tempted by Potiphar's wife, and he ran in the opposite direction.

Do you see trouble coming in your own life? What is your first instinct? Whatever it is, how does it compare or contrast with the wisdom of scripture? If you haven't fully developed your sense of discernment, consider enlisting a godly friend who can help you navigate the situation, and maybe avoid one of the biggest mistakes of your life.

STAYING ON THE PATH

*You lead humble people to do what is right
and to stay on your path.*
PSALM 25:9 CEV

Turn on late night television and you'll see one self-help infomercial after another—ways to lose weight, ways to improve your memory, ways to improve your finances. While all of these are worthy endeavors in and of themselves, none of them leads to a humble dependence on God, which means none of them will bring you closer to Him.

The Bible, on the other hand, says God leads the humble to do what is right, and not only does He do that, but He also keeps them on the right path. Who are the humble? They are teachable, prayerful, gentle people who are lovers of Christ over self. In fact, some translations use the words *meek* or *poor in spirit* in place of "humble," which causes some commentators to refer to the humble as "the afflicted, miserable, or wretched." That would indicate that the humble know hardship—maybe because they have gone their own way before turning toward God, or maybe due to matters that were out of their hands. Either way, they recognize God as the Sovereign of the universe, and they have learned to trust Him.

As their trust in Him grew, their desire to be in His presence did as well. Now they cannot imagine getting through a day without walking and talking with Christ. As they do so, He leads and directs them on the paths they should take.

HEAVENLY CORRECTION

*Our earthly fathers correct us, and we still respect them.
Isn't it even better to be given true life by letting
our spiritual Father correct us?*
HEBREWS 12:9 CEV

We tend to run at the first hint of correction. Correction is humiliating and pride crushing, even when it's justified. When you were growing up and faced the possibility of corporal punishment, or you expected the loss of certain privileges because you did something that was worthy of correction, you probably not only hid, but you also fretted, begged, and pleaded before finally submitting to your punishment.

But, assuming you weren't physically abused, when you were older you were thankful that your earthly father cared enough to correct you, because it made you the man you are today. You probably even respect your father for stepping in when the situation warranted it because now you can see the fruit.

The writer of Hebrews indicates that something much larger is at stake than simply becoming a better person. When we go astray spiritually, our heavenly Father has to step in because *true life* is at stake, meaning eternity in heaven.

God loves us enough to correct us in such a fashion that will keep us from experiencing true death as the result of our wayward actions. If you are experiencing His correction or have done so recently, rejoice! You are being prepared for heaven by our Creator.

WHO, OR WHAT, RULES YOU?

People who are ruled by their desires think only of themselves. Everyone who is ruled by the Holy Spirit thinks about spiritual things.
ROMANS 8:5 CEV

I need coffee. Time for a shower. What should I wear? How am I doing on time? Why doesn't this guy in front of me drive any faster? I wonder how my 10:00 a.m. meeting will go? Who took my parking spot? Why is the receptionist so grumpy every morning? I hope I don't have any difficult problems to solve in my e-mail inbox this morning. I hope Greg doesn't stop by my desk for his typical twenty-minute chat. I have too much to do for that. The meeting went better than I thought it would. What's on TV tonight?

If you were to keep a running list today of every major thought you have, what would it reveal? Would your typical day look anything like the paragraph above? None of these concerns are bad or even selfish, necessarily, but for a Christian to go an entire day without contemplating spiritual things is an indication of a spiritual problem because the Holy Spirit naturally directs and guides us as we go about our daily routines.

As we submit to Him, we see otherwise mundane tasks and situations through spiritual eyes—eyes that want to honor and obey God, eyes that earnestly desire to see beyond our own desires, eyes that want to minister to others. We are quicker to forgive and slower to anger. We long for heaven, rather than the recliner.

ATTRACTING SINNERS

*"If this man really were a prophet, he would know
what kind of woman is touching him!
He would know that she is a sinner."*
LUKE 7:39 CEV

Simon, a Pharisee, invited Jesus to dine with him and some of his friends. But a sinful woman crashed the party after learning Jesus would be there. She broke down in tears when she saw Him and began washing His feet with her tears, kissing them and pouring perfume over them, causing Simon to question whether Jesus was a prophet, as many believed Him to be.

Simon expected Jesus to view the woman the way he did. The religious rules he embraced as a Pharisee didn't allow him to interact with notorious sinners, so surely Jesus wouldn't interact with her either. But the woman wasn't bound by any such rules. She simply saw Jesus for who He was, and she was drawn to Him, knowing Him to be full of mercy. She approached Him from behind, perhaps feeling unworthy to be in His presence, and then lovingly displayed her love for Him. To Simon's amazement, Jesus praised this woman's actions.

Holding to a certain theological bent and then drawing inferences from that theology, as men are wont to do, is of little value if we forget mercy. You will know you have forgotten mercy if the unregenerate are repelled by you and your religious rules, rather than attracted to Christ, who lives in you.

KNOWING GOD

Let's do our best to know the LORD. His coming is as certain as the morning sun; he will refresh us like rain renewing the earth in the springtime.
HOSEA 6:3 CEV

In Hosea 6, the prophet is addressing God's people after a period of sin, saying, "He has torn us to shreds, but he will bandage our wounds and make us well" (verse 1). After we have experienced His discipline, Hosea tells us to do our best to know the Lord. This will look different for everybody.

Some of us will turn to what saints of old referred to as the spiritual disciplines. Richard Foster listed twelve such disciplines in his classic, *Celebration of Discipline: The Path to Spiritual Growth*—meditation, prayer, fasting, study, simplicity, solitude, submission, service, confession, guidance, celebration, and worship. Others of us find the disciplines to be too formulaic and opt instead for a more free form of expression, often focusing on one or more of the disciplines outlined by Foster.

Hosea didn't tell us to adhere to one expression or the other as much as he called us to perform some sort of action to know the Lord. You picked up a copy of this book because you want to know Christ in a deeper fashion. That is a great indicator that you are on the right path. What else are you doing to know the Lord? If a new believer came to you looking for help and asked how you draw closer to God, what would you say?

JUMP-START YOUR PRAYER LIFE

In certain ways we are weak, but the Spirit is here to help us. For example, when we don't know what to pray for, the Spirit prays for us in ways that cannot be put into words.
ROMANS 8:26 CEV

In 2007, researchers from the University of Arizona conducted an eight-year study and determined that, contrary to popular opinion, men and women speak approximately the same amount of words each day: 16,000. It also found that men tended to talk more about technology and sports, while women talked more about relationships. In other words, men talk about things and what other people are doing, while women speak about how they connect with people.

Maybe this explains why so many Christian women are prayer warriors while Christian men are busy talking about theology. Since we struggle to express ourselves in relationships, we struggle to talk to God. We talk about Him instead. But the Spirit is here to help us in our weakness, even going so far as to pray for us when we don't know what to say. That implies we are actually talking to God on some level. Where we fall short, the Spirit takes over. Find both comfort and motivation in that truth to jump-start your prayer life.

HEAVEN'S REGISTER

But don't be happy because evil spirits obey you.
Be happy that your names are written in heaven!
LUKE 10:20 CEV

After Jesus sent out His seventy-two hand-chosen followers to every village and city He planned to visit, they returned to Him and said, "Lord, even the demons obeyed when we spoke in your name!" (verse 17). Jesus acknowledged that fact, but He didn't want their focus to be on the power He had given them. Instead, He wanted it to be on eternity. Their names were written in heaven. That is something to be happy about.

Many of us spend our entire lives trying to get our names known in the business world, hoping to climb the ladder of success as our star rises. And to a degree, there's nothing wrong with this. But if our joy and our satisfaction comes from having our nameplate on an office door on the top floor of a tall office building, it will be short-lived. How much better to derive joy and satisfaction over the fact that our names are written in heaven!

In Revelation 21:27, John gets a peek inside the New Jerusalem and he sees the book that will contain our names: "Nothing unworthy will be allowed to enter. No one who is dirty-minded or who tells lies will be there. Only those whose names are written in the Lamb's book of life will be in the city" (CEV).

If you have been born again, rejoice that your name can be found in heaven's register this very moment.

ENCOURAGE ONE ANOTHER DAILY

You must encourage one another each day.
HEBREWS 3:13 CEV

Motivational speaker Jim Rohn once said, "You are the average of the five people you spend the most time with." You can find a variation of that sentiment in 1 Corinthians 15:33 when the apostle Paul quoted Greek poet, Menander: "Do not be misled: 'Bad company corrupts good character'" (NIV). In a passive sense, we become the type of people we hang out with.

As Christians, we are called to be active in our pursuit of godliness. One of the ways we are to be active is to encourage one another each day. If we don't, sin will fool us, making us easy prey for Satan—much like the lone sheep is easy prey for the hungry wolf. Receiving such encouragement presupposes that we are active members in a congregation and that people there know us well enough to offer and receive encouragement from us.

If that's not the case for you, then find a good, Bible-believing church. Once you have found a place of worship, seek a kindred spirit or two and figure out the best way to encourage one another on a continual basis. Some Christian men exchange Bible verses via text message every day. Others meet for coffee a couple of times each week. And others sneak away during the lunch hour to pray for one another. Find what works for you, and devise a plan.

HEALTHY EYES

"The eye is the lamp of the body. If your eyes are healthy, your whole body will be full of light."
MATTHEW 6:22 NIV

Have you ever woken up in a dark room and been completely unaware of the time or maybe even day of the week? Darkness has a way of disorienting and confusing us, blurring the lines of reality. Conversely, light helps us see what is all around us, allowing us to respond accordingly.

Jesus said our eyes are the lamp of our bodies, and when they are healthy our entire bodies are full of light. In context, He was speaking about storing up treasures in heaven, and this is one of the examples He provided.

In commenting about this verse in his *Notes on the Bible*, Albert Barnes says that if a man who is crossing a stream on a log looks steadily across at some immovable object, he will experience little danger. But "if he looks down on the dashing and rolling waters, he will become dizzy, and fall. So Jesus says, in order that the conduct may be right, it is important to fix the affections on heaven."

The healthy eye stays fixed on Jesus and, ultimately, heaven. As a result, its owner is able to navigate the difficult waters of this life. The unhealthy eye glances from one moveable object to the next. In so doing, its owner treads dark paths in search of meaning in what feels like a maze of confusion.

REJOICE IN HARDSHIP

Dear friends, do not be surprised at the fiery ordeal that has come on you to test you, as though something strange were happening to you. But rejoice inasmuch as you participate in the sufferings of Christ, so that you may be overjoyed when his glory is revealed.
1 PETER 4:12–13 NIV

As Peter wrote these words, Jerusalem was facing impending destruction. Rome considered Christianity a threat, and therefore persecution was heavy. But Peter didn't want believers to lose faith. Instead, he wanted believers to see such hardship as an opportunity to participate in the sufferings of Christ.

Trials and sufferings have a way of causing disillusionment, especially when our expectations include a life of comfort. When you face fiery ordeals, do you see them as a test or as something strange? Or do you rejoice?

In Acts 5, the apostles were arrested, imprisoned, beaten, and told not to teach about the name of Jesus, but that didn't stop them. It also didn't make them bitter or angry. Verse 41 says, "The apostles left the Sanhedrin, rejoicing because they had been counted worthy of suffering disgrace for the Name" (NIV).

Rejoicing in the midst of trials is the power of Christ in us, and that is what the world around us needs to see.

CHASING FANTASIES

*Those who work their land will have abundant food,
but those who chase fantasies have no sense.*
PROVERBS 12:11 NIV

All of us have land to till each workday. It is our lot, and it has been assigned to us to provide for our families. For some, it is physical land; for others, it is a real estate office, a teller window, a delivery truck, a taxicab, or an office. While our tasks may feel like drudgery at times, an attitude of diligence and gratitude can, and should, spur us on.

Just as farmers work in different stages—from cultivation to preparing for the crop to come to harvest—our jobs require constant preparation. Even established real estate agents have to stay informed of current property laws while also meeting with new clients on a regular basis and maintaining relationships with current clients. It's a never-ending, time-consuming cycle. It doesn't have to come at the expense of hobbies or even starting a new small business, though.

When Solomon condemns fantasy chasing in today's verse, he's referring to sloth and inactivity—not hardworking entrepreneurs who are busy tilling new ground. In Adam Clarke's *Commentary on the Bible*, he says it this way: "He who, while he should be cultivating his ground, preparing for a future crop, or reaping his harvest, associates with fowlers, coursers of hares, hunters of foxes, or those engaged in any champaign amusements, is void of understanding."

GOD'S WILL

It is God's will that you should be sanctified: that you should avoid sexual immorality; that each of you should learn to control your own body in a way that is holy and honorable.
1 THESSALONIANS 4:3–4 NIV

The will of God isn't elusive or hidden. We are to give thanks in all circumstances, because this is the will of God for us in Christ Jesus (1 Thessalonians 5:18). It is God's will for us to perform good works so we can silence ignorant talk of foolish people (1 Peter 2:15). And it is God's will that we should be sanctified, or holy, avoiding sexual immorality.

Giving thanks, performing good works, and controlling our sexual urges are not mutually exclusive. When we are thankful and working out our salvation, our sexual urges are better kept in check. On the other hand, when we grumble about our circumstances and are idle and cut off from Christian community, our baser instincts demand attention.

Giving thanks in all circumstances means we are willing to accept the truth of Psalm 16:5: the Lord is our portion; He makes our lot secure. We aren't owed anything more or less than what He has determined ahead of time, including sexual fulfillment. Submitting to this truth is part of the sanctification process.

Performing good works brings a sense of joy that replaces worldly happiness that comes from pleasing the flesh. What good deed has the Holy Spirit been speaking to you about performing?

CHRIST IS YOUR STRENGTH

And he said to them, "I have eagerly desired to eat this Passover with you before I suffer. For I tell you, I will not eat it again until it finds fulfillment in the kingdom of God."
LUKE 22:15–16 NIV

Jesus spoke these words to men who had failed Him. His disciples argued over who would be the greatest. They often misunderstood His teaching. They failed to cast out demons in His name. They fell asleep when He asked them to stay awake to pray for Him. And yet Jesus eagerly desired to eat the Passover meal with this band of misfits before He suffered.

Christ's sacrificial death on the cross led the apostle Paul to refer to him as Christ, "our Passover lamb" (1 Corinthians 5:7 NIV)—the new had come, the old had passed away. Going forward, Paul connects Jesus' final Passover meal with the institution of the Lord's Supper (1 Corinthians 11), in which we proclaim the Lord's death until He returns.

Do you approach the communion table at your church with the same vigor and desire as Jesus? Are you eager to settle your account with God in a corporate worship setting, knowing other believers around you are doing the same thing? If not, it might be an indicator that your faith isn't as strong as it should be. The good news is, He is your strength. The next time communion is offered at your church, approach the table knowing that grace awaits you there.

HIDE THE WORD IN YOUR HEART

I have hidden your word in my heart
that I might not sin against you.
PSALM 119:11 NIV

We hide things for two reasons. We are either ashamed of something or we treasure something so much that we have to hide it for fear that someone will steal it from us.

David knew great sin, but he also knew great forgiveness. In his experience, hiding the Word of God in his heart was the only way to combat his sinful nature and to keep him from falling even further.

To say that he hid the Word in his heart implies several things. First, he went beyond simply owning a copy of God's Word. Owning a copy isn't transforming. Second, he went beyond hiding the Word in his mind. Our memories can fail us. Third, he went beyond simply reading God's Word on occasion. Reading it is helpful. But possessing it in our hearts is transformative.

If you find your faith lacking the power to overcome sin, consider a Bible memory program. It doesn't have to be elaborate. Index cards will work just fine. Look up verses that speak to the sin you are struggling with and jot the verses down on the cards. Carry them with you everywhere, and refer to them throughout the day.

If you meditate, study, and recite the verses often enough, you'll find that they are hidden in your heart—the perfect place for the Holy Spirit to access them for your spiritual breakthrough.

PUTTING ON CHRIST

*Let the Lord Jesus Christ be as near to you as the clothes
you wear. Then you won't try to satisfy your selfish desires.*
ROMANS 13:14 CEV

All of us go through spiritually dry seasons in our
Christian walk. Our desire for Christ and His Word are
lacking. Prayer is nonexistent. We have to make ourselves
attend worship, or sometimes we even give in to the
temptation to stay home. Spiritual truths are hard to
digest. And circumstances don't make sense.

One day our spiritual fog lifts in the form of a word
that is aptly spoken in a song, a book, from a friend, or in
a sermon and we realize that God was there all along. We
were the ones who strayed, not Him. Even in the depths
of our despair, we probably know this to be true, but
knowing isn't enough. In today's verse, Paul tells us we
need to let the Lord Jesus Christ be as near to us as the
clothes we wear.

Think about that for a minute. The clothes you are
wearing are touching your skin right now. They are
tangible. You can feel them. Wherever you move, they go
with you. You don't have to do anything to make them go
with you, other than to move your body. In fact, you have
to remove them intentionally to be free of them.

Can you point to a time in which you intentionally
removed Jesus from your life, chasing after your sinful
desires, as the verse says? Is it possible that your spiritual
dryness began that very day?

Sustaining Grace

Let us then approach God's throne of grace with confidence,
so that we may receive mercy and find grace to
help us in our time of need.
Hebrews 4:16 NIV

Many of us live our entire lives in search of our father's approval. Inherent in his perceived approval is a list of accomplishments he expects us to complete. For some, it's a six-figure income, a seven-figure house, and a beautiful wife. For the more spiritually minded, it could be an expectation to become a pastor, a full-time missionary, or *at least* an elder or deacon.

The problem with all of these expectations is twofold. First, God may not be in any of them. He may have something completely different in mind for us. Second, once we get caught up in seeking our father's approval at the expense of point number one, we end up playing a game of merit. As long as we do what our earthly father wants us to do, we are on track to gain his approval. But the moment we stumble, his approval is withdrawn, and often we become a shell of what we could have been.

God, on the other hand, tells us to approach His throne of grace with confidence. Notice that it is called a "throne of grace," not a throne of rules we have to follow to earn His love or approval. As we approach Him with confidence, we receive even more grace (rather than judgment), and that grace sustains us in time of need.

JUSTIFICATION BY FAITH (ALONE)

*For in the gospel the righteousness of God is revealed—
a righteousness that is by faith from first to last, just as it
is written: "The righteous will live by faith."*
ROMANS 1:17 NIV

In the early 1500s, a German monk and professor named Martin Luther was preparing for a lecture from the book of Romans when he came to the realization that the original Greek language of Romans 1:17 indicated a faith-based righteousness, rather than a works-based righteousness.

Later, he referred to this moment as his "tower experience," and it changed everything, including his rejection of the Roman church's tradition of selling indulgences to absolve sin. He penned the "Disputation on the Power and Efficacy of Indulgences" (also referred to as the "Ninety-Five Theses"), tacked it to Wittenberg Castle church door on October 31, 1517, and caused an uproar from church authorities, who declared Luther a heretic. Under threat of persecution, Luther translated the New Testament into German, giving the common man access to the scriptures, which sparked the Reformation.

Evangelicals embrace the doctrine of "justification by faith alone," but occasionally we attempt to earn God's acceptance or approval rather than simply living by faith—faith that His righteous demands have already been satisfied in the sacrificial work of Jesus Christ on the cross. Start a new tradition this year. Celebrate Reformation Day, and live by faith.

BECOMING A MAN OF NOBLE CHARACTER

But the noble make noble plans,
and by noble deeds they stand.
ISAIAH 32:8 NIV

Would you consider yourself a man of noble character? If so, you're a man who knows God and His calling on your life. You're a man who is value and purpose driven. You're a man with a firm grasp of what's eternal. Sadly, this world is full of bored men. The truth is, at times every man gets bored. Dr. Harold Dodds, then-president of Princeton University, made this counterintuitive observation: "It is not the fast tempo of modern life that kills but the boredom, a lack of strong interest and failure to grow that destroy. It is the feeling that nothing is worthwhile that makes men ill and unhappy." During this month, you will have the opportunity to strengthen your wish, desire, commitment, and resolve to be a man of noble character. Before saying yes to anything, of course, one has to say no to other things. True, some of those other things may not *feel* boring, but they lack any connection to or passion for the Lord God, Creator of heaven and earth—and they lack any lasting honor, let alone value for eternity. The answer isn't to stop everything you're doing. Each established sphere of life is important to God. That includes your continuing education, vocation, marriage, family, church, neighborhood, community, and much more. How do you see God in each sphere? Conversely, how does God see you in each?

WORKING WITH ALL YOUR HEART

*Whatever you do, work at it with all your heart,
as working for the Lord, not for human masters,
since you know that you will receive an inheritance from
the Lord as a reward. It is the Lord Christ you are serving.*
COLOSSIANS 3:23–24 NIV

How strange that the all-powerful, omniscient Lord God, Creator of heaven and earth, allows human hands and hearts to do His will. The man of noble character trusts God to work in and through him. Such a man doesn't waste his time longing for a life without God's calling and purpose. He certainly doesn't waste it longing for a life of excitement, dissipation, pleasure, and ease. A noble man is a God-filled, purpose-driven, and busy man. His hours and minutes are measured and meaningful. "Being busy is not a sin," Max Lucado wisely observes. "Jesus was busy. Paul was busy. Peter was busy. Nothing of significance is achieved without effort and hard work and weariness. That, in and of itself, is not a sin. But being busy in an endless pursuit of things that leave us empty and hollow and broken inside—that cannot be pleasing to God."

Looking back on the past month, what is your experience? To what degree were you a noble man? Granted, God designed us to exercise, sleep, eat. He designed us to shave, shower, dress. He designed us to rest, relax, and recreate with family and friends. But that's not all—as we will continue to consider in coming days.

Doing What Is Right No Matter What

*[He] who sows to the Spirit will of the Spirit reap eternal
life. Let us not lose heart in doing good, for in due time
we will reap if we do not grow weary. So then,
while we have opportunity, let us do good to all
people, and especially to those who
are of the household of faith.*

Galatians 6:8–10 nasb

The noble man knows that he can achieve nothing if he
doesn't love God with all his heart and love others as
himself. He also knows he can achieve nothing without
the Holy Spirit's daily cleansing, filling, and fruit-bearing
work in his heart and life. Why is it so hard to live such a
life? It's difficult, and often impossible, if you are unsure of
the eternal value of your goals, if you are overwhelmed by
the tasks before you, and if you doubt God's greatness,
goodness, and calling on your life. Today, Phillips Brooks
is probably best known for authoring the Christmas
carol "O Little Town of Bethlehem." He was arguably one
of the best known and loved American pastors during the
latter part of the nineteenth century. He loved the Lord,
studied the scriptures, proclaimed the Gospel, lectured
and preached at Harvard, published a number of books,
and helped create one of the nation's most magnificent
church buildings. His clarion call still echoes after all this
time. "Do not pray for easy lives, pray to be stronger
men. Do not pray for tasks equal to your powers, pray for
power equal to your tasks." As you put this book down,
ask God to strengthen you today.

SAYING AND DOING WHAT
THE LORD COMMANDS

*The days of our lives are seventy years; and if by reason of
strength they are eighty years, yet their boast is only labor
and sorrow; for it is soon cut off, and we fly away.*

PSALM 90:10 NKJV

In addition to writing the first five books of the Hebrew
scriptures, Moses also penned Psalm 90. This psalm
appears to have been written between the events recorded
in Exodus chapters 2 and 3. The pleas in verse 13 and other
verses certainly seem to point to a period before the call
of Moses. And the lament of verse 10 seems to correspond
with Moses' age at that time. Of course, little did Moses
know what God had in store for him over the next forty
years. In those "extra" four decades, Moses was more alive
on so many levels than during the previous eighty years.
What made the difference? Moses was saying and doing
what the Lord commanded.

The noble man does the same. He wants to live a
full life infused with God. Then again, he is ready to face
death at a moment's notice. In his advance directive for
end-of-life care, a man added a brief letter addressed to
his wife and eldest daughter. In it he said, "I have enjoyed
life more than most. I have the sure hope of heaven when
I die. I may die later today or fifty years from now. When
I'm near the end, I fully trust whatever decisions you
make. Please never forget how much I love you." May we
be able to say the same.

EMBRACING THE ENORMITY
OF GOD'S CALLING

So teach us to number our days,
that we may gain a heart of wisdom.
PSALM 90:12 NKJV

Few men know which decade, year, month, or day they will die. Then again, at the very end of his life, Moses knew which day he would die. The same can be said for only a small handful of biblical characters. Yet knowing the day of one's death isn't necessarily good news. Like most people, Moses wanted to live longer. If anyone had good reason, he did. After all, Moses longed to enter the Promised Land and enjoy the "milk and honey" awhile. Yet God alone appoints the day of one's death. Not even the best of men is exempt. So it's imperative that we aspire to live nobly before God and others *now*, not some day. Why before "God and others"? Because God's calling almost always extends beyond one's lifespan. In other words, we can't expect to fulfill that calling alone or in our own lifetime. The purposes of God are bigger than we can imagine. That's why eternity always must be in view. A. W. Tozer said it well: "Life is a short and fevered rehearsal for a concert we cannot stay to give. Just when we appear to have attained some proficiency we are forced to lay our instruments down. There is simply not time enough to think, to become, to perform what the constitution of our natures indicates we are capable of." Only by embracing the eternality of God's calling can we face death with nobility.

LIVING WITH THE END IN MIND

*I eagerly expect and hope that I will in no way be ashamed,
but will have sufficient courage so that now as always Christ
will be exalted in my body, whether by life or by death.
For to me, to live is Christ and to die is gain.*
PHILIPPIANS 1:20–21 NIV

Thomas à Kempis's first book, *The Imitation of Christ*, especially the closing three chapters, speaks of the importance of beginning with the end in mind. That is, to think deeply and often when alone about the day of your death. In particular: "How do you want to meet God?" To do this, not once, but as a habit of life, in union with several other habits, creates a God-given sense of purpose and mission. Yet how many people never give serious thought to the end of their life? Oh, they think they do so—they give thought, often excessively, to the way they would like to finish their years in some supposedly blissful retirement. *Then,* they tell themselves, *I'll do what I really want—live in a nice home, travel, write, invest, and do whatever else I please.* Granted, "We must wait for all good things." Yet why wait until the end of life, when the body is frail and the mind may not be as sharp? Pity the man who never decides to live, whose chief excitement is daydreaming, who never dares to passionately pursue his plans now, today, this month, this next year, the next five years, before it's too late and family and friends lament what might have been.

LIVING FAITHFULLY TO THE END

*Oh, the depth of the riches of the wisdom and knowledge
of God! How unsearchable his judgments, and his paths
beyond tracing out! "Who has known the mind of the Lord?
Or who has been his counselor?" "Who has ever given to
God, that God should repay them?" For from him
and through him and for him are all things.
To him be the glory forever! Amen.*
ROMANS 11:33–36 NIV

Today is Billy Graham's birthday. What a life. What a
legacy. Imagine preaching the life-changing Gospel of
Jesus Christ to hundreds of millions of people around
the world year after year, decade after decade. Yet Billy
Graham made it clear in the early 1980s that his ministry
could be over at any point. "If I should ever take any glory
away from God, God would take up His hand off my life
and my lips would turn to clay." It's a sobering thought
that the Lord could nullify what any given man does best.
It's potentially even more sobering to ponder, *What am
I doing that has eternal value?* Fortunately, God doesn't
divide life into "sacred" and "secular." Whether at home
or work, whether in the community or church, the Lord
can work in and through us for His glory and honor and
praise. All a person has to do is ask the all-knowing God,
the Omniscient One, for His wisdom for life here on earth
(James 1:5). The Lord is more than happy to answer such
prayers.

THANKING GOD AGAIN FOR WHO HE IS

"Our God, your name will be praised forever and forever. You are all-powerful, and you know everything. You control human events—you give rulers their power and take it away, and you are the source of wisdom and knowledge."
DANIEL 2:20–21 CEV

Today more than 100 million Americans are expected to cast their vote for the next president of the United States of America. What's surprising isn't how many individuals attempted to win the nomination of the Democratic and Republican parties. It isn't even who won each nomination. What's surprising is that from eternity past God has known who will win and what will happen during that person's presidency. In other words, Election Day is the perfect day to thank God again for His sovereignty (greatness), providence (goodness), holiness (glory), love (graciousness), and mystery (God alone knows). Far from wringing your hands or raising your arms in triumph, this is a day to praise and worship the King of kings and Lord of lords. He alone is all-powerful. He alone is in control. He alone grants political power and takes it away. What's more, He alone knows—let alone fully understands—what has happened, what is happening, and what will happen in the future. Thanking God again for who He is at once frees you from anxiety, worry, discouragement, and undue stress. Like Daniel, you can give thanks to God. After all, "You [God] control human events—you give rulers their power and take it away."

PRAYING FOR OUR NEW PRESIDENT-ELECT

The first thing I want you to do is pray. Pray every way
you know how, for everyone you know. Pray especially
for rulers and their governments to rule well so we
can be quietly about our business of living simply,
in humble contemplation. This is the way our
Savior God wants us to live.

1 TIMOTHY 2:1–3 MSG

Did you vote yesterday? Did your choice for president win or lose? Either way, the noble man takes the apostle Paul's charge to heart: "Pray especially for rulers. . .to rule well." First, each believer is called to pray for the new president-elect, who is scheduled to be inaugurated on Friday, January 20, 2017. You can pray for the new president-elect to be a person who has faith in the one true Lord God, Creator of heaven and earth. You can pray for that faith and love for the Lord to take root deeply, to grow and bear much fruit despite the tremendous pressures ahead. And you can pray for God to direct the many important decisions in the coming days, weeks, and months. Second, each Christian is called to pray for our nation's outgoing president. In seventy-two days he will retire from the nation's most powerful elected office. Again, you can pray for his faith and love for the Lord to take root deeply, to grow and bear much fruit now and in the weeks, months, and years ahead. And you can pray for God to direct his final presidential decisions, including handing off the baton to the new president-elect.

Asking God for Even More Courage

"The thief comes only to steal and kill and destroy;
I came that they may have life, and have it abundantly."
John 10:10 NASB

Life is full of circumstances that test our courage. It doesn't matter that you're honest if you're afraid to tell the truth. Or that you're responsible if you're afraid to try anything new. It's ironic that our society is bent on the idea of trying to become more rebellious, more risk-taking, less inhibited, more outrageous, less self-controlled. Many blame these trends on the 1960s, but the reality is—people have always been bent away from self-control. This bent against self-control, however, inevitably hurts our community, our family, and our friends. Ultimately, it hurts us. If you and I lack self-control, who's in control of our thoughts, speech, and actions? One option is we're giving in to the desires of the nature we were born with. That nature's passions and desires are anything but positive, healthy, or life-giving. Another option is we may be manipulated or controlled by the devil. If we let Satan control us, he will rob us of everything that's good in our lives. He will tempt us to take risky, dangerous, physically destructive, or suicidal actions that could kill us. So what other option is there? It's the option Jesus calls having "life. . .abundantly." Whatever you do today, choose that option! Specifically, ask God to strengthen you in your inner man, to cleanse and fill you, to cause you to be more self-controlled and courageous than ever.

REMEMBERING GOD'S ANSWERS TO PRAYER

Though I walk in the midst of trouble, you preserve my life.
You stretch out your hand against the anger of my foes;
with your right hand you save me.
PSALM 138:7 NIV

In his book *Stories of Faith and Courage from the Korean War,* retired Marine Corps Lt. Col. Larkin Spivey tells the story of Pvt. Ed Reeves. "Lord, if the mortar didn't kill me, the shooting didn't kill me, and the beating didn't kill me, you must want me out of here. But I can't walk. How can I get outta here?" As Reeves lay helpless on the frozen ground beside the now-abandoned and destroyed truck convoy, he continued to pray. Suddenly, God seemed to answer: "You must crawl before you can walk." Painfully lifting himself to his hands and wounded knees, Reeves started crawling over snow-covered fields in the direction he hoped would take him to friendly lines. He passed more Chinese troops who somehow made no effort to stop him. Darkness fell, and he continued his slow, painful journey. He began to sing over and over, "Yes, Jesus loves me!" Finally, he felt the hardness of ice underneath him and knew that he was on the Chosen Reservoir. Exhaustion and the mind-numbing cold were almost overwhelming day after day. Amazingly, the song of his childhood faith kept coming back to him: "Jesus loves me, this I know, for the Bible tells me so." Finally, almost a week after being first wounded, Ed Reeves was rescued. One of his first comments? "Every time I asked God, He answered."

FORSAKING WRONG DESIRES AND FEARS

I eagerly expect and hope that I will in no way be ashamed, but will have sufficient courage so that now as always Christ will be exalted in my body, whether by life or by death.
PHILIPPIANS 1:20 NIV

When are you most at risk of losing courage and feeling ashamed? First, when you pursue wrong desires. Second, when you give in to fear. Wrong desires often revolve around making more money, amassing power, pursuing illicit sexuality, and pouring endless hours into online multiuser games. All four are terribly damaging. Wrong fears are just as bad. Imminent danger—real or perceived—triggers the strongest of human emotions. Fear is hardwired into your brain. It causes you to shut up, freeze up, give up. The good news: you can rewire your thoughts, beliefs, and automatic responses. If anyone proved that, it was Mother Teresa. One of her most haunting prayers:

Deliver me, O Jesus, / From the fear of being humiliated, / From the fear of being despised, / From the fear of suffering rebukes, / From the fear of being slandered, / From the fear of being forgotten, / From the fear of being wronged, / From the fear of being ridiculed, / From the fear of being suspected. / Amen.

THE MOST IMPORTANT THING ABOUT YOU

*"You are worthy, O Lord, to receive glory and honor
and power; for You created all things, and by Your
will they exist and were created."*
REVELATION 4:11 NKJV

What is the most important thing about you? Who you
are? When you were born? Where you live? What you've
done? What you plan to do in the future? What others
think of you? What you think of others? Actually, none of
these take top priority. Instead, the most important thing
about you is your view of God. A. W. Tozer put it this
way: "Without doubt, the mightiest thought the mind can
entertain is the thought of God, and the weightiest word
in any language is its word for God." He goes on to say:
"The most portentous fact about any man is not what he
at a given time may say or do, but what he in his deep
heart conceives God to be like. We tend by a secret law of
the soul to move toward our mental image of God." Sadly,
the images of God prevalent today are "so decadent as to
be utterly beneath the dignity of the Most High God and
actually to constitute for professed believers something
amounting to a moral calamity." If you say you believe
God can do anything but expect Him to do nothing, is it
any wonder you find it hard to pray? Conversely, if you
thank God daily for His greatness and goodness, His
holiness and love, and His mystery, is it any surprise you
like to talk about Him with others? So, what's your view of
God today?

REALIZING GOD IS GREATER THAN WE CAN IMAGINE

*Oh, how great are God's riches and wisdom and knowledge!
How impossible it is for us to understand his decisions and
his ways! For who can know the LORD's thoughts?
Who knows enough to give him advice?*
ROMANS 11:33–34 NLT

How big is God? What does it mean that He is the Creator and Sustainer of humanity, of Earth, of the solar system, of the Milky Way galaxy, of the universe? It means that the Lord God is infinitely bigger than human brains and minds can comprehend this side of heaven. So the foundation of any truths you might state about God is that you don't fully know what He is like. Mere mortals cannot grasp the attributes we ascribe to God, let alone comprehend the total character of God. So many aspects of His nature are mystery to finite man. The thesis of any discussion about theology proper, that is, the study of God, is that He is clothed in both majesty and mystery. Walter A. Henrichsen is right on the mark when he says, "Every problem a person has is related to his concept of God. If you have a big God, you have small problems. If you have a small God, you have big problems." So, how big are your problems? You may be struggling with wrong desires, gripping fears, critical health issues, financial problems, employment stressors, marital strains, parental pains, church issues, few meaningful friendships. Whatever your struggles might be, how big is your God? *How* big? Big enough, to be sure!

ENLARGING YOUR VIEW OF GOD

So who even comes close to being like God?
To whom or what can you compare him?
ISAIAH 40:18 MSG

Nearly twenty years ago, the Los Angeles Times acclaimed best-selling book, *God Is Relevant* by Luis Palau and David Sanford, predicted that militant atheism, which had greatly diminished between 1980 and 1996, would come roaring back after the turn of the millennium. Sure enough, the number of atheists in America has nearly tripled in the intervening years. Is God becoming irrelevant? Just the opposite. A. W. Tozer correctly observes: "What comes into our minds when we think about God is the most important thing about us." Yet even the most sincere Christian has only a limited grasp of God's greatness, let alone a correct theology of how life works. When life falls apart, God cheers. Why? Because God actively longs for us to enlarge our view of His sovereignty, providence, holiness, love and mystery. Tozer continues: "I believe there is scarcely an error in doctrine or a failure in applying Christian ethics that cannot be traced finally to imperfect and ignoble thoughts about God." What's more: "To be right we must think worthily of God. It is a moral imperative that we purge from our minds all ignoble concepts of the Deity and let Him be the God in our minds that He is in His universe." Take a moment to ask God to enlarge your view of His greatness and goodness today.

KEEP ENLARGING YOUR VIEW OF GOD

The LORD is the everlasting God, the Creator of all the earth.
He never grows weak or weary. No one can measure
the depths of his understanding. He gives power
to the weak and strengthto the powerless.
ISAIAH 40:28–29 NLT

Day by day, your view of God grows bigger or grows weaker. One of the easiest ways to measure your view of God is to ponder, How big are my problems? Overwhelming to me? Or no sweat for God? A. W. Tozer wisely points out: "Left to ourselves we tend immediately to reduce God to manageable terms. We want to get Him where we can use Him, or at least know where He is when we need Him. We want a God we can in some measure control." So, who's in control in your life? You? The God in your mind? Or God as He really is? If the latter, how do you know your view if God is big enough? Tozer continues: "We [long for] the feeling of security that comes from knowing what God is like, and what He is like is of course a composite of all the religious pictures we have seen, all the best people we have known or heard about, and all the sublime ideas we have entertained." Laying aside such thoughts, the noble man meditates on the Scriptures, including Isaiah 40:12–31. By doing so, you can keep enlarging your view of God this week.

NOT MISTAKING OUR THOUGHTS
FOR GOD HIMSELF

*For the LORD God is a sun and shield; the LORD bestows
favor and honor; no good thing does he withhold
from those whose walk is blameless.*
PSALM 84:11 NIV

When the Bible compares God to something, it doesn't mean He is literally that. In today's verse, the Psalmist says the Lord is a sun. Does that mean He is made up mostly of hydrogen and helium? That His diameter is 109 greater than our planet? That His mass is 330,000 greater than earth's mass? That His brightness is greater than 85 percent of the stars in our galaxy? Of course not! So, what does the Bible mean by saying God is a sun? It's important to remember we can know the Lord through the scriptures, the life of Jesus Christ, and His creation. When we say God is like the sun, then, it's worth pondering what humanity has always known about the sun. The sun shines whether we enjoy its rays on the beach or lock ourselves in a darkened room with the doors closed, the blinds shut, and the lights turned off. Yet while we lock ourselves in, we can't lock the sun out. Its warmth touches the whole earth and its light shines throughout the universe. The farther we travel from the sun, however, the colder and darker it gets. It is just that way with faith in God. C. S. Lewis put it this way: "I believe in Christianity as I believe that the sun has risen: not only because I see it, but because by it I see everything else."

THANKING GOD FOR HIS WORKS

*"For the Father loves the Son and shows him
all he does. Yes, and he will show him even greater
works than these, so that you will be amazed."*
JOHN 5:20 NIV

How good to know "God never hurries," A. W. Tozer
tells us. "There are no deadlines against which He must
work. Only to know this is to quiet our spirits and relax
our nerves." So, what can you know about God's works?
First, God's works are directive. They are not products
of time and chance. Instead, God actively orchestrated
every detail of creation through His unlimited wisdom
and power (Genesis 1–2). Second, God's works are
selective. God acts in certain ways to do certain things.
For instance, God cannot do evil or create imperfection
(Genesis 1–2 with James 1:13). Third, God's works on earth
are defective, not at all due to God's fault, but due to
the fall of mankind (Genesis 3). Fourth, God's works are
elective. He has chosen to work with and through His
people (Genesis 12, John 1, etc.). Fifth, God's works are
corrective. Ultimately the heavens, earth and humanity
will be restored (Revelation 21). Even now, we can be
"born again." This isn't turning over a new leaf, but radical
correction: we receive a new nature and are indwelt
by the Holy Spirit. This divine transformation will be
completed at Christ's return (Philippians 1:6 with 1 John
3:2). How good that God isn't haphazardly rushing His
work in you!

REMEMBERING WHY WE NEED GOD

Your life is a journey you must travel with a deep consciousness of God. It cost God plenty to get you out of that dead-end, empty-headed life you grew up in. He paid with Christ's sacred blood.
1 PETER 1:18–19 MSG

Scores of times the Bible speaks about emptiness. *Void. Nothing. Nothingness. Empty. Empty head. Empty-headed. Empty life.* How empty? In *Confessions,* Saint Augustine wrote: "Our hearts are restless until they rest in You." Although Blaise Pascal didn't exactly coin the phrase "God-shaped vacuum," he talked about it extensively. In *Pensées,* Pascal said: "What else does this craving, and this helplessness, proclaim but that there was once in man a true happiness, of which all that now remains is the empty print and trace? This he tries in vain to fill with everything around him, seeking in things that are not there the help he cannot find in those that are, though none can help, since this infinite abyss can be filled only with an infinite and immutable object; in other words by God himself." C. S. Lewis wrote a great deal about this need as well. He had started his academic and publishing career as an atheist and agnostic, only to be powerfully converted. In *Mere Christianity,* Lewis wrote: "If I find in myself a desire for something which nothing in this world can satisfy, the most probable explanation is that I was made for another world." What is the longing of *your* heart? Ask God to fill it—with Himself—so you can enjoy life, and enjoy it abundantly (John 10:10).

NEVER FORGETTING OUR
NEED FOR THE LORD

*I am suffering here in prison. But I am not ashamed of it,
for I know the one in whom I trust, and I am sure that he is
able to guard what I have entrusted to him until the day of
his return. Hold on to the pattern of wholesome teaching
you learned from me—a pattern shaped by the faith
and love that you have in Christ Jesus.*
2 TIMOTHY 1:12–13 NLT

The noblest of men are not exempt from abject suffering.
They become stellar examples of faith not because of
how they stay above the fray, but because their trust in
God is tested with fire and proved more valuable than
gold. Even in the face of death, they're committed to
staying true because their foundation is solid and their
convictions deep. Vance Havner could write: "We find
that when Jesus is all we have, He is all we need and all
we want. We are shipwrecked on God and stranded on
omnipotence." Yet secretly many men dread the day of
calamity. Bishop Westcott gave this frank assessment:
"Silently and imperceptibly, as we wake or sleep, we grow
strong or we grow weak, and at last some crisis shows us
what we have become." Like Havner, Westcott actively
sought to be strong in the Lord and to lead others along
that same path. Before this year is out, you can become a
stronger man in the Lord. Go for it with everything inside
you, in all honesty asking God to search (Psalm 139:23–
24), teach (Psalm 86:11), clean (Psalm 51:10), and renew
your heart (Psalm 51:12).

WHAT KIND OF WEEK WILL THIS BE?

*Because of what Jesus said, many of his disciples turned
their backs on him and stopped following him. Jesus then
asked his twelve disciples if they were going to leave
him. Simon Peter answered, "Lord, there is no one else that
we can go to! Your words give eternal life. We have faith
in you, and we are sure that you are God's Holy One."*
JOHN 6:66–69 CEV

This week is Thanksgiving. That doesn't mean it is going
to be an easy week. Over and over again during His
earthly ministry, Jesus performed miracles, preached the
Gospel, celebrated and rejoiced. And over and over again
Jesus faced rejection, ridicule, persecution, and worse.
For some Christian men, this will be a week of rejoicing.
"It's been a great year and I have so many reasons
to thank God." For other men, this will be a week of
reflecting, remembering, and wondering what might have
been. "I don't want to go to church anymore. What do I
say when other guys ask how I'm doing?" Or, "Honestly,
this has been the hardest year of my life. I can't pray
anymore. Not even over a meal." Fortunately, Jesus is our
great High Priest. He was tempted. He suffered and died.
He arose. He ascended to heaven. He earnestly prays to
God the Father on your behalf, and He already knows the
end of your story. What kind of week will this be for you?
Oswald Chambers wisely observed, "Faith is hanging on
very stubbornly to the belief that things are not really as
they seem." What does Jesus see? Ask and believe.

WANTING GOD'S BEST FOR YOU

I, Paul, am on special assignment for Christ, carrying
out God's plan laid out in the Message of Life by Jesus.
I write this to you, Timothy, the son I love so much.
All the best from our God and Christ be yours!
2 TIMOTHY 1:1–2 MSG

What does it mean to want and receive God's best for you? First, it means discarding inadequate, insufficient, ignoble thoughts of God. Herman Melville said, "The reason the mass of men fear God, and at bottom dislike Him, is because they rather distrust His heart, and fancy Him all brain like a watch." Second, wanting God's best means seeing Him as He really is. David Needham writes, "I am convinced that the answers to every problem and issue of life for both time and eternity are resolved through a correct understanding of God." Third, receiving God's best means shedding your intense desire for temporal pursuits and possessions. George MacDonald observed, "Man finds it hard to get what he wants, because he does not want the best; God finds it hard to give, because He would give the best, and man will not take it." Fourth, wanting and receiving God's best means desiring His will over and against your own will. C. S. Lewis put it this way: "There are two kinds of people: those who say to God, 'Thy will be done,' and those to whom God says, 'All right, then, have it your way.'" What did you hope to gain this year? Have you gained it yet? If yes, is it God's best? If no, again, is it God's best?

WANTING TO EXPERIENCE GOD'S NEARNESS

*"If you are tired from carrying heavy burdens, come to
me and I will give you rest. Take the yoke I give you.
Put it on your shoulders and learn from me. I am gentle
and humble, and you will find rest. This yoke is
easy to bear, and this burden is light."*
MATTHEW 11:28–30 CEV

"There is no limit to how close you can get to God." This
has been taught for decades, but is it true? Consider
what the Bible says keeps you from experiencing God's
nearness. Do any ring true? First, unbelief (Psalm 14).
Second, not knowing God's Word (Romans 10:17). Third,
laziness and carelessness (Hebrews 6:12). Fourth, worry
and prayerlessness (Philippians 4:6). Fifth, burdens you
haven't cast on the Lord (1 Peter 5:7). Sixth, unconfessed
sin (1 John 1:7–2:2). Next, consider what scripture says
about experiencing God's nearness. First, Psalm 34:18
says, "If your heart is broken, you'll find GOD right there"
(MSG). Second, Psalm 145:18 says, "The LORD is close to
all who call on him, yes, to all who call on him in truth"
(NLT). Third, James 4:8 says, "Draw near to God and He
will draw near to you" (NASB). Fourth, Hebrews 7:19 says
through hope in Jesus Christ you draw near to God. Fifth,
Hebrews 10:22 urges you to draw near to God "with a true
heart in full assurance of faith" (NKJV). Finally, Hebrews
11:6 says, "Without faith it is impossible to please God,
because anyone who comes to him must believe that he
exists and that he rewards those who earnestly seek him"
(NIV). Jesus is calling. What is your reply?

OFFERING THANKSGIVING TO GOD

*"Thank the LORD! Praise his name! Tell the nations
what he has done. Let them know how mighty he is!
Sing to the LORD, for he has done wonderful things.
Make known his praise around the world."*

ISAIAH 12:4–5 NLT

How can you ever thank God enough? It's a fair question!
Certainly today on Thanksgiving, your thanksgiving to
God mostly will be an overflow from the thanks you
already have expressed to Him throughout the year. You
can't thank God enough for His greatness, goodness, and
glory. You can't thank God enough for His grace, mercy,
and peace. You can't thank God enough for His gift of
freedom from fear, condemnation, guilt, and shame.
You can't thank God enough for His gift of life—new,
everlasting, abundant, and empowered by His indwelling
Holy Spirit. You can't thank God enough for giving you
loved ones and friends and fellow believers to join you
on life's journey. You can't thank God enough for giving
you meaning, purpose, courage, and steadfastness. You
can't thank God enough for using the necessary means of
loss, pain, suffering, and being sinned against to demolish
your wrong theology about God and how life works. You
can't thank God enough for using His Word, the Bible, to
bring comfort, solace, encouragement, strength, joy, and
peace to you in seasons of grief. While you can't thank
Him enough, it is true, do make thanksgiving to God the
hallmark of your everyday experiences here on earth.

ONLY ONE MONTH UNTIL CHRISTMAS

They entered the house and saw the child with his mother,
Mary, and they bowed down and worshiped him.
MATTHEW 2:11 NLT

Are you wondering what to buy your loved ones? Here's a bigger concern: Why is it so easy for many Americans to stop believing in Jesus when they "grow up" and "outgrow" the true meaning of Christmas? It's deeply concerning how aggressively some ridicule the idea of childlike faith. Then again, it's worth thinking about what it must have been like for Jesus two thousand years ago. In complete contrast to the Messianic expectations of the ancient Jewish people, Jesus Christ didn't come out of nowhere riding into Jerusalem as a conquering hero. Instead, He entered this world in a most unexpected way: as an infant child. Have you ever thought about what Jesus did the first ten or twelve years after His birth? That's right: He was a boy. Why in the world would Jesus, God's Son, Creator of the heavens and earth, want to be a kid all those years? Wasn't that a waste of time? No. Absolutely not. First, it was fun being a kid! Jesus got to play with other children. Have you ever noticed that grown-ups sometimes worry too much and don't have enough fun? In contrast, Jesus invented a special plan so that, even though He was God, He could be a kid. Ultimately, of course, Jesus became a child for a much bigger purpose. He entered this world as a child so that you could become like a little child and enter His world. *That* is worth pondering anew today.

LOVING JESUS THE CHILDLIKE WAY

*From infancy you have known the Holy Scriptures,
which are able to make you wise for salvation
through faith in Christ Jesus.*
2 TIMOTHY 3:15 NIV

Have you ever noticed that some grown-ups love to be around kids, and some don't? Even as a grown-up, Jesus loved to be with children. During His three and a half years of ministry as an adult, Jesus gives an amazing amount of priority to ministry to children. Jesus talks with children, something only parents and grandparents usually did in that culture. Jesus commends the faith of little children, who in that culture were sometimes considered unable to truly embrace religious faith until they were almost teenagers. Not only that, but we see Jesus blessing children. We see Him feeding them. We even see Jesus using a little boy's sack lunch to feed the multitudes and send twelve hefty baskets full of leftovers to help feed others. Beyond that, we see Jesus healing boys and girls who are demon possessed and curing others who are sick and dying. He even resurrects a twelve-year-old girl who had just died and an older boy who had died a few hours earlier. In His preaching and teaching, Jesus said that children are a strategic, essential part of His kingdom in heaven and on earth. In so many words, Jesus told His disciples, "Listen! My kingdom belongs to kids!" What's your own view of children and childlike faith?

RECEIVING GOD'S GIFT AS A CHILD

When I was a child, I talked like a child,
I thought like a child, I reasoned like a child.
1 CORINTHIANS 13:11 NIV

Now as in the past, some have the audacity to claim a small child's belief in God doesn't count, but that's not the case. True, children can't understand everything they're taught, yet there is nothing wrong about a child's inadequate concepts of God or of the Christian faith. The Lord and the scriptures certainly don't criticize a child's way of thinking. The One who made us knows us. As we've seen the past couple of days, Jesus loved to be with children. Not only that, but Jesus tells everyone, in essence, "Unless you become like a little kid, you can't even get into My kingdom." What is Jesus talking about? Well, what are kids good at doing? They're good at *receiving.* When you're a small child, your mom and dad give you some food. What do you do? You receive it. Your grandparents send you a birthday card with five shekels in it. What do you do? You receive it. God gives you a sunny day to go outside and play. What do you do? You receive it. The same thing applies when it comes to God's kingdom. You have to receive something. Or, specifically, Someone: Jesus Christ, God's Son, Creator of heaven and earth, the One who decides how life—real and eternal life—works. And, yes, it works in some amazing, sometimes counterintuitive ways.

MAKING IT EASY FOR A CHILD TO TRUST GOD

"And anyone who welcomes a little child like this on my behalf is welcoming me."
MATTHEW 18:5 NLT

One Sunday a pastor had the opportunity to interview more than a dozen third through sixth graders. Each child sat on a "hot seat" and answered questions. The final answer was tough: talk about when it's hard for you to trust God. The pastor was amazed at their responses. First, they had a much shorter list of reasons than adults usually do. Second, several of the children honestly and sincerely responded, "It's always been easy for me to trust God." You should have seen the smiles on their faces. What could possibly ruin such childlike trust in God? Sadly, it's possible for a child to grow up in church, learn many Bible stories, sing wonderful songs, memorize scripture verses, say all the right things, look good—very good—and yet lose his or her faith. Sometimes it's the individual's own choices. Sometimes it is life's harsh realities, which bend and can break a young person. Sometimes it's because of the behaviors of adults the child should have been able to trust. Any adult can cause a child to begin to lose faith—by hypocrisy, critical attitudes, self-centered living—anything that doesn't truly reflect Christlike, childlike kingdom living. Then again, a child's faith grows, not diminishes, when an adult apologizes to the child for, say, losing his temper. What's your story?

PROTECTING AND BUILDING UP THE FAITH OF THE YOUNG

But if you cause one of these little ones who trusts in me to [lose faith or] fall into sin, it would be better for you to have a large millstone tied around your neck and be drowned in the depths of the sea.

MATTHEW 18:6 NLT

Scripture couldn't be clearer—anyone who repeatedly or severely harms a child by sinning against him or her—physically, psychologically, socially, sexually, or spiritually—is in grave danger of God's judgment. Ancient Jewish men feared drowning above all else. Even experienced fishermen like Peter and Andrew, James and John were scared to death of drowning. Sure, some like Peter could swim, but that wasn't a given. There certainly was no Coast Guard at the ready back then. Even if there were, imagine a judge ordering a crew of Roman sailors to take you ten miles out into the Mediterranean Sea, tie a 100-pound milestone around your neck, and send you to the bottom of Davy Jones's locker. Peter and his fellow disciples shuddered at the thought. It should make anyone shudder. Why? Because Jesus warns each and every adult that such a fate would be much better than causing a child to lose his or her faith in Him. The point Jesus is making is clear: don't let your attitudes, your words, or your actions soil or steal the God-given faith of a child. Like Jesus, the noble man cherishes, protects, nurtures, and builds up the faith of the young. In doing so, he builds up and protects his own heart. What could be better?

WILLINGLY RECEIVING GOD'S COMFORT AND BLESSINGS

He has sent me to tell those who mourn that the time of the LORD's favor has come, and with it, the day of God's anger against their enemies. To all who mourn in Israel, he will give a crown of beauty for ashes, a joyous blessing instead of mourning, festive praise instead of despair. In their righteousness, they will be like great oaks that the LORD has planted for his own glory.

ISAIAH 61:2–3 NLT

What a relevant biblical promise for anyone hurting due to financial pressures, job loss, marital strife, and worse. In biblical times, sorrow, grief, mourning, anguish, and despair were expressed in tangible and physical terms. What are some specific ways you can demonstrate your trust and submit yourself to God? First, don't forget seven very important words: "Life is a long lesson in humility." Second, don't forget that in time humility bears rich fruit. Because God is near to the humble, God loves to bless them. Third, remember that humility is not denying the strengths, talents, abilities, blessings, and gifts of God at work in and through your life. Fourth, don't overlook the fact that humility is dependence on Jesus Christ. Fifth, cultivate a strong awareness that God is at work in all His love and power in the other person's life just as much as He is in yours. Sixth, let's not overlook the fact that one of the paths to humility is thankfulness. Seventh, never forget that the Lord promises to comfort those who mourn and provide solace for those who grieve.

JESUS THE CREATOR

In the beginning was the Word, and the Word was with God, and the Word was God. He was with God in the beginning. Through him all things were made; without him nothing was made that has been made. In him was life, and that life was the light of all mankind. The light shines in the darkness, and the darkness has not overcome it.

JOHN 1:1–5 NIV

Here the apostle John mirrors Genesis 1: Jesus was the creative force behind everything that we see, taste, touch, and smell—including our very own eyes, tongues, hands, and noses. The very Creator of the universe, as part of His plan to redeem the creation that had fallen into sin and rebellion against Him (Genesis 3), *literally put on skin* so that He could advance His plan to save the human race. As John says in today's passage, Jesus came to bring light into all the dark places in our world: our hunger, pain, exhaustion, rejection, intense stress, frustration, anger, and temptation.

For those of us living in a complex, lightning-fast, and sometimes frustrating world, this truly is good news. So through this month as we look for places where Jesus shows up in the Bible, let's also look together for places where Jesus shows up, today, in our own lives.

MADE IN THE IMAGE

In the beginning God created the heavens and the earth. . . . Then God said, "Let us make mankind in our image, in our likeness. . ." So God created mankind in his own image, in the image of God he created them; male and female he created them.
GENESIS 1:1, 26–27 NIV

In creation, as an integral part of the Trinity, Jesus formed Adam and Eve into beings that would share the Trinity's likeness and image.

What does being created in the image of God mean to us today? Many thought leaders will say that God's image in us is reflected in our spirituality, creativity, language, relationships, and moral responsibility. Because we are of a higher order than the animals God created, we see the image of God in our own lives whenever we look into the mirror of our intelligence, thoughts, emotions, and spirituality. In other words, there's a big difference between you and Fido based on the way God built His image into you.

So what does that mean for us in practical terms? The Westminster Shorter Catechism simply and beautifully sums up our responsibility in the face of this reality:

Q. What is the chief end of man?
A. Man's chief end is to glorify God. . .and to enjoy Him forever.

COVENANT PROMISES

Now the earth was corrupt in God's sight and was full
of violence. God saw how corrupt the earth had become,
for all the people on earth had corrupted their ways.
So God said to Noah, "I am going to put an end to all
people, for the earth is filled with violence because of
them. I am surely going to destroy both them and the
earth. So make yourself an ark of cypress wood."
GENESIS 6:11–14 NIV

As we look toward Christmas and search for Jesus in the Old Testament, today we see a symbol of salvation in the image of the ark. You know the story: God chooses Noah to build an enormous ship that will save only those in Noah's family. This task takes him 120 years, after which time he closes the doors, the deluge comes, and he and his family spend some 370 days on the ship with all kinds of animals, until God gives him the "all clear" (Genesis 8:15–17).

Then God makes a covenant with Noah (Genesis 9:8-11) that resonates with the one He made with Adam and Eve (Genesis 1:22, 28). And as a symbol of this new covenant, God places a rainbow in the sky as a reminder of the promises He has made.

This story foreshadows God's relationship with Israel, His chosen family, a descendent of whom will become another symbol in the sky that symbolizes another new covenant. Jesus' empty cross is that terrible and beautiful symbol.

GOD SHOWS UP

Abram traveled through the land as far as the site of the
great tree of Moreh at Shechem. At that time the Canaanites
were in the land. The LORD appeared to Abram and said,
"To your offspring I will give this land." So he built an
altar there to the LORD, who had appeared to him.
GENESIS 12:6–7 NIV

As we search the Old Testament for the ways that God
works in our lives, here's an amazing lesson that we learn
time and time again: God shows up. He sees us, He knows
us, and He wants to be in relationship with us.

This particular appearance came to a man named
Abram, whom God had chosen to follow Him. Abram was
the first in a long line of broken, sinful, down-to-earth, and
very real people who became the ancestors of Jesus (see
Matthew 1:1–17). God's appearance to Abram reinforced
the promises God had made to this faithful man. And
Abram was so grateful that he built an altar to God there
so that he would remember this appearance.

In what ways has God shown up in your life? What
are the symbols of His faithfulness to His promises: your
family, your children, your church, your Bible? How has He
provided for you in amazing ways? Like Abram, you can
build meaning into specific symbols in your life that will
help you remember God's faithfulness to you and your
family. Take a moment to think about what one might be,
and teach your family about it, as Abram would surely
have done with his wife and nephew.

MELCHIZEDEK

Then Melchizedek king of Salem brought out bread and wine. He was priest of God Most High, and he blessed Abram, saying, "Blessed be Abram by God Most High, Creator of heaven and earth."
GENESIS 14:18–19 NIV

While the priest and king of Salem (which later becomes Jerusalem) remains a shadowy figure in history, many commentators point to him as a "type" of Jesus in the Old Testament. We know that he was a priest of God who blessed Abram with words that reflected the words of the covenant promises that God gave Abram (Genesis 12:1–3). His name appears again in the Messianic Psalm 110, where David refers to him as well.

The book of Hebrews gives us further definition: "First, the name Melchizedek means 'king of righteousness'; then also, 'king of Salem' means 'king of peace.' Without father or mother, without genealogy, without beginning of days or end of life, resembling the Son of God, he remains a priest forever" (Hebrews 7:2–3 NIV). This incredible description gives rise to the notion that Melchizedek was a Christophany, or a pre-incarnate appearance of Jesus, in the Old Testament.

The writer of Hebrews points to Jesus as the great High Priest of a new covenant, a "better way" to salvation than the old Jewish sacrificial system. As our High Priest, He has sacrificed Himself to pay for the sins of humanity. Jesus was there in the Old Testament, and He will always be with us today. How might that reality change your life today?

A LAUGHABLE PROMISE

*The LORD appeared to Abraham near the great trees
of Mamre while he was sitting at the entrance to his tent
in the heat of the day. Abraham looked up and saw three
men standing nearby. When he saw them, he hurried
from the entrance of his tent to meet them and
bowed low to the ground.*

GENESIS 18:1–2 NIV

Many commentators believe that this particular
appearance of the Lord to Abraham is another
Christophany, a pre-incarnate appearance of Jesus in the
Old Testament. Imagine what it must have been like for
Abraham to have seen God again (reference the devotion
on December 4), and this time in the flesh!

The promise that the Lord made to Abraham in this
story is one that made its hearers laugh—first Sarah,
Abraham's wife (see verses 12–15), and then the billions
of people who have heard this story over the centuries.
It's a wonderful example of how God takes seemingly
unqualified—even unable—people and uses them to
accomplish His tasks. When this first descendent of
Abraham was born, the new daddy was one hundred
years old! Amazing.

If God can use two senior citizens to move His plan
of redemption forward, how can He use you today to
expand His kingdom? God empowers people to do His
work. The Bible is full of stories of God coming through
when human effort and qualification were seriously
lacking. Think big, pray hard, and move forward!

INCREDIBLE SACRIFICE

"Take your son, your only son, whom you love—Isaac—
and go to the region of Moriah. Sacrifice him there as
a burnt offering on a mountain I will show you."
GENESIS 22:2 NIV

Abraham was a man who was used to hearing the voice of God. He had followed it closely and lived by faith. God had promised that Abraham's descendants would number more than the stars in the sky (Genesis 15:5), and he'd been given a natural-born son at the impossible age of one hundred. But this time, when Abraham heard the voice, he must have been stunned.

"Kill my son? The one I waited so long to have? The fulfillment of the promise I heard so many years ago?" But he moved forward in faith and passed the test. Take a moment to read Genesis 22:1–19. It's an incredible story, one that points toward God's sacrifice of His very own Son, Jesus Christ, on the cross. While God provided a ram to be the sacrifice in place of Isaac, the Son Himself would be the full and perfect sacrifice for humanity's sin. No one stayed God's hand when Jesus' time came.

This early picture of the sacrifice of an only son is a vivid foreshadowing of God's plan to redeem the world from sin and brokenness. God's incredible sacrifice of His own Son made it possible for all of humanity to know freedom from sin and eternal life with Him.

Have you accepted that once-for-all sacrifice for your own sin?

WRESTLING WITH GOD

Jacob was left alone, and a man wrestled with him till daybreak. . . . Then the man said, "Let me go, for it is daybreak." But Jacob replied, "I will not let you go unless you bless me." The man asked him, "What is your name?" "Jacob," he answered. Then the man said, "Your name will no longer be Jacob, but Israel, because you have struggled with God and with humans and have overcome". . . . So Jacob called the place Peniel, saying, "It is because I saw God face to face, and yet my life was spared."
GENESIS 32:24–30 NIV

Here, God, through this earthly manifestation (which some theologians understand to be a pre-incarnation of Jesus), names the leader of the family who will carry the plan of salvation forward. When He changes Jacob's name to "Israel," He sets Jacob on a new path from the meaning of his first name ("supplanter" or "one who grasps the heel," which carries the meaning of "deceiver") to "one who contends with God." This would certainly be true for Israel's descendants—which include Christians in the spiritual sense.

Do you wrestle with God's plan for your life? Do you fight to live in a way that honors Him? Mirror Jacob's determination. Pray that God will bless you as you struggle to be His man with your family, in your workplace, and in your church.

THE PASSOVER LAMB

*"Tell the whole community of Israel that on the tenth day
of this month each man is to take a lamb for his family. . . .
Then they are to take some of the blood and put it on
the sides and tops of the doorframes of the houses where
they eat the lambs. . . . The blood will be a sign for you
on the houses where you are, and when I see the blood,
I will pass over you. No destructive plague
will touch you when I strike Egypt."*

EXODUS 12:3, 7, 13 NIV

This story of the deliverance of Israel from Egypt is
loaded with Messianic symbolism. Through the Passover
story we understand that the "lamb without defect"
(verse 5) would be killed for the benefit of God's people.
Those who acted in faith and placed the blood of the
lamb "on the sides and tops of the doorframes" found out
that the blood of this lamb did indeed protect them from
God's wrath against the Egyptians.

The Israelites ate this Passover meal expectantly,
knowing that deliverance was on its way. They acted in
faith, waiting for God to stay true to His promise and
deliver them from slavery. And they experienced God's
delivery.

Was their deliverance easy? No. Was it costly? Yes,
moving forward in faith always is. Read Exodus 12:1–30
and marvel at the symbolism in this passage and how it
points to the One sinless Lamb.

SACRIFICIAL SYSTEM

*"Sacrifice a bull each day as a sin offering to make
atonement. Purify the altar by making atonement for it,
and anoint it to consecrate it. For seven days make
atonement for the altar and consecrate it. Then the altar
will be most holy, and whatever touches it will be holy.
This is what you are to offer on the altar regularly
each day: two lambs a year old."*
EXODUS 29:36–38 NIV

As the people of Israel leave pagan Egypt, God calls them
to be separate from the surrounding countries and to
offer costly sacrifices to Him as a way to atone for their
sins.

The word *atone* appears three times in today's
passage. What does it mean? The dictionary definition
is "to make amends or reparation." The people of Israel
were called to atone for their sins on a daily basis. As they
brought their sacrifices to the tabernacle, the reality of
the needed payment for their sins hit home: animals died,
blood was splashed on the altar, smoke rose up into the
sky. For as long as the sacrificial system was in place, the
people of Israel were never without a reminder of their sin.

Now that Jesus has become the perfect, once-for-all
sacrifice for our sins, our responsibility is to turn to Him
daily in gratitude for what He has done for us. He gave
His life that we might live; in exchange, He asks that we
give our lives in service to Him, telling others about the
hope that we have through His sinless sacrifice.

THE WARRIOR

*Now when Joshua was near Jericho, he looked up and saw
a man standing in front of him with a drawn sword in his
hand. Joshua went up to him and asked, "Are you for us
or for our enemies?" "Neither," he replied, "but as
commander of the army of the LORD I have now come."
Then Joshua fell facedown to the ground in reverence."*
JOSHUA 5:13–14 NIV

Here the commander of the Lord's army surprises Joshua,
who is on high alert as he enters enemy territory. He's
been called to take the fortified town of Jericho, and
he's ready to fight, until the figure identifies himself and
Joshua falls on his face in reverence. The fact that this
commander accepted this reverent act and called the
ground "holy," leads many to surmise that this figure was
another Old Testament appearance of Jesus.

God's commands to Joshua form the most bizarre
battle plan ever. But they leave no doubt as to who is doing
the actual fighting. Again, as we have seen before in the Old
Testament, the command is for Joshua to step forward in
faith and obedience and watch God claim the victory.

And so it is for us today. When we step forward in
faith, we rely on God to win the battles of our lives for us.
Those of us who have seen His deliverance can testify, as
Joshua did when he saw those walls crumble, that God is
indeed the only One who can fight for us, leading us to
victory over our sin and bringing us into eternal life.

DAVID POINTS TO JESUS

My God, my God, why have you forsaken me? Why are you
so far from saving me, so far from my cries of anguish?. . .
All who see me mock me; they hurl insults, shaking their
heads. "He trusts in the LORD," they say, "let the LORD
rescue him. Let him deliver him, since he delights in him". . . .
Dogs surround me, a pack of villains encircles me;
they pierce my hands and my feet. All my bones are on
display; people stare and gloat over me. They divide my
clothes among them and cast lots for my garment.
PSALM 22:1, 7–8, 16–18 NIV

Psalm 22 is quoted from and referred to on numerous
occasions in the New Testament. In fact, no psalm is
quoted more. It is a psalm, or song, of David, written
when he was under pressure from the prolonged attacks
of his enemies. It is a picture of the righteous sufferer, and
as such, it prefigures the story of Jesus' last days on earth
and His crucifixion.

Verse 1 starts out with the words that Jesus used on
the cross as He suffered for our sins. Verses 7–8 reflect
the derision that passersby heaped on Him as they saw
Him hanging on the cross (see Matthew 27:39 and Luke
23:35). Verse 16 points to the nails that would pierce
His hands and feet (see Isaiah 53:5 and John 20:27),
and verses 17–18 predict the soldiers' gambling for His
garments (see Matthew 27:35 and John 19:23–24).

God gave His people glimpses of what was to come.
How does He do the same for you today? Look for ways
that He makes His ways known to you in everyday life.

THE CORNERSTONE

The stone the builders rejected has become the cornerstone; the LORD has done this, and it is marvelous in our eyes. The LORD has done it this very day; let us rejoice today and be glad. . . . Blessed is he who comes in the name of the LORD. From the house of the LORD we bless you.
PSALM 118:22–24, 26 NIV

Here we find another psalm that points to Jesus, this one written in the context of a king giving thanks for victory over his enemies. Verses 22–23 are words that Jesus applied to Himself in the New Testament because He had been rejected by Israel, His own people, yet He was to become the very cornerstone of God's new house, the church (Matthew 21:42; Mark 12:10; Luke 20:17; Acts 4:11; Ephesians 2:20; 1 Peter 2:7).

Verse 26 is the song that the people of Jerusalem sang when Jesus made His entry into the city before His trial and crucifixion. And some scholars believe that this is the very psalm that Jesus and the disciples sang at the conclusion of the Last Supper (Matthew 26:30).

How amazing that we would find such detailed messages about Jesus, the Savior, in these psalms that had been sung centuries before Jesus was even born. It points to the progressive plan of God to save His people that is so carefully laid out in the Bible. Indeed, Jesus is the Cornerstone of our faith, the Rock of our salvation, the only sure footing we have in a world that continues to crumble around us. Turn to Him today and put your feet on solid ground.

THE FIERY FURNACE

He said, "Look! I see four men walking around in the fire,
unbound and unharmed, and the fourth
looks like a son of the gods."
DANIEL 3:25 NIV

The story of Daniel and his three brave friends is a favorite of Sunday school teachers—and students—around the globe.

Daniel and his friends are captives in a foreign land. Their past is gone, their present is difficult, and their future has also been taken away, for as foreign prisoners they were likely turned into eunuchs, dedicated to full-time service to the Babylonian king Nebuchadnezzar. Loyalty was demanded of them, yet they remained loyal to their God.

Their story of defiance is well known, and here we see the pagan king looking into the fire, seeing the deliverance of God, which is just as the men had predicted (Daniel 3:17–18). Having witnessed this miracle, Nebuchadnezzar writes a decree that is simply jaw dropping.

If you've believed in the saving power of Jesus, you know what it is like to be delivered from certain death and an eternity in the fire. Do others who may not know Jesus understand from the way you live your life that you have been saved from this fate? Can they see your faithfulness, your trust in this Jesus who stands beside you in the midst of whatever trial you're experiencing?

DESCRIPTION OF THE KING

*The people walking in darkness have seen a great
light. . . . For to us a child is born, to us a son is given,
and the government will be on his shoulders. And he will
be called Wonderful Counselor, Mighty God, Everlasting
Father, Prince of Peace. Of the greatness of his
government and peace there will be no end.*
ISAIAH 9:2, 6–7 NIV

Up until this point in the month we have been looking for glimpses of Jesus in the Old Testament. For the rest of this month as we head toward the Christmas celebration, we'll marvel at the prophecies of Jesus.

Isaiah prophesied some seven hundred years before the birth of Jesus, and his description of the coming Messiah was jaw dropping. He lived and wrote during a time when Israel was declining and other powers were pressuring the Jewish people. His book points toward the coming defeat and exile of the Jewish people, yet he does not leave them hopeless.

The coming darkness would indeed be hard, as the Jews would have to pay for their disobedience; but, like a candle in a pitch-black room, the King would come. This familiar passage rings through the centuries to inspire us as well—Jesus, the Wonderful Counselor, the Mighty God, the Everlasting Father, the Prince of Peace, is still alive and reigning today in the hearts and lives of those who trust in Him for their salvation. His light chases away the darkness in our lives.

SUFFERING SERVANT PART 1

He was despised and rejected by mankind, a man of suffering, and familiar with pain. Like one from whom people hide their faces he was despised, and we held him in low esteem. Surely he took up our pain and bore our suffering, yet we considered him punished by God, stricken by him, and afflicted.
ISAIAH 53:3–4 NIV

Isaiah 53 continues the amazing description of the suffering Servant that would come to rescue the people of Israel and to save the world from sin. Once again, seven hundred years before the birth of Jesus, we have these promises that describe what the coming Savior would be like.

Despised and rejected—those of us who know the story of the New Testament know that Jesus would be both loved and hated by the people that He came to save.

Have you been "despised" by those in your circle of influence for following Jesus? Understand that Jesus understands. He understands the deepest wounds of our hearts. He knows the ache we feel at the brokenness we experience. He walked the dark path on our behalf, and He still lives today to bring healing where we most need it. Jesus told us, "In this world you will have trouble. But take heart! I have overcome the world" (John 16:33 NIV).

Living for Jesus in this world may bring pain and difficulty, but we have a living Source to help us as we stand firm for Him.

SUFFERING SERVANT PART 2

*But he was pierced for our transgressions, he was crushed
for our iniquities; the punishment that brought us peace was
on him, and by his wounds we are healed. We all, like sheep,
have gone astray, each of us has turned to our own way;
and the LORD has laid on him the iniquity of us all.*
ISAIAH 53:5–6 NIV

Have you ever suffered for something that someone else
did? Perhaps a coworker let his deadline slip and now you
have to work twice as hard to get the project out on time.
Or maybe someone decided to take a quick left in front
of you and you smashed the car that you'd just bought a
month ago.

Life can be hard, but anything we might be going
through because of someone else's poor decisions
can hardly compare to the suffering that Isaiah tells
us about in this passage. Read the passage again: *our*
transgressions. . *our* iniquities. . .punishment that brought
us peace. . .all because a perfectly sinless Savior made the
choice to cover our sins.

Think of the many ways in which we can be like sheep:
stubborn, aimlessly wandering, just following our noses,
eating the grass in front of us without looking for danger
all around. There's no doubt that we have all "turned
to our own way" and rejected the things of God. Then
consider how the sin that you stumble into every single
day is covered—completely wiped clean—by the sacrifice
of Jesus.

SUFFERING SERVANT PART 3

Therefore I will give him a portion among the great,
and he will divide the spoils with the strong, because he
poured out his life unto death, and was numbered with
the transgressors. For he bore the sin of many,
and made intercession for the transgressors.
ISAIAH 53:12 NIV

This picture of the suffering Servant in Isaiah has directed our thoughts toward Jesus as we make our way toward Christmas. Today's passage portrays Jesus almost as an attorney, pleading our case before God, the righteous Judge. It points toward the victory Jesus experiences today because He fulfilled the sacrificial system that the Jews had been following for centuries.

What do you see when you hear the word *transgressors*? Criminals? Prostitutes? Drug addicts? Maybe, but also think of yourself in this context.

Jesus numbered Himself among us, even though He had no reason to. As the sinless Son of God, He could have condemned those who were lost in their sin. And try as we might, we're all lost in our own sinfulness, which darkens our hearts and makes our lives difficult. But, like a lawyer passionately pleading before a judge on our behalf, Jesus continues to make intercession before God. He knows we're guilty, and yet He fights for us every single day. Why? Because He already took our death sentence; He already did the hard time. And because of this, we can live in freedom every single day.

ZECHARIAH'S SURPRISE

*"Do not be afraid, Zechariah, for your prayer has been
heard, and your wife Elizabeth will bear you a son,
and you shall call his name John. . . . And he will turn
many of the children of Israel to the Lord their God,
and he will go before him in the spirit and power of
Elijah, to turn the hearts of the fathers to the children,
and. . .to make ready for the Lord a people prepared."*
LUKE 1:13, 16–17 ESV

Here we find Zechariah going about his business as a
priest, working in an honored position and burning incense
before the Lord. Suddenly an angel appears to him—
Gabriel, one who "stand[s] in the presence of God" (verse
19), telling him that his wife, Elizabeth, in her old age would
have a son, John, who would prepare the way for the
Messiah. Shades of Abraham and Sarah (Genesis 17:19–21)!

Note what a part of John's task would be: calling
Israel back to God but also turning "the hearts of the
fathers to the children." This echoes the last words of the
Old Testament: "Behold, I will send you Elijah the prophet
before the great and awesome day of the LORD comes.
And he will turn the hearts of fathers to their children
and the hearts of children to their fathers, lest I come
and strike the land with a decree of utter destruction"
(Malachi 4:5–6 ESV).

Are you a father? Reread that passage from Malachi
again. Notice that it doesn't talk about mothers here.
Have you "turned your heart" toward your children, so
that they turn their hearts toward you?

GABRIEL COMES TO MARY

*In the sixth month of Elizabeth's pregnancy, God sent
the angel Gabriel to Nazareth, a town in Galilee. . . .
The angel went to her and said, "Greetings, you who are
highly favored! The Lord is with you." Mary was greatly
troubled at his words and wondered what kind of
greeting this might be. But the angel said to her,
"Do not be afraid, Mary; you have found favor with God."*
LUKE 1:26, 28–30 NIV

The angel Gabriel once again gets called up for duty, just
a few months after he had appeared to Zechariah. This
time he appears to Mary, who would become the mother
of Jesus. As far as we know, Mary was an unknown,
normal teenager, perhaps fourteen or fifteen years of
age. And the angel came to her as she was in the middle
of her daily duties—suddenly before her stood an angel
messenger with a shocking, even overwhelming, task for
her to accomplish.

Notice his words to her. He called her "highly favored"
and told her not to be afraid. Did you know that in the
scriptures, whenever an angel appears, the angel tells the
people not to be afraid? Here again Gabriel says these
words of comfort, because his appearance must have
scared the living daylights out of her.

We, too, are "favored" by God because of the saving
work of Jesus on our behalf. And the words that Gabriel
spoke to Mary are for us as well. God has called us to live
and work to build His kingdom, and this passage calls us
to fearless service.

Firsy Day of Winter

An Impossible Calling

*"You will conceive and give birth to a son,
and you are to call him Jesus. He will be great
and will be called the Son of the Most High."*
Luke 1:31–32 niv

If you're a father, you hope for the best for your kids.
You do what you can to help them prepare for whatever
next phase of life they are approaching, all with the hope
that someday they'll be responsible adults who will live
successful lives in the world as followers of Jesus.

Mary didn't have to wonder about what her child was
going to do when He came of age. She had this word from
Jesus that this child, whom she would conceive by the
power of the Spirit, would be a king in the line of David.
How this young girl must have puzzled about this. . .how
could any of this be happening to her? And yet she had
this assurance from God that her Son would lead the
nation of Israel.

Notice that once again God empowered Mary to do
the work. In and of herself, she had no power to do the
work. And the same is true for us. Yes, we've been gifted
with abilities and love for our kids, but we're far from
perfect. Yet we have the same Power Source—the Holy
Spirit—who longs to help us raise our kids to follow Mary's
Son, our Savior.

Mary's task wasn't easy; ours won't be either. But
following God's call means patiently waiting for Him to do
the work through us, as unworthy as we may be.

HIS WORD NEVER FAILS

"For no word from God will ever fail." "I am the Lord's
servant," Mary answered. "May your word to me
be fulfilled." Then the angel left her.
LUKE 1:37–38 NIV

Let's take a moment in this Christmas month to consider the words of the angel Gabriel, the messenger who "stand[s] in the presence of God" (Luke 1:19 ESV). Listen to his words to Mary: "No word from God will ever fail."

Remember the prophecy of Isaiah, spoken seven hundred years before the birth of Jesus? To a people who were oppressed and crushed, they must have hoped and prayed for this king to come every single day. Generation after generation lived and died under this promise, yet God delayed until the perfect time had come for Jesus to be born.

How long have you been waiting for the promise of God to be fulfilled in your life? What promises are you claiming for your life? Maybe it's a job opportunity that you're hoping will come your way; maybe you and your wife have been struggling to have a child; maybe it's a teenager who has walked away from God and you're waiting for Him to work in your child's life in a powerful way.

The Bible is filled with promises from God. Take it from Gabriel, who knows from personal experience: "No word from God will *ever* fail." Waiting can be difficult, but God is faithful. Continue to pray, *I am the Lord's servant*, and look for ways that God is working. Perhaps in ways that you would never expect—just like Mary.

GENERATIONAL MEMORY

*"My soul glorifies the Lord and my spirit rejoices in God
my Savior, for he has been mindful of the humble state
of his servant. From now on all generations will call
me blessed, for the Mighty One has done great
things for me—holy is his name."*
LUKE 1:46–49 NIV

Okay, so Mary has been called to a task that none of
us men will ever have to do: bear and deliver a child.
For most men, this is an enormous relief. We watch our
children being born with wonder, pain, and amazement,
and for the rest of our lives, we give our wives all kinds
of credit for giving up so much of their lives to bear and
raise children.

Mary's faithfulness was rewarded, as billions of people
have heard her story. Indeed, we do "call her blessed,"
because she was faithful to God's call. Her prophecy in
this song of gratitude did come true.

If you're a father, in a very real sense you are a
patriarch, just like Abraham, Isaac, and Jacob. Your
children and your children's children will tell stories
about you. As you approach Christmas, the greatest
memory-making time of the year, are you pointing your
children toward Jesus? During a time when we can all get
caught up in the crush and distraction of preparing for
the holidays, are you reminding your kids that there is a
higher Reason for this season?

Make it your goal to have your children remember you
and call *themselves* blessed for having you as a father.

CHRISTMAS EVE: ANTICIPATION

[Joseph] *went there to register with Mary, who was pledged
to be married to him and was expecting a child.*
LUKE 2:4–5 NIV

Let's go back and visit Mary and Joseph as they complete their long trip toward Bethlehem.

Mary is probably riding on the back of a donkey, and Gabriel's words to her have come true. She is very pregnant and is ready to have this Child—the One who will be King. Joseph has had his own angelic assurances that the angel's words are true (Matthew 1:20–21). The anticipation of this young couple must be hard to contain. They must be so excited to see this baby, the One that the angels have told them about!

Perhaps you remember the excitement of this night when you were a child. If you have children, you can feel the same excitement on this most special night. They breathlessly wait for the morning, when they run into the room where the tree is lit and the presents overflow! On this incredibly exciting night, take the time to turn your thoughts, and those of your family, to this young couple waiting for the coming King to arrive.

Amid all the presents and the fun, be sure that you point your family toward the coming King—the one who first came to an unknown, humble family after a long, long journey—for them, and for the people of Israel.

Christmas Day

INCARNATION

While they were [in Bethlehem], *the time came for the baby to be born, and she gave birth to her firstborn, a son. She wrapped him in cloths and placed him in a manger, because there was no guest room available for them.*

LUKE 2:6–7 NIV

It's a story we all know very well—God becoming man. The Creator of the universe, humbling Himself to come into the world in the same way all of us came.

Imagine being Joseph for a minute. How could he have felt—exhausted after a long trip to register, tired, hungry, dirty; no arrangements made to accommodate his wife, who had to give birth in dirty, chaotic conditions far away from home. How could he feel good about this?

Yet Joseph had a promise from God. A promise that this child would "save his people from their sins" (Matthew 1:21 ESV), that his marriage to Mary would not be in vain. But how could he be sure of this, standing in a dusty, stinky stall with animals standing watch? How could he have known what was to come?

What we know for sure from this story is this: God's plans are surprising. He comes to us in ways we would never imagine. If you're a father, imagine what Joseph must have been thinking and feeling on this history-changing day. Beyond the lights, food, and presents, how are you pointing your family toward God's plans instead of your own?

BLUE-COLLAR CELEBRATION

And there were shepherds living out in the fields nearby,
keeping watch over their flocks at night. An angel of the
Lord appeared to them, and the glory of the Lord shone
around them, and they were terrified. But the angel said
to them, "Do not be afraid. I bring you good news that will
cause great joy for all the people. Today in the town of
David a Savior has been born to you; he is the Messiah,
the Lord. This will be a sign to you: You will find a
baby wrapped in cloths and lying in a manger."

LUKE 2:8–12 NIV

Who was the first group to understand that the Messiah
had come? A group of hardworking shepherds, tired after
a long day of finding suitable food for their sheep. Guys
that stayed close to the earth, who carried their lunch
boxes with them; it doesn't get more blue-collar than that.

Other shepherds had looked forward to this day:
Moses, who spent forty years with his wooly charges
before God called him to free Israel from Egypt (Exodus
3:1–10); David, the shepherd boy who became Israel's
greatest king (1 Samuel 16:1–22). The men who heard the
angels sing on that previously silent night never imagined
that they'd be part of the culmination of history, the
news that the Jewish people had been waiting to hear for
centuries. They had to see it for themselves, and they ran
into Bethlehem to check it out.

God didn't come to kings or politicians. He entrusted
the hardworking shepherds with this Good News.

SILENT NIGHT?

So they hurried off and found Mary and Joseph,
and the baby, who was lying in the manger. When they
had seen him, they spread the word concerning what had
been told them about this child, and all who heard it
were amazed at what the shepherds said to them.
LUKE 2:16–18 NIV

Our blue-collar heroes race into Bethlehem to see if
what the angels had said to them is actually true. And of
course they find this new family and see the child. Have
you ever wondered how long they stayed there? Have
you ever wondered what they did for the family—did they
bring food? Blankets? Did they run to get their wives to
tell them the news? Did they bring their families to look at
this long-promised Savior?

The images that we have of the holy family alone
among the sheep may have been true for a few moments,
but after the shepherds came, they couldn't contain their
excitement. They "spread the word" about what had
happened, and all the townspeople "who heard it were
amazed." The streets were jammed with people who had
come to register. How many listened to the shepherds
and came to see this baby?

This is amazing news! The good news of the Gospel is
meant to be shared. Have you been amazed through this
Christmas season? Have others been amazed at what you
have told them?

SIMEON AND ANNA

*Moved by the Spirit, [Simon] went into the temple courts.
When the parents brought in the child Jesus to do for him
what the custom of the Law required, Simeon took him in
his arms and praised God, saying: "Sovereign Lord,
as you have promised, you may now dismiss your servant
in peace. For my eyes have seen your salvation."*
LUKE 2:27s–30 NIV

It had been eight days since Mary and Joseph celebrated the birth of Jesus with the shepherds in the stable. It was time to dedicate Jesus in the temple, in obedience to the law that had been established after the Exodus (Exodus 13:1-12). They walked the five miles to Jerusalem and entered the temple and found another man and woman who confirmed what the angels and shepherds had told them. How this young family must have stood amazed as these wise servants of God prophesied on behalf of their newborn!

This firstborn, Jesus, was indeed dedicated into the Lord's service in obedience to the law. But unlike other firstborn boys, this baby was destined to become the *fulfillment* of the law, the culmination of Jewish history, the perfect, sinless Savior of the world, and the perfect sacrifice for sin. The baby in the arms of this young girl would, some thirty years later, return to the temple and make some incredible predictions about it (Mark 13:1-2).

Let the wonder of Joseph and Mary color your perceptions during this Christmas week.

TRULY WISE MEN

*After Jesus was born in Bethlehem in Judea,
during the time of King Herod, Magi from the east came
to Jerusalem and asked, "Where is the one who has
been born king of the Jews? We saw his star when
it rose and have come to worship him."*

MATTHEW 2:1–2 NIV

These astronomers saw a symbol in the sky that drew them to seek out the Savior. Recall for a moment an earlier symbol in the sky that reminds us of God's promises in the Bible, given by God to humanity: "Never again will all life be destroyed by the waters of a flood; never again will there be a flood to destroy the earth. . . This is the sign of the covenant I am making between me and you and every living creature with you, a covenant for all generations to come: I have set my rainbow in the clouds, and it will be the sign of the covenant between me and the earth" (Genesis 9:11–13 NIV).

This star stood as a symbol to these pagan astronomers that a historical moment was happening; as with the shepherds, they felt compelled to come and see for themselves.

The star of Bethlehem still stands as a well-known symbol of Christmas, drawing millions to come and see this miracle that God has brought to the world. What better time of year to draw others who don't know about Jesus to Him? The wise men brought luxurious gifts to the holy family; you can bring no greater gift to the God you serve than to tell others about God's promises.

A NEW BAPTISM

The people were waiting expectantly and were all wondering in their hearts if John might possibly be the Messiah. John answered them all, "I baptize you with water. But one who is more powerful than I will come, the straps of whose sandals I am not worthy to untie. He will baptize you with the Holy Spirit and fire."

LUKE 3:15–16 NIV

We read earlier about John the Baptist and how he came to prepare the way for Jesus. This cousin of the Savior never claimed to be the Messiah; he merely pointed the way for people to find Jesus.

John was certainly an odd sight—living in the desert, eating a very strange diet, and passionately urging people to repent from their evil ways and change their hearts. He'd been raised among the Jewish religious elite and represented the ultimate example of a son breaking with his father's occupation with his amazingly countercultural lifestyle.

John was a harbinger of a new era; his appearance signaled a new age, and his message rings through the centuries to those who hope in Jesus for their salvation and who live empowered by the Spirit in the way that God has asked us to live.

John didn't claim to be the Christ; he pointed the way for others to see Him. Does your life point your family, your friends, your neighbors, and your coworkers in the same direction?

A NEW YEAR'S RESOLUTION

*Now, brothers and sisters, about times and dates
we do not need to write to you, for you know very well
that the day of the Lord will come like a thief in the night.*

1 THESSALONIANS 5:1–2 NIV

Throughout this month, we have searched for the Savior through the symbolism, prophecies, and appearances of Jesus in the Old and New Testaments. Throughout this month, we've seen the symbols of the Savior as they led up to the week of Christmas. We've seen the baby in the manger and read about what the angels, shepherds, and others said about Him.

God's plan to save the world, begun so soon after humans fell into sin (Genesis 3), was continued in the birth of Jesus. The Jews had waited for this Messiah to come for centuries, and His life, death, and resurrection give us all hope for the future.

Today, we stand between the two appearances of Jesus. We know He came to walk the earth and to complete His part; we understand that the Holy Spirit came to indwell all those who choose to believe in Jesus Christ alone for their salvation. And we wait for His return.

How will that anticipation change your life as you look toward a new year? Do you wait for His appearance, understanding that He could come at any time (1 Thessalonians 5:1–6)?

This New Year's Eve, resolve to look for the second coming of the Savior, living every moment as if it could be today. Why? Because it could very well be.

CONTRIBUTOR INDEX

Mark Ammerman is a full-time pastor and the author/illustrator of various works of fiction and non-fiction, including the award-winning *Longshot* (of the Cross and the Tomahawk trilogy.) His most recent book is an end-times novel, *Push* (www.eleventhhourpush.com). Mark wrote the devotions for the month of July.

Rev. Robin Burkhart PhD. has served for more than thirty years as a pastor, author, educator, and denominational leader. His varied background includes ministry in Latin and South America, the Caribbean, Europe, Africa, and the Peoples Republic of China. He is the father of three adult children and five grandchildren. Rob wrote the devotions for the month of April

Ed Cyzewski is the author of *A Christian Survival Guide: A Lifeline to Faith and Growth* and *Coffeehouse Theology: Reflecting on God in Everyday Life* and is the coauthor of *The Good News of Revelation* and *Unfollowers: Unlikely Lessons on Faith from Those Who Doubted Jesus*. He writes about prayer and imperfectly following Jesus at www.edcyzewski.com. Ed wrote the devotions for the month of August.

Glenn Hascall is an accomplished writer with credits in more than a hundred books. His articles have appeared in numerous publications including the *Wall Street Journal*. Glenn wrote the devotions for the months of May and June.

Rob Maaddi has been a Philadelphia sports writer for The Associated Press since 2000. He's covered the Super Bowl, World Series, NBA Finals, Stanley Cup Finals, and numerous major sporting events throughout his career. Rob, his wife, Remy, and their twin girls, Alexia and Melina, reside in South Jersey. Rob wrote the devotions for the month of March.

Jess MacCallum is president of Professional Printers, Inc. in Columbia, South Carolina. Author of two previous books, he is father of two daughters and a son. Jess wrote the devotions for the month of September.

David Sanford serves on the leadership team at Corban University, which is consistently ranked by U.S. News Best Colleges as one of Top 10 colleges in the West. Among his many credits, David has served as executive editor of *Holy Bible: Mosaic*, general editor of the popular *Handbook on Thriving as an Adoptive Family*, coauthor of the bestselling *God Is Relevant*, and author of *If God Disappears*. Better yet? David is husband to Renée, dad to five, and grandpa to nine (and one in heaven). David wrote the devotions for the month of November.

Ed Strauss is a freelance writer in British Columbia. He has authored or coauthored more than 30 books for children, tweens, and adults. Ed wrote the devotions for the month of February.

Tracy Sumner is a freelance author, writer, and editor in Beaverton, Oregon. An avid outdoorsman, he enjoys fly-fishing on world-class Oregon waters. Tracy wrote the devotions for the month of January.

Mike Vander Klipp is a 25-year professional writer and editor who has spent the last 20 working in the Zondervan Bible group in multiple roles. He and his wife live with their kids, the cats, and the dog in Grand Rapids, Michigan. Mike wrote the devotions for the month of December.

Lee Warren is a freelance writer published in such varied venues as Discipleship Journal, Sports Spectrum, Crosswalk.com, and ChristianityToday.com. He is also the author of the book *Single Servings: 90 Devotions to Feed Your Soul*, and a regular sports columnist for a Christian newspaper. Lee makes his home in Omaha, Nebraska. Lee wrote the devotions for the month October.

SCRIPTURE INDEX